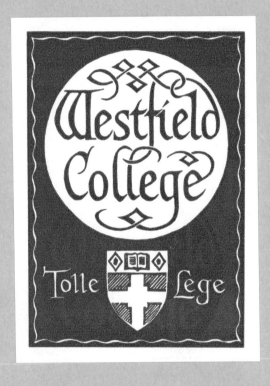

THE AMPLE PROPOSITION

by the same author

COLLECTED POEMS

CHRIST THE HUNTER

ANCESTORS AND FRIENDS

Autobiography

THE WHISPERING GALLERY
(Longmans 1955)

I AM MY BROTHER
(Longmans 1960)

The author at his desk

JOHN LEHMANN

The Ample Proposition

Autobiography III

The ample proposition that hope makes
In all designs begun on earth below
Fails in the promised largeness . . .
Troilus and Cressida
I, iii

Eyre & Spottiswoode
London

First published 1966
by Eyre & Spottiswoode (Publishers) Ltd
167 Fleet Street, London EC4
© *1966 by John Lehmann*
Printed by T. H. Brickell and Sons Ltd.,
Gillingham, Dorset

CONTENTS

ILLUSTRATIONS

Acknowledgement is due to *Harper's Bazaar* for the frontispiece
and to the *Daily Mirror* for the illustrations of the *London Magazine*
launching party.

INTRODUCTION

This, the third volume of my literary memoirs,[1] is concerned with the years immediately following the second German war, during which I built up a publishing firm of my own and lost it at the height of its success; saw my *Penguin New Writing* reach its peak of popularity and interest, fall away and come to an end; launched my experimental literary magazine on the air, *New Soundings*, and lost it, like my publishing firm, when its name and reputation were fully established; and after these reverses was enabled to found another literary magazine, the *London Magazine*, which still exists in different hands. During these years I also travelled and lectured extensively in Europe and America, wrote poems and literary essays and reviews, broadcast all over the world and made more friends in almost every country of Europe and America than ever before or since.

These years were therefore a period of the fullest and most exciting achievement in my life, and also of the most corroding disaster. The afflatus which drove me in full sail through all these experiences has, inevitably, died down. From a life now dedicated to largely different pursuits – though poetry remains a constant thread from the far-off beginnings described in *The Whispering Gallery* – I look back on it, short though the distance may be in the actual count of years, with surprise that is sometimes perilously near self-congratulation, with sorrow sometimes and bitter regret for opportunities missed and chances thwarted; and with a strange kind of almost detached curiosity, as one might look back on the life of a twin brother who had been very close to one and had been killed at the height of his self-realization.

This other life I shall now try to re-create and re-live, in the pages that follow.

---

[1] The first two were: *The Whispering Gallery* (1955); *I Am My Brother* (1960).

ACKNOWLEDGMENTS

Acknowledgments are due to Messrs Routledge and Kegan Paul Ltd for the quotation on p. 54 from *Essays on Contemporary Events* by C. J. Jung. In addition, I must gratefully acknowledge permission to quote from various letters, poems and other works, to the following: Mrs Valerie Eliot, widow and literary executor of T. S. Eliot, and Mr Francis Sitwell, nephew and literary executor of Dame Edith Sitwell; Mr John Betjeman, Mr Paul Bowles, Mr Cyril Connolly, Mr Lawrence Durrell, Mr E. M. Forster, Mr David Gascoyne, Mr Christopher Isherwood, Sir Allen Lane, Mr Laurie Lee, Mr James Michie, Mr William Plomer, Mr William Sansom, Mr Stephen Spender, Mr John Wain, Mr Tennessee Williams, Mr Henry Yorke (Henry Green); and my sister Rosamond.

The line drawings on pages 12, 90, 168, 190 and 208 are designs for *Orpheus* by John Minton; that on page 238 is the design for the *London Magazine* by Edward Ardizzone.

The endpapers are from a drawing by Philippe Jullian inscribed:
> *Souvenir d'un déjeuner place des Etats-Unis,*
> *Olivier, Philippe, Bernard, Dali, Marie-Laure, John*
> *Pour John*
> *Avec tous mes voeux pour 1965*
> *Philippe Jullian*

Part One

I

At the end of 1945, I took two decisive steps.[1] I gambled to win control of the Hogarth Press, Leonard and Virginia Woolf's publishing firm in which I had worked hitherto, and lost; and I moved from my flat in Shepherd Market and took the lease of a house in Egerton Crescent. There I planned to instal my accumulating library and collection of pictures, and entertain the friends, authors and artists, with whom my growing activity as publisher and editor had brought me into contact.

The time, it seems to me as I look back, was one of hope and confidence. Against all odds, we had, with our Allies, destroyed the Nazi and Fascist tyrannies, and a ruined Europe lay at our feet. The cost had been enormous, in lives, wealth, effort, but the full effects of that spending were still to a large extent concealed from us. An atmosphere of triumph as well as of relief reigned, not crude triumph, but a feeling that faith, under inspired and magnaminous leadership, had been fully justified, and that we had taken the key part in freeing the world from the latest monsters the twentieth century had spawned to enslave mankind. The proud bearing, the smiling faces of the soldiers, sailors and airmen one passed in the streets seemed to reflect the mood of the hour. We would rebuild our battered country, remoulding it and our society nearer to the heart's desire, in the image of justice, humanity, and un-self-seeking prosperity. Liberated Europe waited for a lead from us. Wherever I went in my travels, I found, or seemed to find, admiration for, gratitude to, and expectation of the British people. A chance, such as had not been ours for more than a hundred years, lay before us; if only we had the nerve to grasp it and the vision to make the most of it.

[1] See *I Am My Brother*, 308–17.

In literature and the arts, too, I felt almost convinced that a great epoch lay before us. The enormous increase in interest in literature, drama, painting, sculpture, music, ballet, that had grown up during the war years, the new vigorous talent that had emerged in all these arts, promised surely a magnificent harvest. It seemed to me that, as editor and publisher, with the immense good will that *New Writing* had attached to itself, I could play a not unimportant part in the new developments I looked forward to so keenly.

I still had control of *New Writing and Daylight* and *Penguin New Writing*. Books and literary magazines were still selling in quantities that would have seemed incredible when the war broke out. The only difficulty was that I had just been deprived of my position as a publisher. I had been paid for my share in the Hogarth Press, and I therefore had a little money to risk on a new venture; I had plenty of authors willing, in fact eager to throw in their lot with me; but I had been refused a paper quota.[1] I was a rider without a horse, a beaver without a single tree that he could get at.

2

There were only two courses open to me in these circumstances. Either I could try to persuade a big publisher with an ample paper quota to take me in; or I could beg, wheedle or cajole a printer to let me have just enough to start off in a small way with the books I thought most urgent.

Some of the major book printers were, I knew, in the fortunate position, for a variety of reasons, of having paper quotas of their own. Covetous eyes were cast on these quotas by almost all publishers at that time when an edition, or reprint, of any reasonable book (and many almost lunatic books) sold out on publication – or very soon after. The fortunate printers had never been more popular; but very sensibly they used their

[1] See *I Am My Brother*, 316–17.

advantage to strengthen relations with their best customers, rather than with hopeful beggars like myself.

I must admit that as I went the round of printers' offices, my task seemed to me almost hopeless, and more than once I began to doubt whether I was entirely sane in encouraging the authors who wanted to be published by me to wait just a little longer. If it had not, perhaps, been for the rage into which the point-blank refusal of the Paper Control to help my desperate condition had put me, and the sense of injury under which I smarted from Leonard Woolf's decision to drop his war-time pilot, I might have given up. Both, no doubt, had excellent reasons for their actions; but my pride had been sharply wounded, my obstinacy aroused.

Nevertheless, in those first winter months of a peace that was proving austere indeed for Britain, I did manage to extract small quantities of paper (in exchange, of course, for printing orders) out of half-a-dozen sympathetic firms, and also out of a sympathetic paper supplier. I was thus able to send to press an assortment of books I thought would make a good start, at least in order to show my intentions.

Then the first lucky break came my way. I had heard from a good friend in the trade that there was one west country printer, Purnell, who had an exceptionally large quota, and had ambitions to expand into book publishing. They already had one firm, Macdonald, under their control, and I was able to arrange an interview with the son of the chairman of Purnell, Eric Harvey, who was at that time managing Macdonald. He received me in very friendly fashion, and startled me at once by warning me that they couldn't arrange for very large editions, a run of 10,000 copies at the most. Surely there was some gap in our discussions? A river – *the* river – seemed to have been crossed before I knew where I was.

I left Eric Harvey's office with a tentative agreement, which he explained would have to be confirmed by the chairman and the works at Paulton in Somerset, to help me with a few books. For the first time I felt real hope, and the stirring of excitement. A *few* books! As if I had the money to finance any more than a few at the start.

And that was precisely where the crux lay. After the interview, negotiations were taken over by another of the directors, Clifford Gibbs. He came to see me, he was kind, he was encouraging, he promised me support. He explained to me that Purnell had had a rough time before the war, as many printers had, but by a stroke of genius the chairman, Wilfred Harvey, had in 1939 bought up various concerns, not book-publishers, which were able to claim large paper quotas. This move had set them on the road to prosperity, they planned to expand and instal the latest machinery, especially for colour printing, and they wanted to work with publishers in a way that would make it possible always to keep their staff fully employed. This meant, in fact, that they wanted financial control of *my* business. And they weren't particularly interested in *small* publishing.

I felt that I was being taken up on to a high hill. . . . The dilemma was almost intolerable. I saw that if I wanted a decent start, I had little choice except to work with Purnell, but I struggled hard to keep as much independence as possible. Discussions went on all through February and March, a large part of them devoted to the name my new publishing venture was to have. Innumerable suggestions were made, and rejected on both sides; 'The Pericles Press' seemed in the last lap to be leading. I finally agreed to giving Purnell 51 per cent control, if full editorial control was left to me, and I was allowed – provided I could find the paper – to go elsewhere for a small number of books.

Then suddenly, perhaps made uneasy by the obstinacy I had displayed, the chairman said they must have 100 per cent control or nothing. Of course I could have all the finance and all the paper I wanted; but I would become a salaried employee.

I decided to gamble. I refused. I knew the risk I was taking, but I had got on sufficiently well with the directors for them to temper the collapse of negotiations with an agreement to print, and produce paper for twelve books in each twelve months. I had represented to them as strongly as I could that they had at least not dissuaded me from committing myself to a number of books that I should now not be able to publish if they cut off all assistance. Purnell were also probably gambling at this point, on the calculation that I would bite off more than I could chew and have to come back to them. For me, however, the respite – if only respite it was to be – was extremely precious, because it gave me the opportunity to establish the character of my firm before any crisis broke.

There was much to be done, and as fast as possible. I decided to throw in the best asset I had in the literary world, my name, and call the firm John Lehmann Limited. Then came the problem of finance. The money due to me from the sale of my partnership in the Hogarth Press seemed to me to be fairly divisible into the original sum advanced by my family trust (of which my mother was life-tenant), and other sums advanced by my mother and my brother-in-law, Mountie Bradish-Ellames, to help with *New Writing* at one time or another. I therefore proposed that they should be made shareholders and directors in the new firm. My sister Rosamond was keenly interested to take part in the venture, provided some more capital, and also became a director, as well, of course as an important literary adviser. All told, I don't think we had as much as £10,000: an absurdly inadequate sum by present standards, but in 1946 we were still in the middle of the book boom, and my friends, both in the writing and book-selling worlds, were confident that my literary reputation would carry the day. Even so, in spite of my own sanguine hopes and the optimism that surrounded me, I frequently had qualms. I knew I would need a lot of luck.

The most pressing problem after that was organization. The London traveller who worked for me during the war in the Hogarth Press, Ted Sloane, a shrewd judge of a book's commercial possibilities and always full of sympathy and humour, readily came over to the new firm: an inestimable advantage. I joined the newly organized co-operative venture, the Book Centre, to solve my problems of distribution. I wrote to my friends among the publishers in America and had hearteningly enthusiastic replies from them. My friends in the book world in France promised at once to help, and I very soon established close relations in particular with Gallimard, first with Michel Gallimard and then with their charming young foreign rights manager, Dionys Mascolo, who was reputed at one time to be eight hundred letters behindhand. With the *doyenne* of Paris literary agents, Jennie Bradley, known, courted, even some-

B

times feared by every publisher in London and New York, I started a warm friendship which has happily survived the end of my publishing days. Working on my experience at the Hogarth Press, I was also able to find good agents to Australasia, Canada and South Africa.

Next, I had to establish my staff, my band of helpers, keeping it as small as was practicable. No imposing suite of offices, beloved of Americans launching into the glamorous waters of transatlantic publishing, no cohorts of secretaries and office boys for someone starting with less than £10,000. As I had no housekeeper at the time, we decided to use the basement flat at my new house in Egerton Crescent, looking out on the tiny walled garden at the back, with its hydrangeas, camellias and jessamine. Barbara Cooper, who had supported me so devotedly on *New Writing* – which was of course still appearing – took on general editorial work, and helped to read MSS for the firm as well as for *New Writing*. At the time when it looked as if I was to have full backing from Purnell, Cecil Day Lewis had agreed to be a full-time reader for us; but as in the new set-up I could only offer him part-time employment, he had in the end to take a properly paid job elsewhere. Keith Vaughan, at that time just beginning to build up his reputation as a painter, to my delight agreed to come in as book-designer, and had working with him in production and publicity a young man who had been recommended to me, Michael Swan, whose chief passion was the work of Henry James. On the accounts side, Barbara Hepworth, a delicate artist (but not the sculptor), of whom I had grown very fond at the Hogarth Press, joined us; and the happy band was completed by John Hall (whom we called Clive), a young poet I had come to know towards the end of the war. I never thought of them as employees in the strict sense of the word: they were artists, poets, creators in their own right, who enjoyed being associated with the venture – some of them only part-time, to allow them the opportunity to go on writing or painting as the case might be, – and who shared my hopes and anxieties.

I had the good fortune, at the same time, to enrol as an assistant Anne Courtneidge, sister of the famous Cicely, whose gentle charm contributed much to the harmony of our office in the early days. Mention should also be made of Boakie, the office cat, a tabby who, arriving on the scene soon after as a kitten from Susan Ertz's household a few doors away, made a speciality of sitting for long hours on the pile of MSS on Barbara's desk. He was alleged to be able to detect, with uncanny instinct, any MS in which mention was made of fish.

In the matter of authors, there were three things to be done without delay. First, to pick up those authors from the Hogarth Press who were not tied by long contracts and whose loyalty was rather to me than to the Press. I tried without success to get Henry Green to follow me: I had been responsible for his coming over to the Press, and had nursed him, as publisher-editor, through the swift career that had already proved so dazzling. Rightly, however, though full of sympathy for me, he pointed to ineluctable contracts and the awkwardness of leaving half a dozen of his books behind him when there had been no quarrel. He was indubitably *my* author, but I recognized that the loss of him was one of the sacrifices I had to make. I experienced the same disappointment with William Sansom: the appearance of his first novel, *The Body*, under the Hogarth Press imprint a few years later was a painful pleasure to me, for it confirmed me in my consistent conviction, from the start, of his immense original talent, and at the same time aggravated my sorrow at having lost him. No use to say that as things turned out it was better for them to stay as they were; because if I had had Henry and Bill on my list perhaps the catastrophe of 1952 might never have occurred.

With Roy Fuller and Laurie Lee I was luckier. When Roy agreed to come over, he produced, not another book of poems (which came later, as *Epitaphs and Occasions*), but a brilliant adventure story for boys, *Savage Gold*; a marvellous card in my hand for the poker-game with Purnell. Laurie promised me a new book of poems, which came out as *The Bloom of Candles*; and I talked him into promising an autobiography. This took many years in gestation, and my career as a publisher had long been over when *Cider with Rosie* came out, and was an immediate best-selling success. Laurie inscribed my copy: 'This is really your book and you are responsible for it, but I won't blame you.' Another painful pleasure.

Quite apart from *New Writing and Daylight*, which remained my own, there was more than these two authors to pack in my bag when I left the firm. During my last few months there, a remarkable first novel came to me from America, by an unknown young author: *Dangling Man* by Saul Bellow. I was immediately struck by its unusual power and promise, but I did not persuade Leonard Woolf to see it as I did. Saul Bellow had, I thought, a beautiful, incisive style, a penetrating wit, and a wonderful understanding of the solitary imaginative life. As soon as the decision to dissolve the partnership had been taken I raced after it again, and found to my great satisfaction that it had still failed to find a London publisher. I followed this with *The Victim*.

Then again, I had always been deeply impressed by the work of Ivan Bunin, whose *Gentleman from Francisco*, in the translation by D. H. Lawrence, Koteliansky and Leonard Woolf himself, the Hogarth Press had had the distinction of publishing way back in 1922. His autobiographical book, *The Well of Days*, followed in 1933, and had long been out of print. I made up my mind to re-issue it, managed to buy the rights from Leonard and got in touch with Bunin himself, an old and almost starving exile in Paris, who though often (I understood) quietly approached with invitations to return to Russia, continued to treat the Soviet régime with hostility and contempt. This small *coup* had the fortunate result of bringing into my hands, a few years later, one of the most masterly collections of short stories in modern literature, Bunin's *Dark Avenues*.

The second thing to be done was to tie up one or two of the other authors I had supported in *New Writing*, who had either broken with their former publishers or had not yet got a publisher at all. John Sommerfield's wartime stories of the RAF had made a deep impression when they appeared in the Penguin, and I persuaded him to collect them for me to publish under the title of *The Survivors*. As I have described in my two earlier volumes of memoirs, I had made rather a speciality of publishing the younger New Zealand writers in *New Writing*, and I now arranged with the most gifted of the prose-writers, Frank Sargeson, with whom I had carried on a lively correspondence throughout the war, to publish his short novel *That Summer* in one volume with a score of his short stories. In both cases I hoped, as all publishers do when they publish short stories (at least in the Anglo-Saxon countries), for further progeny from the marriage in the more profitable form of novels.

In poetry, Hamish Henderson's *Elegies for the Dead in Cyrenaica*, some of which I had published in *New Writing*, was one of my first choices: I had long felt they were among the most original and beautiful poems to come out of the actual fighting. I also decided to make a volume of John Heath-Stubbs's translations from Leopardi, many of which had also appeared in *New Writing*.

Fulfilling a deep personal debt and an obligation as literary executor at the same time, I set about producing a volume of the poems and essays written in English by Demetrios Capetanakis before his death in 1944, together with appreciations of him by a number of writers he had known. It appeared as *A Greek Poet in England*, and is now completely out of print. Another part of that debt was to continue the translations of the Greek poet to whom Demetrios had introduced me, George Seferis. The team of translators, consisting of Bernard Spencer, Lawrence Durrell and Nanos Valaoritis, went ahead, and when *The King of Asine* was ready Rex Warner wrote a brilliant introduction.

Third, I felt it extremely important to emphasize the European and international line of the new publishing house, in fiction as well as in poetry, by having at least two or three books of living continental novelists, apart from Ivan Bunin. I remembered the success I had had with André Chamson's stories from *Les Quatres Elements* in the earliest volumes of *New Writing*, before the war, and I therefore decided to publish the book as a whole (only four of the five sections had so far been translated). This was to be called *A Mountain Boyhood*.

Elsewhere, I have described[1] the excitement which the arrival in England of a copy of Ernst Juenger's *Auf den Marmorklippen* caused during the war: an allegory of immense imaginative power with what seemed to me to be multiple layers of meaning, one of which could be interpreted as a condemnation of the whole Nazi movement and mystique. One of the first things

[1] See *I Am My Brother*, 325–6.

I did was to go after the translation rights in this book. Negotiations were slow, as they had to be conducted through the
British Control Commission in Germany, but I found an ally
in Gerard Hopkins, who was working for them at the time, and
eventually landed the fish.

I had long wanted to publish a translation of Jean-Paul
Sartre's *La Nausée*, a key book for the understanding of his
philosophical inspiration – and perhaps the best book he ever
wrote except for the short stories in *Le Mur*. When I found to
my delight that Jamie Hamilton, who had bought the English
rights in his new trilogy, *Les Chemins de la Liberté*, was not interested in *La Nausée*, I wrote off to Gallimard, obtained the rights,
and published it a year or two later as *The Diary of Antoine
Roquentin*.

All these translations of novels and short stories went into
what I decided to call my Modern European Library. But I had
an idea for another 'library', a series of reprints of books which,
either because old slow-selling editions had been exhausted
during the war, or for some other reason, were unobtainable.
In the book-hunger of the time, I thought that well-printed and
reasonably priced editions of such books, many of which commanded high prices in the second-hand shops, should go well
and at the same time cater for an important cultural need. I
planned to include not only famous novels, biographies and
even long poems (such as Byron's *Don Juan*), but also specially
prepared selections and anthologies. Henry James was riding
high. His early and middle period works had for long been
special favourites of my own, and I immediately set about negotiating the permissions (they had just come out of full copyright) with Innes Rose, the English agent for the Henry James
estate. I called the series The Chiltern Library, and, perhaps
rather perversely, started off with William Adlington's famous
translation of *The Golden Ass* of Apuleius, for which I persuaded
Louis MacNeice to write an introduction. In the distance, I
envisaged reprints of Mrs Gaskell and Herman Melville.

I was lucky in being able to exploit the good relations I had
established with contemporary English artists through *Penguin
New Writing*, to persuade them to collaborate with me in illus-
trating and designing book-jackets for my first batch of publica-

tions, which came out in the autumn of 1946. At the time, very few original artists were employed for book-jackets, most of which were carried out by designers in commercial studios. Remembering the success I had had with John Banting's designs in the Hogarth Press before the war, I made up my mind that the work of the younger English artists of the day was to be one of the characteristics of my publishing house. Some of the booksellers objected, as they always appeared to object to anything novel; but I think I set a style.

My first book of all, an anthology from the poems which had appeared in *New Writing* during the ten years since it had been founded, had a jacket designed by John Minton, who was also responsible for the jacket of *That Summer*. The seventh (and in fact the final) volume of *New Writing and Daylight*, had Keith Vaughan as its jacket designer, as also for *Poems from Leopardi* and the miniature edition of Melville's *Billy Budd*. Robert Medley illustrated with line-drawings and designed the jacket for *Savage Gold*, for *Dangling Man* and *The Golden Ass*. Stephen Spender's brother, Humphrey, tackled the jacket for *The Well of Days*.

With these nine books, John Lehmann Limited opened its campaign in the autumn of 1946. A recklessly audacious offensive it seems to me now, as all the books were literary, most of them highbrow or near-highbrow. And yet the circumstances of the time, the success of the literary standards set in *Penguin New Writing*, lured forward with promise that would be ludicrous today. My difficulty had not been to find authors or books to suit my ideals, but to get the venture going at all in the face of the bar by the Paper Control, the unlikelihood of the control being relaxed for some time, and the enormous difficulties of staff and materials in which all printers found themselves as accumulating war-born obstacles piled up on one another in the first years of peace. I even sent two small but important books of poetry to New Zealand to be printed by my old friend Denis Glover at his Caxton Press: Laurie Lee's *The Bloom of Candles* and Edith Sitwell's *The Shadow of Cain*.

3

My life in London now became fuller than ever, but I made a point of getting down to Fieldhead for as many week-ends as possible, to talk things over with my mother, and to do some quiet thinking and planning during walks by the river with my mother's large white poodle Chico and a new addition to the household in London, an enchanting golden spaniel with a white muzzle and a white flash on her forehead who was given the name of Carlotta (and called Lottie for short). She was, I think, the sweetest-natured dog I have ever known, and captured all hearts. There was, I fear, a bar sinister somewhere in her ancestry for she had rather shorter legs than a lady of her breed should have developed, but her ears were exceptionally silky and her coat was exceptionally lustrous, points of beauty which made what she lacked in height off the ground of trifling significance. She was, so to speak, the toast of the dogs of SW 3. When, twice a year, she became 'strangely beautiful', her suitors, of all shapes and sizes, assembled from far and wide on the pavement outside the house: Carlotta would appear to them on the first floor balcony, a Juliet fluttering her eyelids at a dozen or so impatiently whining canine Romeos.

My friend Alexis Rassine, the dancer, discovered one day by chance that she was a singer. A Sadler's Wells colleague of his was imitating a prima donna, when suddenly to their astonishment Carlotta cocked her head, then lifted it and produced a remarkable accompaniment to their imitation, emitting a note of the utmost purity, long sustained and without a quaver. From that moment, one had only to act as her tenor for her to join in the duet after a few seconds' rather coy hesitation. Her performances became famous and she was much in demand at parties. In particular, Osbert and Edith Sitwell were fascinated by this gift of hers, and she was frequently invited with me to dinner at 2 Carlyle Square, in order that she should sing to the guests over coffee and brandy. In almost every letter she wrote to me, Edith sent messages. 'Please stroke Carlotta's head from me. What a fancy I have taken to that most sweet dog'. 'I hadn't realized that Carlotta *sang*. But I heard about it from Osbert and David. It is very 1890 of her – I don't think girls do sing much nowadays, do they – I mean as amateurs.' 'Please stroke Carlotta from me, wish her a happy Christmas, with plenty of hunting, and thank her for singing so beautifully at my ghastly supper party.' 'Tell that beautiful (if now somewhat full-figured) young matron who inhabits your house, charming you with the songs the Sirens sang, that I am sorry I hit her, inadvertently, with my bracelet and I hope it won't cause a breach in our friendship.' 'Tell Carlotta I think some of the solos – the arias – from *Wozzeck* would suit her. The girl is a tragedian, in the Grand Operatic manner.' Soon after, however: 'Osbert thinks I am wrong to have recommended *Wozzeck* for Carlotta. He says the girl has a pure melodic line, and ought to keep to *The Bride of Lammermoor*, *The Somnambulist*, and so forth.' 'Tell Carlotta that Tosca is indicated, and should be one of her greatest roles.'

Carlotta and Chico galloped through the grounds of Fieldhead, chasing largely imaginary squirrels and rats, while I wandered round with rather melancholy thoughts oppressing me. For the moment had come to say good-bye to this home that had meant so much to us all in our childhood and youth. It was far too large for my mother, with her crippled thigh and reduced means, to cope with alone, and various plans that were mooted for myself and my sisters to divide it up and live, as it were, in flats there came to nothing. The Red Cross hospital would be closing down, but the W.V.S. was interested in carrying on with the place as a home for disabled old folk. One thing, however, my mother was quite certain about: she would not share her home with an organization any longer. It had been all right, an emergency obligation, while the war was on; but she had lived at Fieldhead too long and loved it too much, to endure having numbers of strange invalids wandering through the flower gardens, orchards and vegetable beds, sitting out by the pavilion, or the lily pool, or down by the river under the wych-elm, indefinitely into the future, in spite of the respect in which she was held and the influence she wielded. She decided to be ruthless, and sell as soon as possible, even though it was the worst time for getting rid of property such as Fieldhead, not really large but large enough to have serious staffing and fuel problems.

So in 1947 we put it into the hands of house agents, and set about looking for a smaller property roughly within a ten-mile radius. Disillusioned though my mother was with the inroads of national political parties into local administration which the 1945 upheaval had brought with it – staunch liberal though she was, she had always believed in the old tradition of unpolitical, unpaid service by those who could afford the time to devote themselves to these local problems – she wanted to keep her ties with various county council committees and other bodies where her work had for so long been appreciated.

Eventually we found a house on the high ground just outside Beaconsfield to the west, which she could run with the help of her devoted housekeeper Maud Deeley. The grim business of sorting through cupboards and drawers and chests in a house that had been lived in continuously for fifty years began. What papers to destroy? What furniture, curtains, carpets to take with us, what to sell? My mother faced all these problems with a slow, steady New England patience, sometimes looking desperate and exhausted, but sustained by her sense of humour and the feeling that life would be easier when the task was done. To move house at any time is a burden, but to have to go through the experience in old age – my mother was over seventy – is especially hard. It is as if one is packing up everything for the grave. She had already done a great deal of work on family letters and diaries (from which I was to benefit many years later when I came to explore the family past for my book *Ancestors and Friends*), but odd, and often rather poignant mementoes of my father's athletic, political, and writing life would continually turn up: old rowing photographs, medals, cuttings about famous regattas, drafts for political speeches, illuminated addresses of thanks, menu cards of notable *Punch* dinners, and bundles of clippings of poems and articles. And then there were the memorials of the childhood of my sisters and myself: lockets of hair, laboriously written fair copies of compositions produced before we had even reached our teens, the earliest school reports, girl guide badges, photographs of amateur theatricals in which we had taken part, and programmes of afternoon entertainments we had put on ourselves; all preserved by our parents with a fond and amused piety. Many went into the wastepaper basket, only those with the rarest flavour were preserved. And then, the forgotten, stuffed-away toys, albums, christening presents going back several generations, dog-collars, treasures of every sort fit only, for the most part, for Autolycus's tray. In dismantling the defences of the wine cellar, which had pretended to be our air-raid shelter during the war, my mother discovered in the remotest recesses an overlooked bottle of Château Margaux 1870. Alas, its contents, unlike its label, did not conjure up the 'fine dew, sweet yet tart', that glistened on the boy Rimbaud's brow as he wandered through the war-ravaged French countryside that year; they were pretty well undrinkable.

Curiously enough it was the hidden corners of the garden that moved me with the sadness of parting rather than the formal flower beds, the ornamental centres of urn, bird-bath and sundial set in their expanse of green cropped lawns and paved rose enclosures, the long vistas of pergola dripping their purple clematis, pink rosebuds and never-ripening vine clusters. I went down and talked to the old head gardener, Mr Goodman, in his pungently smelling garden shed that was also an apple store, and encouraged him to tell me of his boyhood days in the valley. I crept up the wrong side of the bank at the end of the garden, planted with poplars, from which I had, with my chums, busily noted engine numbers as they thundered across the railway bridge in my childhood, and tried to recapture a long lost magic and dreams of being an engine-driver. I sniffed for the last time the peculiar, mixed, musty smell of the long boathouse, and let my fingers slide over the punts, canoes, skiffs and slim rowing craft I should never see again. I looked up to see the martins speeding out of their nests in the rafters beside the blades of the closely-ranked oars, as I remembered them doing for years and years into the past. I opened the kennel gates that had once housed Great Danes, St. Bernards and mastiffs and had then been made into 'houses' for my sisters, and tried to find some fragment in the scattered straw and broken boxes that would bring those days back in a vivid flash of memory. I lingered in the now rankly overgrown dogs' cemetery, re-reading the engraved names of animal friends just remembered from earliest childhood, and others buried before I was born and part of my sisters' mythology, and trying to put names to those 'sad little hummocks in the ground',[1] which had never received a stone.

The lilac and laburnum came into flower in the shrubberies in front of the house. Gradually the bookshelves in the library were emptied of their gold-lettered sets of famous authors, leaving a dusty, bookless vacancy behind them. The ancient apple trees were in pink and white blossom once more, the walnut trees putting out their tender leaves, but we should not crop the fruit. My mother dug up a few plants especially precious to her, and put them in boxes, ready for the van. Yes, the time had come and we must be off.

Rosamond wrote: 'I went over to Fieldhead last night and looked my last on the garden with feelings indescribable.'

The departure from Fieldhead was the cause of almost the only poem I wrote in those years, 'The House', which I described as an 'Eclogue for the Air, on themes suggested by living in an age of transition'. It was commissioned by Robert Gittings at the BBC, as one of a series of long, semi-dramatic poems by living poets. My life was too fully absorbed again in hunting for other authors and looking after their work, as it had been in the early days of the Hogarth Press, for me to be able to listen more than fitfully to the small voice of my own muse.

4

One event of the winter of 1946–7 brought the contrast between past and present into sharp focus: Christopher Isherwood's first visit to England since he had left with Wystan Auden almost exactly eight years before. It made me, and I think his

[1] *The Whispering Gallery*, 122–3.

other friends, suddenly see the distance we had travelled since before the war, in certain experiences that had perhaps matured us and others that had undoubtedly impoverished us.

Christopher wrote from Santa Monica in December, announcing his coming visit towards the end of January, and asking if he could stay with me for a couple of nights before going up to Cheshire to see his mother at their old family home. He added: 'I'm a Yank now – but don't be alarmed – you'd never know it.' Perhaps he didn't realize that his accent and some of his mannerisms had changed as much as we noticed at once. These changes did not, however, show themselves continuously: I had the impression, talking to him during the three months of his visit, that he was, in spirit, being pulled to and fro across the Atlantic all the time.

In his article in the 'Coming to London' series, published in The *London Magazine* some years later, he writes of his arrival at my house the night he landed: 'There a welcome awaited me that I shall never forget. Looking around me at the faces of my old friends, I discovered a happy paradox – namely that, while England seemed fascinatingly strange, my friends and our friendship seemed to be essentially what they had always been, despite the long separation. That was what was to make my visit so wonderful and memorable.'

Christopher was excited, during those two days, a little confused by the wartime changes he had already noticed, and nervous about the way he would be received. We soon, I think, put him at his ease: as many of his old friends as could be mustered to meet him in person, and others who were on the telephone almost at once. None of us had joined the scapegoat chase in which politicians and journalists who had never known them had tried to vilify him and Auden as 'escapers'. We had been sorry not to have him with us during the weird, sometimes apocalyptic and frightening experiences we had been through; we had been a little sceptical, while the bombs fell, of his mystical exercises in Yoga temples; we were immensely glad to have him back, even in this slightly transmogrified form. We noted that the face, tanned by the Californian sun, was a little more lined; but that the deep-set eyes, though opened wide in respectful amazement or horror at the tales we had to tell, would twinkle with the same old impish appreciation of anything comical or fantastic. We noted that his favourite talk was of Hollywood and movie stars; and we wondered sometimes whether he didn't in fact see us as characters in a film – an American film of little old England heroically carrying on through all trials and tribulations.

Christopher's sharp observation of the altered London he encountered made us see ourselves more objectively. We realized we had become shabby and rather careless of appearances in our battered surroundings. That we had become crushed as civilians to accept the ordering about of officialdom. That we had become obsessively queue-forming, and were priggishly proud of it.

That winter was in any case worse than anything that had been experienced since the first winters of the war – and it was worse than that. It was also worse because we were no longer sustained by the sense of shared danger in the face of an enemy we were determined to destroy. The adrenalin was no longer being pumped into our veins. We endured with misery and loathing the continual fuel cuts, the rooms private and public in which we shivered in our exhausted overcoats, while the snow blizzards swept through the country again and yet again. Were there to be no fruits of victory? The rationing cards and coupons that still had to be presented for almost everything from eggs to minute pieces of scraggy Argentine meat, from petrol to bed-linen and 'economy' suits, seemed far more squalid and unjust than during the war when we knew at least what they represented in the mortal perils of ships and sailors.

Worse still, to my increasingly disillusioned eye, was the kind of mean puritanism that the newly triumphant Labour MPs and their officials appeared to have decided was the proper wear of the day. Too many of them seemed to think there was a virtue in austerity and shabbiness, in controls and restrictions; to delight in cutting one off from foreign travel, especially in view of the assumption that it was only the parasitic and un-patriotic rich who would want to spend their money in the contaminated countries beyond the English Channel. In *Edwin Drood* when the fatuous auctioneer who became mayor of Cloisterham, Mr Sapsea, 'had once declared anything to be un-English, he considered that thing everlastingly sunk in the bottomless pit'. Mr Sapsea seemed to be having too much say in our national affairs. It was perfectly obvious that, owing to the fact that we had drawn so heavily on our national resources and reserves to win the war, and that the Truman administration in Washington had cut off lend-lease, we were going to have to count our pennies pretty carefully for some years; but one couldn't help feeling sometimes that this awkward situation was a source of satisfaction rather than regret to our new rulers, and that it was being unnecessarily protracted by muddle and bungling. Above all, if one had felt, as I had, that the national unity of the war was a deeply moving experience, the revival of crude class hostility and demogogy, in the midst of the building of a welfare state that had been agreed by all under Churchill's wartime administration, was just plain nasty. And that, in spite of my sincere admiration for many of the things the Labour Party was trying to do, and my kindly respect for many of the leaders, such as John Strachey. That spirit of generous hope and confidence, which had seemed to me to be abroad immediately after the peace in Europe, was fading away, and its place, I could not help feeling, was being taken by a spirit of envy and petty self-righteousness.

Christopher retired, after a few days of happy reunion with his friends, to the rigours of Wyberslegh Hall in Cheshire. 'I was never meant for these latitudes,' he cried in his first letter to me, 'and I huddle miserably in front of a blue gas-fire. London seems almost as remote as America. If only we lived there still! . . . I spend most of the time reading my old diaries (goodness what energy I had in those days! It's a marvel I'm not impotent) and washing dishes. My mother hasn't changed a bit. She does all the cooking. But Nanny is very, very old. . . .' And in the next: 'Being up here is like a steamship journey. You just screw down the porthole and weather it out. I have all my letters, photographs and books to amuse me. Turning over the pages of *Evil Was Abroad* I wished so much you'd write another novel. Will you? Please!' Later on he went down to Cheltenham to stay with his old friend Olive Mangeot and with the original of Sally Bowles. He tried to get over to Stratford to see my sister Beatrix who was that season playing leading lady in an astonishing assortment of parts,[1] and to whom he had long been deeply attached, but swirling floods cut them off from one another.

Before he left in mid-April, he came down for a final party at my house, at which I managed to gather many friends with whom he had not yet been re-united, and many others, younger people who were eager to meet the legendary 'Herr Issyvoo'. I had introduced him in particular to John Minton and Keith Vaughan, and their paintings, some of which he had already seen in reproduction in *Penguin New Writing* during the war. He became a keen fan of Keith, and carried off with him several samples of his work, which he intended to show to everyone in California. And he promised to act as an unofficial talent scout in America for my new publishing firm, a promise he never forgot, as many letters of tip-off advice (and warning) about the younger generation of American writers witness.

On arrival in New York, he wrote: 'Just to let you know that I arrived on Friday, after a bugger of a voyage, with strong head-gales. I avoided being sick by doggedly over-eating and dosing myself with whisky. We were all vaccinated, which made me a bit sick after landing but I'm fine now. . . . In a few days I hope to start driving the plough over the terrain for my new novel. I have terrible stage-fright about this, but the only thing is to make a start. At all costs, I'm resolved this time, not to be funny. I don't care how dreary and boring it is, as long as it isn't the kind of book anybody could possibly read for pleasure on a train. People resent being amused more than anything, I've decided.'

The World in the Evening was interrupted by his journey to South America and the writing of *The Condor and the Cows*, and seven years passed before it appeared in England.

---

[1] These included Viola, Portia, Isabella, The Nurse in *Romeo and Juliet* and The Duchess of Gloucester in *Richard III*.

5

With the nine books I had published in the autumn of 1946, and with the others I had signed up at about the same time, I had at least made a blue-print for the future pattern of my publishing venture. I now had to consider very carefully how to go about laying down more solid foundations. I had gobbled up what had been lying about for my picking in the aftermath of my career with the Hogarth Press. And I had started The Chiltern Library as a medium for the more highbrow reprints which particularly interested me, and which seemed to be in demand. Michael Swan undertook to look after the Henry James reprints, to prepare the selection of stories, to write all the introductions to these selections and to write the forewords to the novels which were to have James's own introductions as published in the definitive New York edition. Rosamond agreed to advise on the reprints of Mrs Gaskell, each volume of which was to have an introduction by a different expert, including an introduction of her own to the unfinished masterpiece *Wives and Daughters*. Taking advice from William Plomer, I decided to look after the Melville reprints myself. At the same time I started the poetry side of The Chiltern Library with an anthology of the poems Shelley had written in Italy. All this was immense fun.

Now I had to lay my snares beyond what I had already taken on, for (1) the new British writers, (2) the new writers in Europe, and (3) the new American writers. I began to believe that my 'nose' would lead me to where they were lurking in the coverts.

It was not only literature in the shape of fiction and poetry I envisaged, but new writers of travel books, autobiographies, biographical criticism, and experts on the theatre, the opera and the ballet. In fact I wanted the list of John Lehmann Limited to look, in some ways, not unlike one of the recent copies of *Penguin New Writing*, with all the arts given their place. Novels cannot be commissioned: you can only encourage the

c

authors to carry on. Commissioning, however, is more or less essential to those other books that need research and illustrations. I therefore urged Norman Marshall to write what turned out to be one of the most successful books we ever published, *The Other Theatre*, an account of the avant-garde theatre movements in England since the end of the first world war. Norman had been in most of the experiments in one form or another and had made his name as director of the famous Gate Theatre from 1934 until it was destroyed during the air-raids. Back from the wars, he threw himself with enthusiasm into the writing of this neglected piece of history, which he accomplished with thorough scholarship and a keen critical appreciation. I think many people were surprised to find how many experimental theatre groups had existed between the wars, how immensely varied and lively this endeavour had been; and I am sure the book had an important influence when avant-garde theatre began to be revived.

Norman's book was the first of a number of books I published about plays and actors. Meanwhile I encouraged William Chappell who had written so well for *New Writing* while he was in the army, and had invented the grotesque figure of 'Carmen Miranda's Aunty' to entertain the troops, to write the book about ballet he obviously had in him. Billy had had an astonishingly varied experience, as dancing partner of famous ballerinas from Karsavina to Margot Fonteyn, as designer of scenery and costume to many of the earliest native ballets in this country in the days before the Sadler's Wells had been recognized as a national cultural asset, and as a witness of all the difficult beginnings of which that was the triumphant culmination. *Studies in Ballet*, when it was ready, was less history than what in fact its title indicated, a series of essays on the art of ballet, on the dancer's physique, and on the problems of the association of music, plastic design and choreography; but it was valuable on both counts, was written in an uniquely personal style and had the considerable advantage of being illustrated not only with precious photographs from Billy's archives but also with his own imaginative line drawings.

My friend Eric Walter White, now genial and devoted assistant secretary of the Arts Council, had, in my earliest Hogarth days, written a short but remarkable book called *Stravinsky's Sacrifice to Apollo*. He now undertook to write a much longer critical study of the composer's developments and changes of style, which was published, also by the end of 1947, simply as *Stravinsky*.

Finally, in this department, I suggested to Alan Ross, some of whose earliest poems I had published in *New Writing* while he was serving in the navy, that he and John Minton should go off to Corsica together and write a travel book, illustrated by John. This was in many ways the most ambitious of my early projects for a single book, for it was to be an extremely lavish, anti-austerity production. Without the magnificent facilities put at my disposal by Purnell, I could not, of course, have attempted it. *Time Was Away*, more a poet's notebook on holiday than a conventional travel book, is a very beautiful book, with its lavish black-and-white and four-colour illustrations, an evocatively sultry and arcadian jacket by John, and its elegantly original typography and spine-design by Keith Vaughan. It is also now a rare and much sought after book.

6

I had for some time been feeling that the formula of *New Writing and Daylight* was wearing a little thin, and that something new was needed. I have always disliked, and been aware of the danger of carrying on with one formula too long, of letting things slip into a rut. In complete contrast to this, Barbara Cooper hated any kind of change, and I think she was shocked and deeply disappointed when I announced that I was going to kill NWD and start a new book-magazine in its place.

If *Time Was Away* had been planned as a book to startle with beautiful design and brilliant colour in the drab hour through which we were passing, *Orpheus* was to be even more an out-and-out anti-austerity production. I handed over the designing in its entirety to Keith Vaughan. He was to be responsible not

merely for the three-colour jacket and the decoration of the
whole cover, including the spine, but also for the general interior
decoration in the form of black-and-white almost abstract tail-
pieces to go wherever there was space at the end of a contribution. The result, I think, was exceptionally beautiful. When I
opened the first advance copy to reach me from the works, I
experienced a thrill of pleasure; a thrill that is still renewed
today, whenever I take the volume out of the shelf. And at this
point I must pay tribute to the work Keith did for my publishing house in the early years as a transformer of what can so
easily remain the plain informative utility of the spine of a
book   that is, what is seen when the jacket is taken off and it is
put into the shelf – but in his hands became an enchanting
series of imaginative inventions. Set side by side in a long row
they are poems: but when, alas, except in a publisher's library,
are they set side by side? Keith Vaughan has since become so
famous as a painter that his early applied work, as jacket and
cover designer and illustrator of a number of books for my
publishing house, which include the first volume of *Orpheus*, and
P. H. Newby's story for boys, *The Spirit of Jem*, is largely forgotten. One exception, much sought after now by connoisseurs,
is the edition I gave him to design a year later, of Rimbaud's
Une Saison en Enfer, with the French on one side of the page and
Norman Cameron's English version on the other. The book was
exquisitely produced by James Shand at the Shenval Press, and
Keith's colour lithographs are, not in my opinion alone, masterpieces.

The second volume of *Orpheus* I gave to John Minton, with the
same freedom of over-all design, except that I kept the Vaughan
cover. I gave him my copy of Pine's 1733 edition of Horace,
with its engraved decorations of the utmost classical refinement,
and asked him, not of course to follow them, but to let himself,
if possible, be inspired by them as a starting point. The result
surpassed my expectations: a series of tail-pieces in which classical motifs were married to John's romantic lyrical fantasy.

My idea was that *Orpheus*, which I had originally thought of
calling *The Nine*, should be a magazine of *all* the arts; an expan-
sion of the idea that had been developed in *Penguin New Writing*,
in the later years of the war, beyond the limits that a paperback

was held to at that time, and without the element of topical
semi-reportage that had been so popular when its readers were
scattered over all the continents and all the oceans and were
looking for some common denominator of spiritual experience.
'There are admirable magazines devoted to literature, or drama,
or music separately,' I wrote in my Introduction. 'There should
be more when they can all come together in a *Festspiel* of the
printed page, proclaiming their kinship by proof and lighting
one another with interlinked fires.' Deep down, I think, I still
hankered after the equivalent in a magazine of what the ballet
had achieved under Diaghileff: the marriage of several arts in
one coherent creation – music, dancing, decoration, painting,
even spoken poetry. Only of course a magazine could never be
as unified as a ballet or theatrical production (I am thinking as
I write of Karolos Koun's magical production of *The Birds*),
and could only *suggest* the coming together of the arts by in-
direct means. Poems could be printed, pictures could be reproduced and paper decorated, but music and theatre and dancing
could only be commented on critically.

Nevertheless, even this limited ideal, even this Dionysian
illusion seemed to be worth attempting, and celebrating, a little
defiantly, in the face of the prose of our age. 'The deep need
today,' I wrote in the concluding paragraph of my Introduction, 'is to assert the lyrical and imaginative spirit against
materialism and the pseudo-sciences. This is not new, for it is
what Shelley and the other great creative minds of his time were
proclaiming one hundred and fifty years ago, but it is even more
urgent in our own lives upon which the same dangers can act
so much more frightfully and more swiftly. Nor is it new that
it should be equally urgent to assert the rights and dignities of
the individual human being against the pretensions of the state.
It is one of the oldest of wars, but the enemy has returned to the
offensive armed with far greater powers than the spies of
the Inquisition ever knew, and the encroaching sahara of his
paperasserie is far vaster and more chokingly arid.'

Bunin – Seferis – Elytis – Supervielle – Queneau: contribu-
tions from these European authors, together with an article by
Bernard Denvir on modern French tapestries, another by John
Fleming on the Roman artist Renzo Vespignani, and a third

by Harold Acton on modern painting in Mexico justified the claims I had made that *Orpheus* would 'know no national boundaries, but will everywhere choose what is visionary rather than what is merely realistic, what rejects the dogmas and looks at truth every day with fresh eyes.' The programme did not, however, find favour in Moscow, where literature and art were groaning at that moment in the deepest Stalinist darkness. A certain Comrade Zenkevitch, writing in *Soviet Literature*, threw a good bucketful of abusive words at *Orpheus*. He called it artificial, reactionary, useless, epigonic, decadent, stale, stilted, a hopeless void, just a phantom, and a plateful of gilded nuts. It was exhilarating to have hit the target so exactly, particularly as a fellow-crusader against the decaying culture of the west, Comrade Elistratova, was weighing in against *Horizon* in the same number, and unmasking the hideous face of American imperialism behind it.

The gilded nuts did not last beyond a second helping. The press notices of *Orpheus* were good, some very good indeed, and private comment was enthusiastic; but the sales did not seem to me to justify the heavy expense involved. If I had been personally rich, and had had no other irons in the fire, I might well have devoted myself to it; but my decision to abandon it after the second number, albeit with a heavy heart, was also influenced by changes that were taking place in the world of books as a whole and in the fortunes in particular of my own publishing venture.

7

By the middle of 1947 I became aware that dangers were looming ahead. I had known too well the publishing conditions of the 'thirties not to sense a change of wind early on. The fuel crisis of the long winter, the breakdowns in production at the factories which were still short of labour, meant that one had to space out the publication of books whose profitability had been calculated in a more concentrated form. At the same time the conditions of book-selling, far too good to be true during the war, began to change back to normal. The returning soldiers were putting money aside to buy new homes, new equipment for living, though leisure had not yet been exploited by mass travel and television. No longer was it possible to calculate that an edition of 5,000 to 10,000 of a new book of any merit whatsoever would sell out on publication – or within a few weeks. No longer could one reckon on those urgent telephone calls from big wholesalers and libraries: 'Can you make our order 5,000 instead of 2,000?' The empires were breaking up. Hard, and harder work in selling lay ahead. And stocks would have to be held longer. That meant money, capital locked up.

I had embarked on an ambitious programme in 1946, partly because I felt the conditions to be favourable, partly because I knew that to take full advantage of my literary position I must move fast. Authors cannot be kept waiting for long, however loyal or grateful they may feel to one personally. To a certain extent my advantage was mean: with no back list to keep in print like the big established publishers, I had been given the chance to exploit a fairly large allowance of paper to bring classics back into circulation. Seeing, however, how the dice were loaded against me in other ways, I did not feel oppressed by guilt about this; particularly as I noticed no striking impatience among the relevant publishers to do anything about the authors I was interested in.

The programme, then, was building up; but my capital, in the changing situation, was running out. Between the wars, an ambitious new publisher had once observed that in order to start a publishing house one needed £100,000 – and that would only serve to establish one's imprint in the first five years. With my Hogarth Press background, I had always considered this a bit of an exaggeration; but I now saw, only too clearly, that even so the £10,000 odd I had mustered was far too little. What was I to do? I considered that I had made all the demands that were fair on family and friends. The problem was urgent: to slow up my plans even more than the fuel crisis had made necessary might risk the whole grand design. I had never dealt with capital finance problems before in so isolated a position, and I passed many anxious hours of reflection, many sleepless dawns in trying to decide on the best course. I realized in the end that I was, in a sense, at the mercy of Purnell, however unwilling they might be to put the screw on: my paper came from there, and I had no quota right to a single ounce of it. If I found new backers from elsewhere, how should I answer their reproaches if Purnell for their own good reasons, suddenly cut down on the paper they allowed me? My room to manoeuvre was small, but if I went to the directors now, at least I was in a stronger position than I had been eighteen months before. The publishing house was *there*, it had established its character, it had had its successes and its honours. I had manufactured editions of several of my books – my anthology of *French Stories from New Writing* for instance – for America. Three of my books had been chosen for the National Book Exhibition to be held in 1948. The Denyse Clairouin Prize had been awarded to Rosamond for her translation of Jacques Lemarchand's short novel *Geneviève* which I had brought out in the summer. Recommendations from the Book Society were coming in fast, accolades that inspired respect if not necessarily sales. All these were strong arguments I could use in order to be left in full control of editorial and artistic policy. I decided – I should really write 'it was decided for me' – to swallow the bitter pill.

I found that Clifford Gibbs was very willing to re-open negotiations. He acted, during the autumn months of 1947, as liaison between myself and Wilfred Harvey, and very soon brought me the news that Harvey was indeed still interested in backing the firm with the full resources of Purnell, but only on the terms which had caused the collapse of our discussions at the beginning: 100 per cent. financial control. This was no surprise to me, and I did not, could not object. The agreement that was finally worked out allowed me to pay my relations, my mother, my sister, my brother-in-law, in full for the money they had so bravely put up. That at least was a tremendous load off my mind. It allowed me to remain as managing director on a fixed salary, and to engage Rosamond as a salaried reader. Two good advantages. Another advantage was that it allowed me still to have one or two special books produced from time to time outside the Purnell group – books that would only be a nuisance in a factory designed for straightforward, large-scale operations.

I could now go full-steam ahead with my plans for extending The Chiltern Library, and for founding two other libraries, or series. The first was to be called The Library of Art and Travel, and was to consist of reprints of notable books, long unobtainable, as elegantly produced as possible, such as Robert Byron's *The Station*, Geoffrey Gorer's *Africa Dances*, and Sacheverell Sitwell's *The Gothick North*. The other, The Holiday Library, was also to consist of reprints, but of between-the-wars fiction and biography in a format rather similar to that which had made The Travellers' Library and The Phoenix Library so popular in the 'twenties and 'thirties.

I am inclined to think that The Holiday Library was my great mistake. Purnell were very keen to acquire, through me, as many copyrights as possible, and I let my judgment be swayed too easily by their enthusiasm. The publishers were very much more reluctant to let these titles go, and in many cases I only acquired a licence limited to a short term of years. There was, I believe, nothing much wrong with the choice: the first dozen volumes included Anthony Powell's *From a View to a Death*, Edith Sitwell's *I Live Under a Black Sun*, Rose Macaulay's *Going Abroad* and Rosamond's *A Note in Music*. Nor was there anything wrong with the look of the books: they were extremely pretty, both inside and outside, and I considered the design one of Keith Vaughan's outstanding successes. Unfortunately, however, there was something wrong with the whole conception – as a money-making proposition. Even three years before I think they would have sold out; but as things gradually returned to normal in the publishing world, it became clearer and clearer that the time was over for such reprints, at a price of 6s. instead of the 'new' price of a novel at 8s. 6d. or 10s. 6d. The future was with the paper-back revolution. Too much of the capital sunk in The Holiday Library was to remain locked up.

The prospect ahead of me seemed full of exciting possibilities. Perhaps, as the New Year of 1948 dawned with its rosy hopes, I was a little too ready to ignore the fact that the powerful tanker which had re-fuelled me in mid-air had also hooked me.

It was the end of the beginning. But a small voice somewhere inside me could sometimes be heard whispering: 'Is it also the beginning of the end?'

8

I have already described, in *I Am My Brother*, the excitement of my first post-war visit to Paris in September 1945. Ever since, I had dreamed of following this up with visits to the countries beyond the Rhine that I had come to know so well before the war, especially Austria, which had for so long been a second home to me. In immediate post-war conditions, the idea seemed far harder to realize, more exciting but much more alarming also. What would Vienna and Prague look like after the bombardments and the battles? How many of my former friends should I find alive, and what would be their attitude towards me? Would they have become embittered by all the anti-English propaganda they had been forced to swallow by the Nazis, and by the possible sufferings they had endured at our hands? Or would they greet me as a long-lost friend whose return they had steadfastly hoped for through all the silence? I dreaded, yet longed to know.

Luck favoured me in a remarkable way. It seemed that *Penguin New Writing* had followed the troops into the occupied countries, and the British Council decided that I was just the chap, especially with my knowledge of central and south-European Europe, to go and lecture for them in the centres they had already set up in the main cities. As a matter of fact, the first visit, to Czechoslovakia, came as much from the Czechs themselves as from the British Council. With the founding of *Daylight* during the war,[1] I had become very closely associated with the Czech intellectuals who were in exile in England, and had made a particular friend of one of them, Jiři Mucha, the son of the famous *art nouveau* artist. Jiři himself, with several of the others,

[1] *I Am My Brother*, 156–9.

had already returned to Prague, and got to work at once to engineer an official invitation. It came in the late summer, and I set off in mid-November in an uncomfortable, semi-converted bomber, with a contract from a Czech publisher for an anthology of stories from *New Writing* in my pocket.

As we sank beneath the mother-of-pearl cloud sea, out of the sunlight, and saw at last the snow-sprinkled forests of Bohemia below us, a Czech in the seat next to me peered out tensely. His eyes filled with tears: it was six years, he told me, since he had seen his homeland. I was met by Jiři and some other Czech friends who had returned a few months or weeks before, and that evening I told them how moved I had been by the little episode. To my surprise they laughed scornfully, and patted me pityingly on the back. 'Now get this clear,' they said. 'He was weeping for sorrow, not joy. *We* know: we were outside the prison ourselves not so long ago.' They were not very serious, and in the general atmosphere of festivity that evening, during which they displayed anything but the furtive habits of those who live in police states, it was not very easy to take them seriously. But I had been gently warned, and I kept my eyes and ears open.

My first shock of pleasure was to find that Prague, like Paris, had been practically unharmed by the war. The allied bombers had done some efficiently destructive work in the great industrial centres, Brno, Pilsen and Kolin; but in Prague the main damage seemed to be confined to the gutted town hall where the Germans had put up a desperate last fight, and a tall building in the Wenceslas Place had been ripped open by a random American bomb. It was more than I had dared to hope. At night the city was illuminated for an international students' congress, and as one rattled down the hill in the tram (with about fifty people standing – and always room for half a dozen more) all the famous domes and towers glowed against the night sky. The baroque statues on the Charles Bridge were mirrored darkly in the trembling water. The noble conglomeration of palaces and churches that form the Hradshin glittered under the arc-lamps as enchantedly as Buckingham Palace on VE night. I remembered the poems in celebration of the beauty of Prague, written by the great modern poet, Vitezslav Nezval, – which I had published in translation in *Daylight*, – and whom I was now to meet. And I thought to myself: the evil dreams and murderers have gone, and the rightful owners are back:

> The toasts are raised, the dancing shakes the floor,
> And that tall stranger with the eyes of ice –
> Look round, and laugh, for he is there no more
> To drain the tankard with the skull device . . .

This impression of the all-smiles ending to the grim story, of living happily ever after, was increased when I went to a big reception and was able to meet Jan Masaryk again, home at last in the Republic his father had created. He was his characteristic cheerful, joking self, but I thought he looked unusually care-worn.

Then the doubts began. The euphoric mood of my arrival faded, to give place to a more anxious, uncertain assessment. I began to notice that too often there was a green look about people's faces, and their clothes were appallingly threadbare. I learned that fats, vegetables and many other foodstuffs were terribly scarce, real coffee and tea and chocolate almost unknown. The gas only came on two or three times a day, just strong enough to cook a meal, but not to have a hot bath. Transport had broken down. Not enough lorries, not enough rubber, not enough petrol; rolling stock smashed in the railway sidings, bridges blown up and lying (as I saw with my own eyes) in jagged chunks in the valleys and streams. All this was understandable enough. But there was something worse.

The Red Army was leaving. Or so they said. The joke in Prague was that they left in uniform, with bands playing, at one gate, and came back stealthily, in civvies, at another. One or two people I met muttered despairingly: Why, why did the allies allow the Russians to occupy Prague? With the Red Army had come the indoctrinated Czech communists who had spent the years of exile in Moscow. They were powerful, strongly favoured by the Russians, in spite of the coalition National Front government that seemed so democratic and amicable on the surface. They were deeply suspicious of the *other* Czechs, such as my friend Jiří Mucha, who had spent the war fighting with the allies in the west. Totalitarianism is a disease that lurks in the bloodstream when the spots have gone. After nearly seven years of subjection to the Nazis, one may find it easier, and even natural, to substitute one kind of police control for another rather than breathe the difficult air of democratic freedom. Gradually, I found that some Czechs, of a fine record untainted by any form of collaboration, still looked over their shoulders to make sure that no one else could hear when expressing criticism of the way things were going. Perhaps it was a hangover from the days of the Gestapo: perhaps *not*.

Then there was the case of the weekly journal *Obzory*, run by Pavel Tigrid, an intelligent young Czech who had worked with the government in exile in London. Ostensibly, there was complete press freedom in liberated Czechoslovakia, each party being allowed to publish its own papers without interference. *Obzory* was one of the papers sponsored by the popular Catholic People's Party. I had a particular interest in it, not only because I had known the editor for some years, but also because he wanted to publish one of my lectures. Tigrid had been outspoken in his criticism of the new political set-up in his country and had commented unfavourably on the behaviour of the Red Army. Everyone admired his courage, *Obzory* was popular and its circulation increasing. By the time I was leaving, however, it was clear that its policy was the subject of furious criticism within the government, and that influential totalitarian-minded members of the bureaucracy were trying to find a way to stifle it. A warning shot was fired on the Prague radio, with an announcement that the authorities were considering its suppression, though there was no law that would in fact permit this.

What left an even nastier taste in the mouth was a story I heard in the British Embassy where my old friend Philip Nichols, brother of the poet, was doing his best to further British interests in a situation which he obviously considered extremely tricky. A guest at luncheon talked of the case of a certain count, a young man belonging to the old aristocracy, of partly German origin, who had been flung into prison on charges of collaboration. I was assured that these charges were entirely trumped up, and he had never been brought to trial. The real reason, my informant asserted, was that the communists wanted to confiscate his estate, which they thought would make an ideal rest-home for writers. I discussed this story with several non-communist writers, and found that they knew it and were deeply shocked. It is important to remember that this was before the communists actually took over the republic lock, stock and barrel, and before Masaryk's tragic suicide when he saw that he had been cheated of all that he had worked for.

The story had a disagreeable if slightly ludicrous sequel. I was asked if I would like to be taken to the castle, and refused. A couple of mornings later I was visited in my hotel by a woman of cold and sneering aspect. After a certain amount of beating about the bush, she revealed that her mission was to persuade me to visit the castle after all. My refusal, she explained unsmilingly, might be misinterpreted. If I didn't. . . . She astonished me so much that I was at first tongue-tied. I could not imagine what she, or those who sent her, thought they could do to an Englishman and an officially invited guest. Then I pulled myself together and told her to go away. I thought a great deal about the incident. It seemed to me a very bad omen.

I flew to Bratislava very soon after reaching Prague. There, even more than in the west of the republic, my first impression was that Russian influence was far stronger than British or American. I had been warned by Jiři that the trauma of Munich had not yet been overcome; and I remembered Beneš's words during the war about the great Russian brothers, friends to all the Slavs in their tribulations. When flags were out in Slovakia, in nine cases out of ten they were the Russian and Czechoslovak flags alone. From shop-windows still decorated for the liberation (and for want of goods to put in them) huge portraits of Beneš and Stalin stared out at me – not of Churchill or Attlee, not of Roosevelt or Truman. But the further I scratched below the surface, the more evidence I came on that, so far from having rejected us, these people were keener than ever to be our friends.

In Brno and Bratislava I was lecturing on the European idea in English literature during the previous ten years. Not a subject, I realized, for everyone; and I spoke in English. The arrangements had been hurried, owing to a change of date. We expected quite small audiences, but in fact the halls were filled to overflowing. I did not flatter myself that more than a few people in my audiences followed what I said at all closely. I soon understood that the applause that greeted the lectures simply came from their happiness at hearing an Englishman speak to them at last in the flesh, after the long separation. And I was moved to discover that everywhere there was an enormous interest in everything Anglo-Saxon, and a great keenness to learn English. My impression was confirmed by Martin Blake, who had recently arrived to direct the British Council, and by the gentle poet Edwin Muir who headed the newly formed British Institute. If I were asked to name the major responsibility for this state of affairs, I would say unhesitatingly: the BBC European Service.

In Slovakia, however, the shock of the arrival of the liberating Russian troops had been much greater (or so it seemed to me) and this had been another reason for revulsion towards the western allies. From the Russians' point of view it was unfortunate that the first Red soldiers to arrive had been Malinowski's armies, poor in quality and far weaker in discipline than, for instance, Zhukov's armies. Some of the stories were very funny, others horrifying; but the burden of the complaints I heard over and over again was that the soldiers had seemed incapable of distinguishing between friend or foe, and that the standards of living they found – even after five years of war – had simply gone to their heads. Pillage, rape and wrist-watches: I had already heard the same stories about the Red Army's behaviour in *enemy* Germany.

I had often spent week-ends in Bratislava when I was living in Vienna, and knew it well. I went up to where I could look along the Danube into Austria. There, in the haze, was the city I longed most to visit again. I felt a terrible pang of nostalgia. But directly before my eyes was an astonishing sight that drew me sharply back to the realities of the present. Some rough pontoons had been thrown across the river in place of the shattered bridge, and there, lumbering slowly over, with what seemed an infinite patience, was straggling column after column of Russian troops, fur-capped and dishevelled, with their carts and camp-followers. I might, I suddenly thought, have been watching the hordes of Genghiz Khan or Tamburlaine. Asia had at last broken through, where nearly three hundred years before Prince Eugen had held the Turks at bay and rescued the western civilization to which Austria and Bohemia truly belonged.

Vision and fantasies of a November afternoon in 1945 . . . but the more I talked with the Czechs, the more certain I became that the Russians were not popular except with the dedicated Communists. One evening at dinner I met an industrialist, director of one of the biggest concerns that had been obliged to work for the Nazi war machine. He spoke gloomily of the future, and expressed his fear that another war was brewing. 'And who will you support in that war, if you can choose freely?' I asked him. 'England, of course,' he replied with a quiet smile. 'But why do you say "of course"?' 'Well, your country hasn't lost a war for about three hundred years, has it?'

This man, like many other Czechs, deplored the orgy of assassination and imprisonment without trial that had swept over the republic at the moment of liberation, and was convinced that many innocent people had suffered, especially among the Sudeten Germans. 'But you must remember,' he said, 'that our people had justification for their hatred of these Germans. The Nazis always gave them priority of all good things in the shops, and they took the lead in torturing Czech patriots in the prisons and concentration camps.'

Some years later, when the last of the frail bastions of genuine democracy had collapsed in Czechoslovakia, I met one of the innocent people, a prince of the old aristocracy, at an international gathering of writers in Venice. He had been flung into prison and vilely treated, merely for the accident of birth, though he lived to tell the tale in freedom. I questioned him about his experiences, and he said: 'You may be surprised to hear me say it, but I came out of prison more convinced of the worth of human nature than when I went in. Whatever the cruelties we endured at the hands of our gaolers and on the instructions of their political bosses, the prisoners themselves were wonderful. They were from all walks of life, and it was the poorest and simplest who showed the greatest kindness to one another – and to me.'

9

It was two years before I was able to visit Vienna again. Meanwhile, as soon as peace in Europe was declared, I had been able to get in touch with my friends who still remained in Austria; above all, with my friend Toni, who had been my secretary and chauffeur in the old days, and his family.

The first letters were full of excitement and relief. He was alive – we were both alive – and he now had a little boy who had been born to him and the art student, Gretl, whom he had married at the beginning of the war. They had lived all the time in my old flat in the Invalidenstrasse, right up to the last moments when Vienna came into the firing line between the Nazis and the Russians. All the family were alive, his mother, his sisters, it seemed almost incredible. But their survival had not been easy.

When I got to Vienna, he was able to tell me the story. I had been fearful, when I left in the summer of 1939, that the Nazis might turn suspicious of his connection with me. If their intelligence was efficient, they would surely know that I had been associated with the international anti-Nazi movement. In my experience, however, the secret police of totalitarian states are, contrary to what is generally believed, remarkably inefficient. Not a rat stirred for a long time. Toni joined the Reichswehr, did his training successfully, and had a good posting. It was months before the blow fell. He was suddenly arrested, and while under guard found it totally impossible to discover what the charges against him were. Finally he was brought before his judges, and accused of having been closely associated with 'the notorious British agent John Lehmann'.

Luckily, Toni had the Viennese gift of the gab and of bluffing it out developed to a high degree. He was able to persuade the court that the charges were ridiculous, that he had only been my secretary without any knowledge of what I was doing. He was released, marched with the German troops on their entry into Paris, then later with the first wave of troops that invaded Russia. For a long time he was stationed in Minsk. He told me some of the horrible things he had witnessed. He would never forget, he said, seeing Russian partisans bundled into a lorry. Gallows were set up beside the lorry, nooses were fixed to their throats, then the lorry drove off at full speed, and they were left dangling.

Later still, he was invalided home, owing to ill-health. By then the nightmare disaster of Stalingrad had overtaken Nazi arms, and enthusiasm for the war, which had never been re-markable among the Viennese, dropped almost to zero. Even-tually I was to learn that two or three of my former friends, including Richard, the art student who had painted my flat, had 'never returned from Stalingrad'. Toni told me that he discovered a secret organization had been created in the city to cause crippling accidents to soldiers, on ordinary leave or on sick leave, who were about to be sent back to the Russian front. A friend of his, revolted by the senseless slaughter, had got in touch with them. He had been taken to a room where he was laid out on a table, and his leg smashed. He was then bundled into a taxi, with a helper on either side, and driven to one of the bathing places on the old Danube. There he was told to walk as normally as was possible for him in his acute pain, jump into the water and then call for help. To all appearances he had broken his leg by stupidly jumping in at the shallow end. He got away with it.

When the Russian armies were approaching Vienna, Toni was still in my flat with his wife and little boy, Peter. As the fighting raged over the Danube bridges and in the Prater, once the scene of carefree summer amusement and amorous encounters among the twilit bushes, he decided to evacuate his family to his father's home on the other side of the city. Gradually the gunfire died down; and one day he felt it was safe enough to return to the city and attempt to get back into the flat, in order to collect various belongings he had left behind. Scarcely had he reached the city boundaries when the fighting flared up again, now in the more central districts. With infinite difficulty, dash by sudden dash, and using the knowledge of Russian he had acquired in Minsk in order to get past the Soviet posts, he made his hazardous way to the Invalidenstrasse. To that day, he told me, he didn't know how he had managed it.

Dusk was falling when he reached the flat. He found that in their flight they had left a basket of eggs in the kitchen, and he cooked himself what he described as 'the biggest omelette I have ever eaten or am ever likely to eat in my life'. He sat in front of the great circle of windows looking out over Vienna north and north-westwards, the same windows from which I had watched the torchlight procession of the jubilant Nazi youth in March 1938, and later, in the summer of 1939, the trains rolling through the Hauptzollamt station just below, crammed with troops for the Polish front. Bombs and shells were falling. Fires were blazing everywhere, and he saw the Stefansdom suddenly ignited like a giant torch. 'I couldn't bring myself to go away,' he told me. 'The whole war, all we had experienced seemed to be summed up in what I saw before me. What an end that fiery panorama was to the mad, stupid adventure that had started when the Nazis took over, how ghastly a tragedy it had been for our beloved Vienna.'

Finally, he decided that he must make an attempt to get back to his father's home. As he opened the front door of the house, a bomb whistled down nearby, and blew open the iron shutters of a bicycle shop, revealing several glittering new machines. The temptation was irresistible: he seized one of them, swung himself on, and made off. He had hardly gone a few hundred yards when he heard a Russian voice challenging him. He looked round, and could just see a Soviet sentry with a raised rifle. 'That's a nice machine, just give it here.' He had no option, and proceeded gloomily on foot. At a big cross-roads a few minutes later, he saw coming down towards him two Soviet soldiers on horseback, very drunk and singing noisily. He took a chance, shouted to them in Russian, and was told to jump on behind. So, swaying through burning Vienna, he eventually found himself on the western outskirts, jumped off, waved the drunken soldiers goodbye, and made the rest of his way on foot.

When the fighting was at last well and truly over, he went back again, his wife Gretl pushing a cart made out of a wooden crate in which their little boy Peter was installed, and found that the flat had been commandeered by an officer of the Russian Danube fleet. He never got it back. One day the Russian officers left, as the Invalidenstrasse was declared part of the British zone. Immediately, however, his neighbours on the same floor, whose flat had been damaged by shrapnel, broke through the wall and occupied it. If I had arrived in uniform in some capacity attached to our occupying forces – and almost everyone seemed able to do this at that time – I could no doubt have bundled the man out and reinstated Toni and his family. As it was, I had no time, and could only find Toni a good lawyer to help him through the labyrinthine complications of the laws about living space at that time. The case went on for years, and Toni eventually won it, only to be deprived of the fruits of victory by the Wohnungsamt, where the bureaucrats decided that as he already had a flat he couldn't have his old one back. How they imagined he could have lived in the interval without a flat, they didn't explain.

So I never saw my Viennese pied-à-terre – about which I wrote in *The Whispering Gallery* – again. Toni had, however, taken the books I had left and one or two pieces of furniture with him. It was curious to look through those English books, and to think they had been waiting for me behind the enemy lines all through the war.

Toni took me one day to call on his mother, the redoubtable Frau Chval, who had looked after me so devotedly while I was in the Invalidenstraase. She was living still in an apartment in an old tenement house not far from the Danube Canal. I took with me some small parcels of goods that were unobtainable in Vienna at that time. When she saw me she burst into cries of joy, and then into tears, and began, rather incoherently, to tell me about the miseries of the war and the cruelties and stupidities of the Nazis; and only a moment later about what she called the Russian terror that had followed the German defeat.

Apart from the wrecked Prater, the damage in central Vienna was confined mainly to a few outstanding buildings, which had suffered in the very last stages of the war: the charred and collapsed roof of the Stefansdom, the Opera House and the beautiful baroque elegance of the Albertina Museum behind it, and the Burg Theatre. It was strange that these dominant symbols of Austria's civilized past should have been hit in the orgy of destruction that Hitler had willed, thus completing – so it seemed then – the ruin of a once great country. I had been given a room in the British-occupied Sacher Hotel, through whose corridors mad Nijinski had wandered after his rescue from Hungary two years before. Even under military occupation it had not completely lost its atmosphere of a vanished aristocratic world. What had happened to that world? Who had survived the war that destroyed the Habsburg empire, the inflation that followed it, the economic misery in which the grim and pointless struggle between Dollfuss and the social-democrats took place, the Nazi terror against Jews, socialists, Roman Catholics and humanists, the new war and the bombardment and the street fighting, the Russian invaders and the terrible new inflation? One step after the other in the descent to the hell of the present. It seemed impossible that central Europe would ever recover. Those Viennese who still held on to any decent life were selling their last possessions to buy food on the black market. They seemed dazed and adrift. They hadn't much time to think of rebuilding the shattered world of the mind and the spirit. Nor was the 'cold war' helping them to find their bearings again. One morning I came out of Sacher's to see that a new display had been mounted in the windows of the American reading room at the corner of the Kaerntnerstrasse. It accused the Russians of having conspired with the Hungarian communists to carry out the political coup in Budapest the year before. It even had carefully captioned photographs of the Russian military authorities responsible – and no beating about the bush at all. And yet at that time, the representatives of the four occupying powers, sitting stiffly in a jeep side by side, were still making their daily rounds through that central part of the city which had been declared common to them all.

One day I went exploring through the Third district, where I had lived and which I knew so well. I walked through a square in which I had once had my earliest flat. It had been a charming square in those days, inhabited by middle and upper class families, many of whom had come down in the world from grander abodes after the inflation of the 'twenties. In the middle of the square, among the trees, had been a *Kinderfreibad*, one of the attractive open air bathing places for children that the enlightened social-democrat municipal government had built all over the city. I was looking forward to seeing it again; but when I came into the square I saw nothing but ruin. There was no bathing place, there were no trees, and the houses had been half-destroyed by bombs or shells. What sent a shudder of horror through me, however, was an anti-aircraft tower that rose, a monstrous growth of green concrete, where the bathing place had been. With its smashed searchlights on top and the battered, deserted shelters at its base, it was a vision of pure nightmare.

Just before the war, the Swiss philosopher Jung had written a remarkable essay which he called *Wotan*. One of the most striking passages came back to me: 'Germany is a land of spiritual catastrophes where certain facts of nature never make more than a pretence of peace with the world-ruler reason. The disturber is a wind that blows into Europe from limitless and primeval Asia, sweeping in on a wide front, from Thrace to the Baltic . . . It is an elemental Dionysus that breaks into the Apollonian order. We call the creator of this storm Wotan.' Jung saw the Nazi movement as the latest and most destructive storm created by Wotan. The Austrians had been caught up in this tremendous primitive storm and tidal wave; and then the counter-wave that it provoked in Asia had come crashing down on them. It was Wotan's own tower, I suddenly thought, that stood before me.

And I remembered also a picture of horror I had carried away from Czechoslovakia. The ancient castle of the Spielberg dominated the city of Brno, and in the heart of that castle, used as a barracks by the Germans, was a Greek Orthodox chapel. Under it were the mediaeval dungeons. The Nazis were just completing the streamlining of those dungeons to satisfy all their most revolting refinements of barbarism, when liberation came. They *had* completed the alteration of the chapel on top of their torture-hell. They had torn down the crucifix and erected in its place a sculpture of a German eagle, clasping a wreathed swastika in its talons. Where the altar had been they had placed a reading desk, and on it a copy of *Mein Kampf*. They had made it into Wotan's altar. There the faithful were to come to worship the inspirer of the thousand-year Reich, while the victims groaned below.

I have said that the Austrians still seemed dazed and adrift. Nevertheless, theatrical and musical life had already begun to revive, and to show that Vienna's high traditional standards in these arts had not been lost. I rejoiced to see that enchanting actress Paula Wessely again in the exquisite and undamaged *Theater in der Josefstadt*. I heard Clemens Kraus conduct Strauss's *Salome*, with Hans Hotter as Jochanaan and Maria Cebotari as Salome, in the *Theater an der Wien*, and was amused to find the programme notes in four languages. And I attended a superb performance of Verdi's *Requiem* by the Vienna Philharmonic, with John Barbirolli as guest conductor, given in aid of the fund for the rebuilding of the Stefansdom and the Opera House.

After I had given my two lectures in Vienna, to the English Seminar of the university and to the Austro-British Society, I took the British military train down to Graz and Klagenfurt, passing out of the Russian zone and into the British zone at the Semmering. This was a comparatively simple operation compared with my final journey, from Vienna to Innsbruck by the ordinary international express. Nothing could have illustrated more vividly the ordered chaos of the aftermath of war and the jealous way the four powers stood on their rights. I had to show my *laissez-passer*, the well-known 'grey card' issued to visiting foreigners and stamped by the four separate authorities, three times during the night, once at the Russian demarcation line, then at the American line, and again at the French line before we reached Innsbruck. The longest and most anxious wait was, needless to say, at the Russian line, at the cold and sleepy hour of 3 a.m. The young Russian frontier guard was brusque, suspicious and disagreeable. I do not think he could read, because he appeared to be looking at some of the travel documents up side down, but he spotted something that seemed to him to be wrong – perhaps the colour – in the permits of an Austrian couple sitting opposite to me, poured out some violent objections in Russian which they did not understand, and then bundled them off the train. I was glad that I was not an 'enemy' national.

I was discouraged when giving my lectures, to find how un-responsive the audiences were. My lecture technique may well have been ghastly, but I don't somehow think it was my own inadequacy that made the Austrians who faced me so blankly incapable of asking questions at the end. The teutonic univer-sity tradition is for the professor to pronounce his words of wisdom from on high and for the awe-struck students to take them almost as if they were receiving punishment. Added to this, the Nazi experience had made the sort of people who formed my audiences even more submissive to command and authority. It was painfully different from the technique of dis-cussion groups, which had developed so vigorously in Britain during the war.

Apart from the lectures, the British Council officials in Styria and Carinthia provided me with the opportunity to meet some of the younger poets in informal gatherings where the ice could be broken. I found these young people charming and interest-ing; but it became pretty clear to me that, down there in the provinces at least, the vast majority were still Nazis at heart.

It was not on this occasion, but on a second visit a few years later, when life, at any rate on the surface, was beginning to return to normal in Vienna, that I had a curious experience, a moment of agonizing vision, complex and yet heart-rending in its meaning. I was strolling through the streets on one of those soft, golden September afternoons that I have always as-sociated with Vienna. On the opposite pavement, coming to-wards me, were a group of friends, young men in *lederhosen* (they had not yet discarded them in favour of jeans), with their girl-friends in *dirndl*, looking exactly as they might have done twenty years before when I first came to know the city. At that moment, bells began to peal from churches nearby, and in the familiar music of the bells I became conscious, almost simultaneously, of two sensations. I imagined, for the flash of a second, that I was my younger self, and that these young men approaching me were the friends I had known two decades ago. In that same instant of transformation, 'instant of knowledge and des-pair', I realized that those friends were lost, had vanished with-out trace, had 'never returned from Stalingrad', were leading crippled lives somewhere, and the young men confronting me

on the other side of the pavement, though so bewilderingly like
them, were their sons, a new generation that had never known
what we, their fathers and myself, had known and been through:

> For nothing in their eyes foretells
> The mirror fate my friends would find,
> These are their sons – they are not there.
>
> Stillness appals, where life goes on:
> Called I in anguish, ruined stairs
> Would echo only stone by stone,
> And no halloo assuagement be
> Across those soft, September airs.
> Out of the dark ancestral tree
> The dragon roared, and they are gone.

I walked on, feeling more ghostlike than real, conscious almost unbearably of the wreckage of the age in which I had
lived, and of the bitter fruits of allowing one's affections and
interests to be divided between two countries. I was also, not
altogether happily, conscious of the speed with which the appearances of things are mended. But it was not the appearances
that worried me. Had something been fatally changed and
ruined deeper down, in the spirit of men?

10

In between those two excursions into the past, I had visited
Greece, for the first time. This was certainly a highlight of the
post-war years for me. I had always been deeply interested in
everything Greece could mean to an imaginative Englishman
brought up in the classics, her art, her civilization, the impression she had made on our great poets of the Romantic period
while she was fighting to free herself from the long Turkish
domination. My visit to the Naples museum in my last year
at Eton had brought this idealization to its highest point of

enthusiasm but, unlike so many of my Greek-struck contemporaries, I had never set foot in the country itself. Partly this was
due to my obsession with central Europe and the social scene
of the 'thirties, partly to the fascist cloud that hung over political Greece at that time. By 1946, however, I had learnt a great
deal about modern Greece. Owing to the chance of meeting
Demetrios Capetanakis at Cambridge during the winter of
1940–41, I had discovered not only the heroism of her resistance to the Italian and German invaders, but also her contemporary literature and art. Sikelianos, Seferis, Elytis in poetry,
Ghika, Tsarouchis in painting, seemed to me among the most
important and exciting names in the creative arts of the time –
not to mention Demetrios's own writings. I had had the opportunity during the war of publishing translations of their poems,
illustrations of their paintings and studies of their work. Now
I was keyed up to meet them in their own country, to experience the effect of Greek light and air on my own senses. Demetrios had taught me to keep my mind and imagination open to
Greece, not as an isolated far away phenomenon of the sixth
century BC, but as a constant, ever changing but fundamentally
unvarying presence throughout history, right down to our own
day, in which the battle with the fascists, the occupation and
the famine, the liberation and the civil war that had accompanied it, were merely new manifestations of the eternal Greek
struggle for identity. 'What matters,' he had written in 1941,
'is not history as history, but human beings. What matters is the
Greeks of today and what will become of them. . . .'

The opportunity came when, during the summer of 1946, the
British Council, at the suggestion of Steven Runciman who was
their representative in Athens at that time, invited me to travel
out to give some lectures. Some tentative suggestions had been
made by the Greeks themselves at about the same time. So I
knew that I would be welcome. In addition my friend Rex
Warner had been appointed Director of the British Institute in
Athens the year before, and I knew that he would see that I
had at least a good and probably a thoroughly uproarious time,
as far as local conditions permitted.

My plans and papers were finally in order by the end of
October, and I arrived in Athens on November 1st. I have

always regretted that I did not keep a diary of this visit, because it was one of the most passionately interesting episodes in
my whole life, so crowded with incident that only a day-to-day
journal would bring everything back to mind. Though I left
in a state of total exhaustion, which was, alas, not entirely sober,
it acted as a terrific tonic on a war-wearied citizen of London,
thirsting for renewed contact with the vibrant, life-enhancing
sources of the Mediterranean world. In my mind, as a keynote
of my expectation, ran the opening lines of Odysseus Elytis's
Age of Blue Memory:

> Olive trees and vines spreading to the sea,
> And, beyond, red fishing-boats as far as memory,
> The golden sheaths of August over our midday sleep
> Full of sea-weed and shells. . . .

Undoubtedly my visit was made by Rex, and the band of
young ex-soldiers, lecturers and enthusiasts all for Greece, who
were working with him or in one of the offices of the British
forces still encamped on Greek soil to help the Greeks put their
country into order after the ravages of the German occupation
and the murderous civil war that followed it: Maurice Cardiff,
Steven's predecessor in the makeshift organization that was
set-up after the liberation, who, under the pseudonym of John
Lincoln, wrote a remarkable account of his war-time liaison
with the Greek partisans as *Achilles and the Tortoise*; Ronald
Crichton, expert in many facets of Greek art and the traditional
dancing of the Greek sailors; and Brian de Jongh, student and
lover of Pausanias in the forefront. They were supported, on a
higher level, not only by the wordly-wise, amusing, scholarly
personality of Steven who was *persona grata* with the Greek
Royal family, but also by the charming ambassador, Sir Clifford
Norton, and his wife 'Peter', who had a passionate interest in
modern Greek art and also in the art of young Englishmen, in
particular John Craxton, who were in love with the Greek scene.
Gigantic, brilliantly coloured pictures of young Greek shepherds, in curious perspective with their sheep and the Greek
landscape, decorated the august walls of the reception rooms
in the British Embassy, where elegant eighteenth century portraits had hung before. Britain was fortunate in having these

men and women to represent her at that particular time: if
their appointment was not the result of extremely skilful choice
by some anonymous genius in the Foreign Office, it was certainly an exceedingly lucky chance. They had managed to
make themselves intimately popular with the Greeks, and indeed gave the impression of being on holiday with them rather
than working in their midst as members of a foreign mission.
Those were the halcyon days of the Anglo-Greek honeymoon,
darkened before a decade had passed by the bitter Cyprus dis-
pute.

Rex took charge of me at once, introduced me to all his Greek
friends, who always seemed in the highest spirits when in his
company, arranged my expeditions and lectures, frightened
me by the glowing terms in which he described me as I sat
cowering beside him on the platform with a sea of unknown
Greek faces before me, and took me off to carouse in tavernas
when official duties and ordeals were over. His good humour
never failed. The atmosphere in his office when visitors called
– and they called very often – was indeed more like that of a
taverna than a centre of administrative organization. This the
Greeks immensely appreciated, knowing that they could argue
exactly as they pleased in his presence, on politics, literature,
history and sex, while Rex chuckled continuously at the quips
that flew around and made genial but shrewd ripostes whenever necessary. He imposed authority as much by his sturdy
physical build as by his obviously deep classical learning, his
devotion to Greek civilization, and his reputation as an outstanding imaginative author. In his *Views of Attica* Rex observes
that when offered the job originally he felt neither particularly
interested nor particularly well equipped for it. Perhaps that is
the way to start on an exceptionally successful mission.

I have been to Greece several times since 1946, as a simple
visitor and as a member of the British team at the meetings of
the Anglo-Greek Mixed Commission, and on each occasion I
have seen more and learned more about that wonderful country. But on each occasion I have found tourists in even greater
swarms, and the countryside, especially in Attica, a little more
spoiled by frenzied and graceless building, of hotels, residential
suburbs, factories, bathing establishments and petrol stations.

And on each occasion, therefore, I am even more grateful for the invitation that allowed my first impression to be so unencumbered, at the time when, for instance, the coastline between Piraeus and Sunium and the scenery along the road to Eleusis and Daphnis could be appreciated in all their natural and awe-inspiring beauty, and fragments of prehistoric pottery could still be picked up from the tangled flowers and weeds in the excavations of Mycenae's citadel. In fact it seems to me now extraordinary that I was able to visit some of the most beautiful sites with no one about at all, except for our own small party and perhaps a shepherd piping in the heather of a nearby mountain slope. The roads were often atrocious, and the accommodation simple in the extreme: but the gods were at home.

This numinous quality, which is now so rapidly vanishing as the eager young students clamber in their hundreds every week over the ruined columns of the temples, and the ministry officials in Athens seriously discuss the possibility of removing them altogether and substituting concrete replicas, affected me very deeply. I had a dream the night before visiting Sunium, that a strange creature, like a winged insect and yet indefinably resembling a human being at the same time, appeared to me. Inexplicably in my dream. I knew it was the goddess Demeter. The next day, while strolling through the grass that surrounds the floor of Poseidon's temple, I suddenly observed a creature at my feet that recalled the dream with a shock: I had never seen a praying mantis before. Again, after visiting Eleusis, I dreamed that I was present, as a ghost or in some former incarnation, at a ceremony of initiation in a huge theatre-like cavern below the rocks. Music, with an insistent hypnotic beat, was rising to a climax, while on a stage lit by streaming torches and in front of awed, upturned faces crowded row after row into the darkness at the back of the hall, actors in gigantic effigies as gods were performing a mysterious dance.

I was even more deeply affected by my visit to Delphi. At the best, even today, the journey from Athens is long and tiring. Then, in 1946, the roads were full of potholes and shell craters, some of the bridges were in an extremely precarious state, and for long periods a car was only able to crawl, throwing its passengers violently up and down as they attempted to fix their thoughts on timeless art and myth. At first the authorities were unwilling to let me go, muttering about the dangers of bandits on Parnassus. I replied that I had long been familiar with this situation and did not care. Eventually we set out one morning early, lunching in Thebes (which seemed to me then, my head full of Oedipus and Aeschylus, a totally absurd thing to do), and gradually penetrating deeper into the wild and lonely country beyond. My head swam, my pelvis ached, my conversation became more and more monosyllabic and inane, and I wondered on several occasions whether I could restrain myself at the next pot-hole from scrambling out of the car and taking to the maquis. Then, on the last lap, amid the increasing grandeur of the mountain scenery while twilight fell, my spirits began to revive. A thunderstorm was gathering over the peaks, and opaque black clouds seemed to be whirling ahead of the car like manifestations of spirits from Pluto's kingdom. As we came round the bend of the road, that suddenly reveals on one's right the gigantic arena of the mountains which the ancient Greeks looked upon as the navel of the earth and chose as the stage for their most sacred religious ceremonies, the storm broke. Lightning played on the broken columns of the temples in livid searchlight flashes, and thunder-claps reverberated with deafening echoes. For that experience alone the journey, a long operation without anaesthetics, would have been worth while. It was, I thought, as if Apollo were revealing himself in all his terrifying majesty: I could well imagine the effect the phenomenon would have had on pilgrims in ancient times approaching the famous shrine from distant parts of Greece, to consult the Pythian oracle.

The next morning, the scene was totally changed. A dazzling November sun of Greece blazed in the cloudless blue of the sky, and below me I discovered one of the most amazing sights of my life. Far, far away, down beyond in the south-west, a tongue of hazy blue sea indicated the edge of the Gulf of Corinth; and I saw descending towards it, in almost unbroken multitudes, forest after forest of olive trees like a vast silver-green glacier. On the other side, like the back of some great cyclopean theatre rose the sheer wall of Parnassus, and over it, as it seemed in the remote depths of the sky, eagles were slowly circling and gliding, keeping up their ceaseless search for prey.

We met no bandits on our journey, nor did any partisans descend to encircle and kidnap us. But the warning we had received before we left was a sharp reminder that the unhappy country was still not entirely at peace. In Athens itself it was difficult to believe that the orderly streets one saw had so recently been the scene of a ruthless, brutal civil war. If you swallowed the free fantasy of the Paris left-wing press – and even some of our own – you pictured restaurants closed, papers outlawed, armed police with British troops beside them patrolling the streets and preparing to fire whenever two or three starving people gathered together for what might be clandestine plotting, lorries mounted with machine-guns racing past under the shadow of the Acropolis, and picking up defenceless, struggling victims for the next fusillade against the barracks wall.

I knew that all this was malicious or misguided exaggeration, and had in fact been appalled at the readiness with which influential left wing, or even liberal elements in England, ever up in arms to defend foreign causes they misunderstand, had fallen for the propaganda picture of ELAS as heroic guardians of justice – even after Churchill's memorable dash to Athens in 1944. But what I found in Greece was so different, at the same time far better in some ways and rather worse in others, that I found it difficult at first to adjust myself to the reality.

There was no famine in Athens. The shops were full of goods, many of the kind that had been unobtainable in London. The restaurants, even quite small ones on the outskirts of the city, were capable of producing dishes that devotees of Greek cooking pronounced delicious, washed down with *retsina* (poison to me). You could buy papers of socialist or even communist leaning at the kiosk outside your hotel – if you could dodge the attentions of eager small boys with their shoe-shine apparatus – and voice any opinion you liked at your café table. I never saw, or heard of a policeman threatening anyone with a revolver while I was there, nor did the British troops cause anything worse than mild traffic jams when changing the guard outside their headquarters. The Athenians in fact seemed thoroughly grateful to the British police mission for having taught their own police to handle difficult crowds and demonstrations without firing on them.

This was the first surface impression; but of course one soon saw that there were qualifications underneath. The smell of the police state *did* sometimes creep under the door, though far less noisomely than my well-trained nostrils had recognized in countries before the war. If the royalists were criticized for harshness, they could with reason point to the massacre of the anti-communists when ELAS was in control in Athens, to the seizure of hundreds of innocent hostages who had disappeared for ever with the retreating communists, to the foreign fingers pulling the strings. Greece had simply become one of the chief battlegrounds for the new war that had supplanted the old, the war for world power between the Soviets and the west. Out in the provinces, particularly near the frontiers, many friends told me things did not look as pretty as in Athens or Attica. There political vendettas were still violent, and murderous. Some of those who were lumped under the general description of 'bandits' might indeed be old-style brigands profiting from the aftermath of international and civil war. Others, however, were the irreconcilables of ELAS who neither expected nor wanted a pacification as things were. Others again, the most tragic of all, were those who had been enrolled in one capacity or another with the communists, who would have liked to be reconciled but dared not trust the royalist authorities into whose hands they would have to surrender, or dared not disobey secret mobilization orders from the communists, for fear of the vengeance of terror. Indeed terror and blackmail for political ends, the worst and most corrupting disease of any society, had taken a firm hold in Greece; it was not surprising that it broke out a few years later in Cyprus.

There was, as I have said, no famine in Athens; everyone had enough to eat, but for the majority it was the simplest fare, and if the shops were loaded with luxuries it was because only the rich and those who had profited on the black market could afford them. Against that, one had to make an odd counter-qualification. The rich were not always those you would have expected to be rich. The retired civil servants and widows with pensions were the worst hit, while the dock labourers in Piraeus

Alexis Rassine, Christopher Isherwood, and Gore Vidal

The author with Carlotta

Rosamond with Carlotta at Lake Cottage

Alexis Rassine, Beatrix and Taffy at Lake Cottage

probably earned more in that topsy-turvy time than most em-
ployers who were trying to run their own small businesses.

Nevertheless, the mood in Athens was exuberant enough, at
least when Greeks and British met together. If I had known the
country before the war, perhaps I would not have been so surprised that social intercourse seemed so animated, so full of en-
joyment of life and interest in all things intellectual and artistic.
How different, I thought, from the atmosphere in Paris, in
Vienna or even in Prague. I fell under the spell.

My friends took me down to the Piraeus to see the sailors
dancing in some of the simple tavernas. I had never seen Greek
dancing before, and even managed to consume a large quantity
of *retsina*, so hypnotized was I by the insistent rhythms of the
bouzouki music, the clapping of hands and the waving of hand-
kerchiefs, the strange leaping and twisting of the linked performers as if in a trance, now surging in line to and fro like
waves on a beach, now a pair caressing one another as if half
in an agony of love, half in sensuous hate, now a single sailor
breaking away to perform a spontaneous *pas seul* in utter obli-
vious concentration, as if every step had a symbolic meaning,
as if in their sequence they were lines of a poem he was creating
from his imagination that had its inspiration far, far back in
history. In comparison, all dancing I had ever seen before
(apart from pure classical ballet) seemed almost empty of meaning and degenerate. I was sad, on a visit to Athens fifteen years
later, to find that the march of sophistication had pushed the
tavernas where one could see such authentic demonstrations
many miles further away.

I was introduced to George Katzimbalis, the liveliest talker
and most fantastic *raconteur* in Greece (and perhaps in the
world), stout, balding, formidable yet entirely charming, with
a voice that was more like a roar when he reached the climax
of one of his incredible stories and a chuckle that reverberated
through any room where he was entertaining his friends. He
was at that time editing the *Anglo-Hellenic Review*, under the
benevolent eye and with the financial support of the British
Council; not a propaganda sheet but a serious cultural review
with first-class contributions, and a larger circulation than any
other similar paper in the country. The Council was performing

E

at that time an immense and indispensable service with its pro-
vision of English teachers and English books, its lectures and
exhibitions and theatrical performances, but nothing it did
struck me as more valuable and fruitful than its support of Katzimbalis as editor.

Many other meetings enlivened almost every day. I had long
talks again with Panayotis Canellopoulos, at that time out of
office but waiting in the wings with intense concentration on
not only Greek politics but also the whole international scene of
power manoeuvring. I had not seen him since Demetrios's
death, and had to relate the whole sad story of his last illness
and the impression he had made in my own country. I met
Demetrios's relations for the first time, in particular his brother,
John Capetanakis, distinguished specialist at the Evangelismos
Hospital, and his pretty wife.

One evening in a taverna I was brought to the great poet
Angelos Sikelianos, whose *Death-Feast of the Greeks* I had published in *New Writing*. He was in the company of Rex and
Lawrence Durrell, the latter over on a visit from Rhodes where
he was working for the British mission. Sikelianos's health had
been undermined by his privations during the war years, but
his talk, of poets and poetry and experiences of his life, was full
of fascination and wit, and I was struck by the dignity of his
bearing, the sweetness of his expression, and the gentle warmth
of his manner. He had been a legendary figure in his generation,
organizer of great poetic festivals at Delphi before the war in
1927 and 1930, and an inspiration to his countrymen during
the Italian invasion and the German occupation. The story was
often told how, during that grim time, he and George Katsim-
balis had led the singing of the Greek national anthem – then
of course forbidden – as the poet Palamas was carried to his
grave.

Larry took a number of photographs of the occasion, and
wrote from Rhodes afterwards: 'The meeting with Sikelianos
will have some of that smoky historic poignance that one gets
from the Manet painting showing them all there, Rimbaud,
Verlaine, etc – or do I mean the Toulouse Lautrec?'[1] I feel the
locale was perfect with the wall of gaudy biscuit tins behind,

[1] He meant, in fact, the Fantin Latour *Le Coin de la Table*.

and the once great Sikelianos – a sort of phoenix huddled in the ashes of his overcoat.'

The poetry of Sikelianos is deeply impregnated with a sense of Greek history, of Greek religion and myth, as a responsibility and consciousness that the modern Greek cannot escape; in that resembling, though more mystical (his belief has been called Christian orphism), the poetry of the younger George Seferis, who has now received international recognition as recipient of the 1963 Nobel Prize. I had first met Seferis[1] after our mutual friend Demetrios's death, when he came to London as adviser to Archbishop Damaskinos during the crisis of the winter of 1944–5. I had already published some of his poems, and had in mind the volume that was eventually to appear as *The King of Asine*. During that autumn he was resting, in an interval of his diplomatic labours, on the island of Poros, and the miracle-working Minister of Information, Baltazzi Mavrogordato, managed to get a gun-boat of the Royal Greek Navy put at our disposal to take us all out there.

On the way, we put in at the island of Hydra, and saw the cliff-built villa (now alas destroyed by fire) of the painter Nico Ghika, and were able to observe how lovingly he had used the features of his island home in his paintings, so that they seemed to combine, in one impression, modern Greek island landscape and classical and Byzantine idiom. How far away from the work of his elegant contemporary Tsarouchi, with his Matisse-like sailors and bicyclists, their muscles and masculinity bulging out of the framework of his canvasses.

When we reached Poros, we found the poet awaiting us in genial mood. He discoursed to us learnedly, wittily, endlessly, and showed us his remarkable collection of walking-sticks, many of them *objets trouvés* from his walks inland and along the shore. He looked more relaxed than he had at the time of the Damaskinos episode, and more relaxed, too, than he was to look during his difficult London mission as Greek ambassador at the height of the Cyprus troubles. Then, as before and later, I was struck by the high-domed head and the look in the brown eyes when at rest, as if brooding over the destiny of his country and the ruin of modern Europe – the Europe of his so-admired T. S.

[1] See *I Am My Brother*, 280.

Eliot's *Waste Land* – like the mask of an Ionian merchant captain, one thousand, two thousand, or three thousand years ago, a Tiresias who had seen everything and known too much:

> Here terminate the works of the sea, the works of love.
> Those who shall exist here some day where we end,
> If the blood should overflow to darken memory,
> May they not forget us, the weak souls among the asphodels,
> May they turn upon the mysterious darkness
> The heads of the victims.
> We who owned nothing shall teach them peace.

On the way to the islands George Katzimbalis, standing up in the gun-boat like an archaic statue that had been dressed in modern clothes for a lark and was being transported to a museum, made an impassioned oration on the subject of the great past of Greece, claiming that in Alexandrian times 80 million people had spoken Greek – 'a nation of 80 millions!' he roared, not entirely consequentially, to the waves and the wind and the uncomprehending, rather scared young sailors. Thinking about this when I woke next morning, I wondered whether we British too would be filled with such intense, proud, almost intoxicated national consciousness if the order of history had been reversed and *we* had fallen from a nation of 50 millions with a glorious past to a small nation of 5 millions, pawn of the intrigues of greater powers, upstarts in the longer historical perspective. Demetrios had said that the Greek had an 'unheard of pride'. Was it that pride that made the air of Attica so electric, or something in the climate, or both? Reflecting on the great poets of modern Greece I had met, and on the violence of political life that all my friends had made me aware of since my first contacts during the war, I began to see the Greeks as bearers of a double identity: on the one side the heroically inspired, unforgetting heirs of the great civilization from which our own evolved; on the other, a passionately politically minded people who were capable of pursuing the power game with a blind Balkan ferocity and disregard of any rules – except winning.

I I

Elsewhere,[1] I have described how the success of *Penguin New Writing* crept on in a way that astonished me as much as my publisher, Allen Lane, during the last year of the war, and how a new series, with more pages, improved lay-out and colour plates as well as photogravure illustrations, was launched in the spring of 1946 with No. 27. By this time the first printing order had been increased to 100,000 copies, which could easily mean a readership of at least 250,000, a figure which made me feel rather dizzy. Nothing seemed able to stop it; and yet the tide was already imperceptibly turning here too.

Underneath the surface of mounting success, there were often difficulties, struggles and even heated exchanges between myself and Penguin Books – which were as often amicably resolved within a few weeks. Partly this was due to my continual pressure in favour of making *PNW* a regular magazine, appearing at least at fixed quarterly intervals, if not six times a year, or even at best as a monthly. Allen Lane rejected the idea of making it a monthly, and, later, a bi-monthly, on the grounds that such regular publication did not suit his organization, and was not in any case feasible under the still rather higgledy-piggledy conditions of post-war printing and binding. In these decisions I think on the whole that he was right (in a cautious fashion); but the disappointment at my end was great. It was not only that I had always wanted a monthly or bi-monthly but also that I felt certain it would be much simpler and cheaper for me to organize on that basis. In addition, the material that was now pouring in at a torrential pace would have provided enough contributions for at least six numbers a year, even if only a minute fraction of it were used.

As well as arguments about how often *PNW* should appear, there were also arguments about its price, about whether advertisements should be included to help the finances, and

[1] See *I Am My Brother.*

whether it should be available on subscription. Perhaps everyone's temper had been a little frayed by the long war. We were
certainly all more exhausted by then than we realized. It seems
a little absurd that everyone who was involved in handling a
literary and artistic publication whose circulation had reached
six figures should not have been wreathed in smiles; but in fact
almost immediately after the climax that was reached in the
spring of 1946, some of the great success began to slip away.
Other magazines were feeling the same change, but I had hopes
– and I think Allen Lane had shared them – that we had discovered an untapped source of mass appreciation; that given
the right formula an enormous public was now ready to devour
what would have been considered almost entirely highbrow
fare before the war. But war is like one of those machines that
build up terrific temperatures, under which certain substances
are transformed into others. Without the pressure the substance
remains obstinately as it always has been. In 1947 the printing
figure had dropped to 80,000. Eighteen months later it was
40,000, and in spite of all the new features we had introduced
the circulation was still falling.

To have a readership that can be estimated as somewhere
between 50,000 and 100,000 is something most editors of literary magazines in Britain during the last half-century would
find intoxicating. If, however, you have tasted the keen air of
the peaks, the lower slopes are apt to be disappointingly un-
stimulating. As we toiled away at the huge piles of MSS at our
desks in Egerton Crescent, as we read through the still so enthusiastic letters that poured in from all over the world, it seemed
very difficult to believe that the change was taking place, that
the temperature which had altered so much during the war
years was dropping fast. It was not that the hard core of enthusiasts had abandoned us, nor the true converts we had made.
What we had underestimated was the ease with which the great
outer circle of those who had become readers, and often eager
readers, when there were few competitors for the occupation of
leisure hours, would slip away. Now, as I write twenty years
after the war, I do not think I am speaking from a purely selfish
or injured point of view, or for literature alone, if I say that the
low level commercial exploitation of the increased leisure that

the British people have won themselves since 1945 has been one of the great post-war disappointments.

By January 1949, Penguin Books decided that they must reduce the number of pages to 128, with 16 pages of photogravure. and some months later they felt that they could only produce two numbers a year. From my end, with an assistant and office expenses to cope with, however much shared with my other professional earnings as broadcaster and journalist, this decision meant – as my accountant was not slow to point out to me – that I was actually losing on *Penguin New Writing*. Publishing was taking up more and more of my time, which meant there was less time for profitable journalism.

I still felt that if Allen Lane were to allow it to have an impact as a magazine with regular publication instead of occasional appearances, and were at the same time to admit advertisements, it could be saved. I felt this particularly keenly as at exactly this time the foundations of *Horizon* were beginning to crumble under the same change of wind. We still had a circulation several times as large as *Horizon* at the same date. If we both disappeared, what would be left in the way of literary magazines? The price of *PNW* had been raised in 1948 to one shilling and sixpence. Though we had started at sixpence, this still seemed to me in post-war conditions to be extraordinarily cheap for a finely illustrated literary and artistic magazine. We had also had the cover re-designed once more, in order to display the contents more effectively. This final design, which was used for Nos 39 and 40, was, in my opinion, a beautiful and skilled piece of typographical ingenuity.

All was in vain. By the beginning of 1950 Penguin Books had come to the decision that they could not under any circumstances produce it more than twice a year, and perhaps only once. I did not doubt their good faith; only I was bitterly disappointed that they did not share my belief that it still could be saved by a change of publishing conception. I knew that I could not continue to run it on the basis they proposed. I also felt that even if I could find the money, to do so would spoil my chances of finding backers for a monthly or quarterly elsewhere.

So it came about that No. 40, published in the later part of 1950, was the last. We had survived, in our hectic, extraordi-

nary and rather romantic career, as a 'little magazine' that had
had the public of a very big magazine indeed, for ten years.

This last number was rather interesting. In the photogravure
plates, we had not only reproductions of new paintings of John
Minton, and new sculpture and drawings by Barbara Hepworth, but also photographs of some of our American contributors. These were: Lionel Trilling, Paul Bowles, J. F. Powers,
Tennessee Williams, Saul Bellow, Nelson Algren, and Eudora
Welty. Not a bad roll-call, I think, of the names that were
making American literature at the time – and several among
those who are still making it vigorously today. The text itself
was remarkable for a first story by a new English writer of
clearly outstanding gifts, Frank Tuohy, and an extract from a
first novel by a new American writer, William Goyen. I am
glad, looking back, that our last number kept up so well our
reputation for introducing the future. Perhaps the most striking
contribution, from this point of view, was the last of all: an
article by the twenty-five year old John Wain, scarcely known
at that time outside university circles, on the poetry of William
Empson. This was, in fact, a revolutionary appeal that was
deeply to influence the new 'movement' of poetry that started
not long after *Penguin New Writing* came to an end. The concluding words were as follows: 'Whether Empson will ever write
any more poetry is not my business. If he does, it will be interesting to see whether the landslide in English literary taste has
left us with a public capable of appreciating him. For the plain
fact is that many of the reputations which today occupy the
poetic limelight are such as would crumble immediately if poetry
such as Empson's, with its passion, logic, and formal beauty,
were to become widely known. If the day ever comes when
poems like *This Last Pain, To An Old Lady, Manchouli, Notes on
Local Flora*, are read and pondered, and their lessons heeded, it
will be a sad day for many of our punch-drunk random "romantic" scribblers. But I suppose it never will.'

The long enforced ban on the publication of new magazines
had come to an end earlier in the year, and it seemed to me
that new groupings and new attitudes – such as John Wain's
article foreshadowed – were bound to emerge soon. The doubts
I had were whether in the changing climate that was withering

Penguin New Writing, a purely literary magazine would be able to survive. In my Foreword to No. 39, I had proposed an imaginative vision of the future: 'A group of young ex-service-men had founded at last the monthly to propagate the artistic ideals of which they had vowed themselves devotees seven years before in the Middle East. The bolder wits, both male and female, of Oxford and Cambridge, had joined together to produce a magazine appearing twice a term which glittered with all the lively exercise of intelligence and imagination the elder critics had long declared moribund in the land. Three poets of a middle generation, remembering how closely allied, in English literary history, the finest criticism and the finest poetry have always proved themselves, had issued the first number of a quarterly that was to establish the criterion of ex-cellence in the arts of the 'fifties. An entirely unknown young man, with no credentials except enthusiasm and flair, suddenly appeared to bewitch the jaded *littérateurs* of London into writing as they always dreamed they could have written, in a magazine he named *Pluto's Cave*. . . . Alas, as we lifted our eyes from the crystal, the old gloomy doubts assailed us. Would it pay? And if not, would benevolent uncles and guilt-ridden heirs of pri-vate enterprise still be able to stand the racket? Would even the toughest, the most inventive newcomer be able to overcome the gradual seeping away of subscriptions amid the usual chorus of polite but sterile praise? Would one be driven to introduce a Woman's Page, a Week-end Gardening Talk, and a Film-Star Competition? Would it need – most terrible thought of all – a new war to revive interest in the battle of the spirit, the arts of peace? . . .

With No. 27, *Penguin New Writing* had at last become what we had always hoped it could be: a magazine primarily de-voted to literature – and offering opportunities to young writers above all but also covering the other arts, with articles on the theatre, the ballet, music, cinema, radio, as well as on literary themes, and illustrations to complement those articles. All this, of course, on an international not merely British scale.

This more ambitious scope added considerably to the work of preparation, but enormously increased the fun of it at the same time. Later on, when new magazines could be started, it was obvious that more specialized reviews would appear; but at the time we were moving in to what was almost a vacuum, and the response we found, from artists, producers and choreographers was correspondingly eager and co-operative. I think I have enjoyed all my days as an editor, but no period more than this, when my house was filled, not only with huge piles of MSS but also with drawings, paintings, and photographs of plays, operas, ballets and their creators, all waiting their turn for selection and reproduction. We had articles on London theatre during the war, on the arrival of the Sadler's Wells Ballet at Covent Garden, on violence in the cinema, on the interplay of French and British traditions in painting, on the poet and the stage, on Paul Klee, on Renato Guttuso, Peter Brook (then at the beginning of his adventurous career) on style in Shakespearean production, Michael Ayrton's controversial article on Picasso, Keith Vaughan's declaration of a personal credo in his *A View of English Painting*, Jacquetta Hawkes's remarkable *Art in a Crystalline Society*, J. P. Hodin on the Cornish renaissance in painting, reproductions of all the young English painters from Robert Colquhoun to Francis Bacon, of the new school of tapestry design in France, and of those painters and sculptors who were leading the post-fascist Italian renaissance, Guttuso, Dalla Zorza, Saetti, Santomaso, Campigli, Marini, Manzu. I doubt if we missed any development of real significance of those years. What is curious to reflect is that this marvellous opportunity came my way at a time when I was most truly in sympathy with what was going on. Ten years later, at the height of the vogue for non-representational painting, and for the Marxist theatre of Brecht, for instance, I could not have felt the same afflatus, or had the same imaginative understanding to guide me.

In my farewell words I pointed out that *New Writing* had been honoured to number among its editorial assistants and advisers, at one time or another, Virginia Woolf, E. M. Forster, my sister Rosamond, Christopher Isherwood, Stephen Spender, Demetrios Capetanakis, Keith Vaughan 'and all the time of nine years Barbara Cooper'. Barbara was in tears when the decision to call it a day was made, and tears continued to flow while the depressing business of sending back the MSS that could no longer be used went on. I do not think they were tears only for the end of an enterprise she had so whole-heartedly identified herself with. She felt, as I did, that with *Penguin New Writing* added to the lengthening list of literary magazines that had folded, the future for young writers looked decidedly black. 'Already,' I wrote, 'the creeping frosts have claimed *Horizon* and *Life and Letters* as their victims, and a number of other less talked about magazines that performed a specialized but valuable function. *World Review* has deserted the straight path of literature; soon there will be hardly any address at all to which a young poet or writer of short stories can send his MSS in the hope of advice and publication – and that immediate and so necessary settling of roots that publication can give. Such a state of affairs cannot be endured for long, because a healthy literature demands a centre of growth and ferment, of appreciation and criticism by intelligent and imaginative standards. . . .'

When the story broke – within hours in the London Letter of the *Manchester Guardian* and the *Evening Standard* – the letters and telephone calls of regret began, and soon swelled to a flood. Stephen Spender wrote: 'It is the worst loss so far, and for the greatest number of people. Isn't there anything we could do? Isn't the failure of these magazines partly due not just to the public but to the failure of talent? Wouldn't it be possible now to start a magazine of all the talents? Couldn't we, say, try to draw up a list of those who are simply the best writers in England and try to get the collaboration of all of these, old as well as young and new? . . .' This idea was, indeed, very much the inspiration of the *London Magazine* three years later, but by then Stephen had branched off in a new direction of his own. Bill Sansom wrote: 'Let me say . . . how valuable were your own comments and suggestions, for you are one of the very few editors I have known who have troubled to make criticism in detail in the hope that a work might be improved – which in my case it always was.' And Laurie Lee: 'I have learned with dismay about *PNW*. I feel it a public as well as a personal loss. Yet, I suppose it had to go, if only to make room for the new magazine which I am confident you will create in its place.'

Out of the past, too, came a letter from Fred Smewin, a literature-loving sailor, shy, tied-up, but full of impulse and nervous energy, who had sent me poems from distant seas during the war; to tell me that he was running a boys' club in Bristol, to voice his bitter regrets over the end of *PNW*, and to say with passionate sincerity how much it had meant to him and how much he thought it had done, beyond calculation.

I may perhaps be forgiven for remarking on the extraordinary legend that *New Writing* appeared to have created. I have continually come across people hitherto unknown to me who have been eager to tell me how much it meant to them. Of course this pleased me; but it also, quite genuinely, astonished me. Once, when I was lecturing in Copenhagen, some years after *PNW's* decease, a young West Indian got up, and announced that he didn't want to ask me anything – but to tell me something. As usual I was galvanized into despairing attention, bracing myself for denunciation on count after count. The young West Indian, however, plunged at once into a panegyric of *New Writing*, informed the audience that he and his friends in Jamaica had been keen readers and had followed it throughout its career. He wanted me to know how much they had appreciated it, and he was sure they would be pleased to know that he had had the opportunity to thank me personally. Taken completely by surprise, I blinked and stammered, while the audience clapped and Her Britannic Majesty's Ambassador gave me a huge grin from the front row.

Equally astonishing has been the number of letters I have received over the years from people who wanted me to know what an important part *New Writing* played in their lives at one time or another. As I write this – fifteen years after the appearance of the last number – a letter has come in from someone I have never met, in Canada, who writes that at the age of eleven, during the war, he was given a copy by his father, and was 'literally dug out from the pages of *Biggles* and *The Wizard* and *The Hotspur* and transplanted into the world of literature. A world that occupies all of my free time now.'

12

One of the first bonuses that came to me from the new arrangement with Purnell, was the opportunity to visit the USA. A
group from the firm was going over in April of 1948, mainly to
study printing methods and machinery, and they managed to
get me included without difficulty. This immensely simplified
the problems, peculiarly complicated at that time, of permits
and allowances. Also if I had still been on my own, I rather
doubt whether I would have thought the heavy expense justified.

I was very much excited about the visit. I had many friends
in America, especially in the publishing and literary world, and
I knew that they would make my introduction to the novel
scenes and experiences of their country as pleasant and stimulating as possible. I hoped that both John Lehmann Limited
and *New Writing* would derive considerable profit from it. But
above all I was excited by the thought of at last getting to know
my mother's homeland and seeing the places where my New
England ancestors had spent their lives.

American hospitality is renowned, but even so I was amazed
at the immense amount of trouble taken by friends and relations
to organize everything for me as nearly perfectly as possible.
Blanche Knopf immediately got me a hotel booking, and she,
Eugene Reynal who had been Rosamond's first publisher in
Reynal and Hitchcock, and Frank Taylor, a charming young
publisher then working at Random House who had been one
of the first to visit Europe after the war, arranged parties and
prepared introductions with indefatigable zeal; while my cousin
Harry Ransom Davis appointed himself travel agent for that
part of my visit that was to be spent in New England, warning
all relations and family friends of my approach, working out
the most ingenious time-tables to see that I missed as few of
them as possible, inviting me to stay with him and his family in
Worcester, and arranging for a room to be reserved for me at
the Harvard Club in Boston.

I left by air early in April, with a good luck telegram from Edith and Osbert Sitwell in my pocket. At that time the transatlantic trip was still rather an adventure. When we took off from Shannon for Gander it was already night, but I only slept in snatches. Every time I woke up it gave me an odd feeling in the pit of my stomach to think that below me there was nothing but thirty thousand feet of air that ended in the limitless black waters of the Atlantic. Then the change of time began to play its tricks. Darkness before dawn in Gander, but my watch informed me that it was just breakfast time in London – and a generous Canadian breakfast I had in the airport huts while we waited for refuelling. As we flew over Boston another breakfast was served on the aeroplane. When we arrived at La Guardia it was time for a late New York breakfast. In spite of this accumulation of breakfasts, in my keyed-up state of eager anticipation I found myself quite ready for lunch when the time came round.

It is, I think, a common experience of British publishers visiting New York that the first few days are a delightful round of handshakes, drinks, invitations to lunch and dinner and to the theatre, and an occasional passing reference to a book, as something quite on the side. Then it begins to get serious. Catalogues that have been slipped into one's coat pocket have to be carefully examined, items are marked for further enquiry before one switches out the bedside lamp, and the second time round the discussions begin to turn professional. Advance copies of 'winners', proofs of novels or biographies that their publishers are convinced will break the sales records, arrive in parcel after parcel at one's hotel. One struggles to cope with them all, but as by this time hospitality has got under way with a vengeance, it is a losing battle. The telephone never stops ringing, one reads later and later into the night. In the end one abandons many of these offerings unread, and arranges for the bulkiest of those others that seem to promise something special to be sent on by post, after having made desperate attempts to pin down options on them. Like many other visiting Englishmen I found there was some champagne quality in the Manhattan air that makes the burning of the candle at both ends tolerable, and even enjoyable. It is when one leaves the city that the kick-back hits one, and one is suddenly prostrate.

I shall always be grateful for the way in which my New York publishing friends – who turned out to be far greater in number than I realized – initiated me into their extraordinary closed society. I could not have had more marks of attention and affection lavished upon me if I had been a long-lost brother or son. I marvelled at the ruthlessness of their behaviour to one another, and at the same time at the way they kept together in spite of their cut-throat scheming. I marvelled at the way in which authors were treated as if they were mere raw material for editorial and sales departments to work on, if necessary entirely transforming original, cherished versions. I marvelled at the tremendous organization involved in promotion campaigns. After all, was it not true that far too much money was involved for anything to be left to chance? Since then, British publishing has gone some of the way down the same road; but in 1948 I felt like a cottage weaver confronted by the vast machinery of modern textile industry.

Before I left, I had already made up my mind to capture as many of the new post-war generation of American writers as possible. They seemed to me to have qualities of vitality, self-confidence and keenness to explore new territory that were much rarer in Britain, where the exhaustion of the long struggle still appeared to inhibit experiment and invention. A reputation for talent-spotting and disinterested encouragement of youthful adventurousness, founded on my record as editor of *New Writing* and associate of Leonard and Virginia Woolf in the Hogarth Press, had preceded me; sometimes I felt it was a little difficult to live up to, but it opened all doors to me, and I found it far easier than I imagined to pounce on the authors I wanted. In some cases I had been anticipated by a shrewd colleague. Little Truman Capote shook his head, or rather his fringe, and announced that he was very very sorry, honey, but he had already had a very grand interview with A. S. Frere of Heinemann's, so grand that he had felt obliged immediately to agree to go on Heinemann's list. I regretted this because I felt that *Other Voices, Other Rooms* showed an extraordinarily original poetic talent; but perhaps it was as well that he was engaged elsewhere, because I decided to take a chance on Gore Vidal, whose homosexual novel *The City and the Pillar* had just caused a

considerable stir. Gore, I discovered, considered himself to be in
an unique rivalry relationship with Truman, almost like infant
prodigies banging away at the piano against one another in different parts of the same concert hall. Later, when Gore came
over to London and I was preparing the publicity for his book,
I asked him whether it was true that he was only twenty-three.
'No, John,' he said, with a pained expression on his face, 'I'm
twenty-*two*. It's Truman who's twenty-three.'

It was already perfectly clear to me, in those early meetings,
that Gore had limitless ambition and confidence in himself. I
have never known any young author keep a malicious and witty
eye so assiduously trained on the careers of his contemporaries.
The full betting odds on their futures appeared from time to
time in letter after letter, as preliminaries to the descriptions of
the work he was engaged on himself. I grew fond of him, but in
spite of my estimate of his abilities and energy I could not then
have envisaged his blossoming out, a decade later, as one of the
most successful American writers of plays for television and the
stage, author of extremely clever and successful film-scripts, and
even a controversial figure in Democratic politics of the Kennedy
era.

There were several passages in *The City and the Pillar*, a sad,
almost tragic book and a remarkable achievement in a difficult
territory for so young a man, that seemed to me, my travellers
and the printers to go too far in frankness. I had a friendly
battle with Gore to tone down and cut these passages. Irony of
time and taste! They wouldn't cause an eyebrow to be lifted in
the climate of the early sixties.

I was taken to Tennessee Williams's *Streetcar Named Desire*
which was running with great success on Broadway with Marlon
Brando as Stanley Kowalski, and felt at once that he was too
good an author to be missed, even though the publication of
plays has never been a very profitable line of business. I was
amazed to find that the English rights were available, settled
the contracts when I returned to London, and started the series
with *The Glass Menagerie* the same year. We did well with them;
we did even better with his short novel, *The Roman Spring of Mrs
Stone*, which we published in 1950, causing a furious division of
opinion among the critics, some of the female critics being

An apology

*Two pen and ink
drawings by
John Minton
for the author*

Banished to Elba

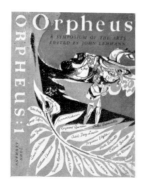

A montage of
John Lehmann Ltd
jackets

uncompromisingly hostile. Like Rosamond, however, Barbara Cooper was enthusiastic from the beginning, saying that she thought him 'the Puccini of modern literature'. *The Glass Menagerie* was produced a few months after I returned at the Theatre Royal, Haymarket, by John Gielgud, a production which brilliantly inaugurated Tennessee's reputation on this side of the Atlantic.

In general, my American trip was more valuable in getting to know publishers and agents, and in clinching deals that had already been proposed, than in actually finding new authors. I already had Saul Bellow on my list, and had arranged to publish Merle Miller's *That Winter*, the best novel written about the struggle of soldiers to re-adapt themselves to civilian life at the end of the second world war. I had already taken a short story by J. F. Powers, whose work remains unique in the American scene and in his generation, and tentatively agreed to publish his remarkable first collection of stories *Prince of Darkness*. Calder Willingham's *End as a Man* and Chandler Brossard's *Who Walk in Darkness*, the first 'hip' novel of all, were to come a little later, though I heard much about Calder's reputation on the trip. There were, however, three notable exceptions.

It was odd to pick up an English novel in New York, but the curious fact of the matter was that Humphrey Slater's *The Conspirator*, a novel that was to appear extraordinarily prophetic when the Burgess-Maclean scandal broke a few years later, had not found an English publisher. My friend Bob Giroux, percipient 'editor' at that time with Harcourt Brace, brought it to me. It was having wonderful reviews in the American press, and the film rights had just been bought; but still no proper bite in London. Perhaps English publishers thought the theme too farfetched and absurd. In any case neither Rosamond nor I did, and we arranged to publish it at once.

Before I left New York, my agent Mike Watkins told me of a novel that had great difficulty in finding a home, though James Laughlin of New Directions, famed for encouraging 'far-out' highbrow and experimental writers, had at last shown interest. The author of this novel, however, was not in his twenties, but had known Christopher Isherwood in Berlin in the thirties. He had just had a remarkable and macabre story, 'A Distant

F

Episode' published in *Horizon*. He had also written the incidental music to *The Glass Menagerie*. Paul Bowles, in fact, was a musician by reputation and *The Sheltering Sky* was his first novel. 'It's a pretty strange book,' observed Mike. 'And I'm not going to say anything more than that. Except that I don't see it on anyone's list in England except yours!' When the typescript arrived, I read it with mounting enthusiasm: I had not been so struck by an American novel since Saul Bellow's *Dangling Man*. We all agreed that it must be on our list, whether it could have been on anyone else's list or not. It proved one of our greatest successes. The *Evening Standard* chose it as its Book of the Month, and George Malcolm Thomson wrote of it: 'This is writing with an "edge" on it, derived from the author's command over words, his uncomfortable insight into the elusive mainsprings of human action and human failure . . . a novel touched with genius.'

The third notable exception was Theodor Roethke. Donald Elder, sensitive and witty 'editor' at Doubleday, whom I had got to know well during his stay in Europe, showed me some of his poems which they had published, a *succès d'estime* but not much more. I was immediately attracted by the earliest group, and felt that if a young writer (but he was in fact, as I learned later, only a year younger than me) could create so completely convincing a poetic world out of greenhouses, potted plants, camellias, weeds and moss, he was a poet indeed. I could not resist a poem that seemed so completely on my own wave-length as 'Child on Top of a Greenhouse':

> The wind billowing out of the seat of my britches,
> My feet crackling splinters of glass and dried putty,
> The half-grown chrysanthemums staring up like accusers,
> Up through the streaked glass, flashing with sunlight,
> A few white clouds all rushing eastward,
> A line of elms plunging and tossing like horses,
> And everyone, everyone pointing up and shouting!

We made a book out of these and a selection of the later poems, and published it under the title of *The Lost Son*. Roethke, who was a professor of English at Washington, was soon to be recognized as one of the most gifted poets of his generation, with Wystan Auden among his most enthusiastic admirers. His early death, only a few years ago, was a disastrous loss to American literature.

As my aeroplane took me away from the fabulous city, I made a small inventory of things that had particularly struck me. I noted the rather grim, quite definitely not contented look on the faces of the crowds that poured in and out of offices four times a day. Keeping up with the Joneses seemed especially difficult among the skyscrapers: however well you did, there was always somebody richer and more amply endowed with the material furniture of success. I noted the smart modernity and cleanliness of apartments and offices; and the filth that blew through the narrow canyons of the streets. I noted the prevalence of a cynical, wisecracking habit of comment, often very witty and semantically inventive; which nevertheless co-existed with a spontaneous, warm-hearted concern with the plight of friends in trouble. I was touched by the generous impulses that were aroused in people the moment they heard one was a 'limey', and the rather awestruck respect they had for our sufferings in the blitz; and amused by the way these impulses struggled with a traditional suspicion of our diplomatic and commercial craftiness and of concealed, unassuaged imperial ambitions. I was appalled by the habit of drinking several extremely dry double martinis before a meal, and of subsequently taking iced coffee and water with it. Any knowledge of wine was as rare as the classification of orchids. I was driven mad by the inability to get my shoes polished by putting them out in the corridor when I went to bed. And I was more entertained than perturbed to find that the general criterion of worthiness, the alpha plus in the examination for American excellence was the ability to *sell* – whatever it was to whoever it was. I shall never forget going into a shop to buy a pair of socks, and the look of despair on the face of the young salesman when he failed to sell me at the same time two other pairs of socks, several drip-dry shirts and a dozen underpants. It was, for him, as if all thumbs had been turned down against him in the American arena.

Boston was made especially pleasant for me by the behind-the-scenes attentions of my cousin Harry, by meeting Dorothy Hillyer of the Houghton Mifflin Company, F. O. Matthiessen, the great Henry James scholar, Billy Abrahams, young novelist friend of Dunstan Thompson, and my old friend the poet Richard Eberhart, at an evening in Cambridge. The Harvard Club astonished me by maintaining the traditional character of an eminent London club more successfully than any Pall Mall establishment that had survived the blitz, and by the way extremely elderly members would rise shakily from their armchairs on hearing my name and deliver glowing nostalgic eulogies of my father as legendary rowing coach of long ago.

My expedition into the New England countryside began a few days later. I stayed in Worcester, where my mother had lived as a young girl, with Harry and his enchanting family. His wife Eleanor made me feel at once as if I had known her all my life; a gift I think peculiar to the nicest kind of Americans – even when they are not one's relations. They took me out to their little beach house in Montauk, far up on the north-eastern end of Long Island. There was a light sea-fog when we got there, but the sea made itself known by the endless beating and toppling and foaming of the waters: Harry's wife said she could never have enough of it. And the moment the fog lifted and I saw the house on the sand-cliff, I felt it was exactly the kind of house I had been looking for myself. I became much attached to them all, and was horrified when tragedy struck some years later. A typhoon came raging inland, and the alarm was sent out that it was approaching Worcester. Dear, kind, gentle, responsible Harry went up to the roof of his business offices to see that everything was battened down, and was whirled off into the street, as if by a demon of destruction, and was dead in a few moments.

I was taken to see cousin Forest, an eccentric, extremely rich old bachelor who lived alone in what looked like an enormous Greek temple. He greeted me genially, but with a certain canny reserve, as if he thought I might well be a conspirator in some plot against his possessions. I could not help remembering that many years before, on a lightning visit to England, he had come over to see me as a young boy at Eton. In those days an Eton boy when visited by a rich relation expected a tip to be pressed into his hand as goodbyes were said: a £1 note at least, to be spent in an orgy of banana messes among his friends the next day. Cousin Forest demanded almost at once to be taken to my hosiers, the famous shop of Devereux. He then proceeded to indulge in a riot of spending, ordering practically every item of clothing he set eyes on, in half dozens, dozens and more. The assistants raced around the shop almost hysterically, and my hopes rose higher and higher. £1? £5? Perhaps even more? But there was absolutely nothing in the hand that so fondly shook mine as he went off to catch his train.

I stayed in Milton with Rosamond Hamlin, one of the two Peabody girls my mother had been teaching when my father first met her, and still deeply devoted to her. I spent a night in Exeter, with my mother's sister Aunt Jessie and her husband Jack French, in their home, one of the beautiful clapboard houses that seem to me one of the great architectural achievements of Anglo-Saxon civilization. I had never seen them before, and they prepared an enormous repast for me the next morning, with eggs and meat and waffles and every other conceivable delicacy of the American breakfast. I felt ashamed not to do justice to it with my war-shrunken English stomach. They drove me up into the mountains beyond Concord to visit the old family farm of Cliffhead, on Saddleback, wild, lonely and romantic among its overgrown orchards, with a famous pink quartz fireplace in the living room that my grandmother had added; an expedition that moved me deeply, for it had loomed very large in my mother's childhood memories of endless summer holidays, picnics, blueberry picking and burning juniper bushes on the mountain at night.

Before my last few days in New York, I went to stay with Archie Clark-Kerr, by then Lord Inverchapel, at our Embassy in Washington. Archie proved himself as delightful a friend and conversationalist as ever; but I got the impression that he was not altogether happy in Washington. After his outstanding successes in Chungking and Moscow, Washington should have been the crown and triumph of his career. Instead, there seemed to be a slight air of disappointment about him, as if he had lost his touch and didn't quite know why. The new assignment was very different from the other two, where his forthright way of dealing with all and sundry, his salty humour and his quick, imaginative understanding of people who came from simple backgrounds had been invaluable assets. In Washington he found a highly sophisticated, rather ingrown society, where the fact that his wife Tita was only rarely with him told against him. 'Don't expect too much of Washington,' he had written to me. 'There are only two *Weltmenschen* in the whole town. I am one! My God, I shall be glad to get home, much as I love these people.' Rumour was that jealous voices in the French Embassy had suggested that the Russian valet he had brought back with him from Moscow – Stalin graciously conceding that he could let one citizen go out of 150,000,000 – was a spy. They had nothing to go on; but throw enough mud and a little of it sticks.

The other guests in the Embassy while I was there were Lieutenant Oliphant and his new bride, whom he had brought to introduce to Archie. The story of the 'lonely loot'nant' was one of the remarkable phenomena of war-time London, comparable only with the story of 'the sergeant', Stuart Preston.[1] Towards the end of the war the cry went round, in Emerald Cunard's circle and elsewhere, that a young American naval lieutenant, of good family and connections, was coming over to London. He knew no one, he would be very lonely, and we must all befriend him. The next thing I knew was that I received an invitation to a party given by Lieutenant Oliphant. As I entered the room I saw a dense and heaving crowd of almost everyone who was anyone in London society, with the slim and personable lieutenant handing round drinks himself in a white jacket.

Archie, on leave from Moscow, came to know him in these social circles and they struck up a close friendship. When Archie was given the Washington Embassy, the 'lonely loot'nant' established himself there as a kind of unpaid social secretary. His services were of great value to a newcomer to the Washington scene, but his presence caused some confusion. Now his charming bride seemed a little confused, in a strange world her young husband knew so intimately, and she not at all.

My farewell week in New York passed in a haze of parties and last interviews with authors, publishers and agents. No one could be gainsaid: neither my cousins Georgene and Helen, living together in a smart apartment on Fifth Avenue, nor my new American friends, who now included the melancholy,

[1] See *I Am My Brother*, 186.

sensitive but witty and intensely social Leo Lerman, who had the
reputation of being able to collect a party of notabilities faster
than anyone else in the city; nor any of my London friends who
seemed to have gathered there at that moment in abundance,
Alice Harding, Stuart Preston 'the sergeant', George Dix the
elegant and anglified young artists' agent, Harold Acton, Alexei
Solomos the young Greek theatrical director, Hugh Gibb and
many others. Henrietta Bingham, my sister Beatrix's old friend
and daughter of Senator Bingham, invited me to the ballet, but
by the time we got there, we had drunk so many martinis that I
was deeply struck by the number of dancers the stage could
accommodate; when eight were on performing, according to the
programme, I saw sixteen. My agent Mike Watkins and his
attractive ash-blond secretary Jean Parker whirled me round
the editorial offices, fixing up contracts for articles and arrangements for the transatlantic use of *New Writing* material. I had
one small, but important agent's job to complete myself on be-
half of Rosamond. I went to see Katherine Brown at MCA,
and broke to her the fact that the sales of *The Ballad and the
Source* in USA had now passed well beyond 600,000. This meant
that a new clause in Rosamond's film contract with Walter
Wanger came into operation by which she was due for a further
very large sum in dollars. Katherine Brown took this news gallantly, but not without flinching; for the project had run into
trouble and one after another of the great film stars had failed
to agree, or be free, to play the leading role. Bowing her head
for a moment she quickly turned to another topic. Did I know,
she asked, what her favourite book was? Why, of course, *Dusty
Answer*, and Walter Wanger agreed with her. They renewed
their agreement on this matter every time they rang one another up on the long-distance telephone. What a film it would
make! They agreed enthusiastically on that, too, but . . . if only
the young people in it, so lovable, could enjoy a little *human
happiness* at the end. . . . Judging it not to be my business to
recommend my sister to make the answer less dusty, I sighed
and took my leave.

Part Two

I

Since the end of the war, what I have described in *I Am My Brother* as the 'almost stable society' of the literary world of London, gradually expanded as the warriors returned home to discard uniforms and take up the broken ends of their private lives, and in some cases to launch themselves on literary careers of which *New Writing* and *Horizon* had seen the first tentative steps.

Prominent among these, in especially close association with myself, were Alan Ross, who only several years later, and after more than one operation, fully recovered from the face injuries he had received in the Fleet Air Arm; Roy Fuller (in fact a young veteran of the 'thirties), who, as I have already noted, blossomed out beyond his poetry as an ingenious writer of boys' adventure stories, seeds of the future novels; and Christopher Kininmonth, a companion-in-arms of my dear friend John Lepper, who was to write a fascinating book for me about the Greek islands – long before they became fashionable for tourists – *The Children of Thetis*.

Looking back on those years of the late 'forties and early 'fifties, it seems to me that some of the chief focal points of metropolitan intellectual and artistic life were created, first, by the French Embassy under the dazzling régime of René and Odette Massigli, by Edith Sitwell, supported by her brothers Osbert and Sacheverell, by Jamie Hamilton and his enchanting – and enchantingly outspoken Italian-born wife Yvonne; and, of course, by Sibyl Colefax.

Sibyl's strength, however, was failing. The famous 'ordinaries', the dinners to which one was invited but for which one paid one's own bill later on – still went on for some years, and, naturally the cocktail parties in Lord North Street. Then came the time when one only saw Sibyl in bed, looking frailer and frailer, as if she were made of matchsticks and old wool, but somehow or other keeping up her appetite for celebrities with heroic determination. Her latest enthusiasm was for the Oliviers, Larry and Vivien, twin stars at the height of their joined brilliance in the theatre. I think Sibyl almost literally worshipped them. I remember one occasion when I was bidden to visit her in hospital, and found when I arrived that a large company of her friends had already arrived in her sick room. She enquired as ever, with eagerness about my doings, and began introducing me to other people whom I already knew. Then, suddenly, the door opened and Larry and Vivien came in. Even in her enfeebled state, Sibyl's eyes brightened as if a hundred-watt bulb had been switched on behind them. Instinctively, the rest of us retired to our corners, turned our backs and engaged one another in conversation, while the ceremony of worship began.

Sibyl died at the end of September 1950. I went to the memorial service, at 12.30 one morning, in Wilton Place. There was gathered a large company, many familiar faces and many known to me only because I had seen them time and again at Sibyl's parties. Even with those intermittent acquaintances I felt I had a kind of bond, and I was sad because I knew in my bones that I should rarely, if ever, see them again. Rose Macaulay was beside me, and just before the singing began she whispered to me: 'This is Sibyl's last party.'

It is said that when that other great hostess of the time, Emerald Cunard, departed a few years later, she was under the impression as she lay on her death-bed, that she was making her way into the crowds of a large party. 'I can't make out,' she said, 'who the host is.'

Brilliant ambassadors of France, and ambassadresses who made brilliant hostesses, have come and gone in London; but for those of us who were fortunate enough to be in town at the time, and on the French Embassy's invitation list, there will never be a period as brilliant and stimulating as the long reign of René and Odette Massigli.

Odette once confessed to me that she had never believed herself fitted to be an ambassadress in a great capital such as London; and that she always had a feeling of shrinking and inadequacy when entertaining and being entertained by intellectuals. Be that as it may, she certainly gave no impression of shrinking at her great parties, but rather of formidable attack, of extraordinarily adaptable sympathy and glittering social charm and wit. Dressed always with an elegance such as the war-weary British had almost forgotten to be possible, she dazzled London just at a time when it badly needed to be dazzled as a counterpoise to the prevailing glum austerity, the régime of restrictive ordinances; and in so doing she served her country well. René let his wife lead socially, and was not one of the easiest persons with whom to enter into a casual conversation; but he was, and is, I believe, not only an extremely shrewd diplomatist, but a man who cares deeply for the intellectual life. He was aware of all the latest developments in the French literary world, and read all the most important quarterlies and monthlies. I remember being pleasurably startled when, a few years later, he revealed to me that he always took the latest number of the *London Magazine* to read in bed, as soon as it came out.

The champagne parties, the evening receptions, often with music, the great luncheons and the intimate dinners, at which the food was always delicious, were a tonic that all thirsted for, whether politicians, financiers, newspaper magnates, duchesses, women of influence in full sail, or mere actors, musicians, and writers like myself. Part of the secret, I am sure, of Odette's success, was that she had not only strikingly good looks, but also under her attractive femininity a strong masculine streak. There was something of male comradeship between her and René: she did not want simply to be a great hostess, but *au courant* with everything that was going on in the world, so that she could discuss the important affairs of the day with her husband. I have seen her at breakfast in bed, deeply absorbed not only in political but also financial papers. When René was ambassador at Ankara before the war, her great pleasure was to take a horse and ride out into the wild countryside. General Weygand dubbed her Penthesilea – Queen of the Amazons.

On one occasion, she arranged a 'private' dinner at the Embassy, as she said when she invited me, 'for the Queen Mother to meet some intellectuals and literary people'. There were about thirty of us gathered there when the Queen Mother finally arrived; but Rosamond and I murmured to one another in slight dismay that dukes and duchesses, earls and countesses appeared to be in the majority. We could only see Harold Nicolson and Vita, Kenneth Clark, Pierre Brisson of the *Figaro* and Maître Garcon on our side of the line. Nevertheless the party was a great success, partly because food and wine were absolutely tip-top, partly because Odette was in tremendous form as hostess, never losing control and looking sensational in her coronation dress of white velvet-satin with a royal blue wrap; also because the Queen Mother was enjoying it all so gaily and naturally.

After dinner I sat in the little circle round the Queen Mother with Harold Nicolson, Kenneth Clark, Lord Salisbury, the Duke of Wellington and the Duke of Buccleuch for the last hour and a half. Harold managed to steer the conversation round from the inter-relations of the nobility to Byron and Shelley. The Queen Mother showed herself intensely curious, amused and intelligently interested, and suddenly professed the strongest views about not putting any more busts in Westminster Abbey. I remember one incident in particular. The Duke of Wellington turned to Harold Nicolson, and said: 'Tell me, Harold, have we got to take this chap Dylan Thomas seriously?' Harold replied: 'Yes, of course' – and was firmly supported by the Queen Mother.

True to the tradition of the French, great parties were given whenever distinguished French men of letters were visiting London: Jean Schlumberger, Jacques de Lacretelle, André Gide. Odette was unshockable, and liked to draw her guests out, whether English or French, into reckless indiscretions. She also had the engaging trait of not caring in the slightest if she appeared ignorant or ill-informed, and would sharply question if at a loss. In the spring of 1951 the Tate Gallery put on an exhibition of the famous eighteenth century Eton 'leaving' portraits. A reception was held one evening, one of the most desperate scenes of jostling pandemonium I have ever witnessed. It was impossible, in those near-hysterical crowds, to savour again the haunting beauty of the pictures I have always loved so much. The Duke of Wellington attempted to make a speech of welcome which was reduced to an unintelligible boom by the loudspeakers. This did not daunt Eddie Marsh from leaning

over to me, and saying: 'He's such a good speaker, don't you
think?' Struggling through the milling bodies, I came up to
Odette, who said she felt seasick. I made an idiotic remark im-
pelled by I don't know what demon of fatuity: *'L'ardeur des
enthousiastes pour l'art et l'histoire monte comme une fumée qui étouffe!'*
She immediately looked serious and perplexed, and said: '*Tiens,
c'est une citation?*'

The next morning, I rang up Osbert Sitwell, who said: 'It
was like the revolution, don't you think?'

Edith still used as a base for her sallies on London from
Renishaw the Sesame Club in Grosvenor Street, and there she
would hold what she called her 'monster tea-parties', her more
intimate luncheons and occasional suppers after a theatre or a
concert. She was an exotic figure in this respectable middle-
class ladies' club and as she swept through in her long dresses
and bizarre hats designed to emphasize her patrician looks,
strange gold ornaments round her neck and enormous semi-
precious stones on the rings that covered her fingers, a hush
would descend on the conversation at tables where other members were entertaining their guests, and eyes would be raised
from newspapers where ravaged solitaries were huddled in de-
crepit armchairs. They did not look in the least imperial figures
or pioneers – the full name of the club was the Sesame Imperial
and Pioneer Club – but Edith *did*, and curiously enough the
two words, so grotesquely associated with the club's name,
represented the two sides of her nature: the aristocrat always
conscious of background and breeding, and the daring, icono-
clastic pioneer in the arts who had shocked conventional
London with her early poems and the public presentation of
them.

Edith's policy at these gatherings was to mix old friends and
almost total strangers who happened to have written to her
about her poetry or *their* poetry – with visiting relations and
the inevitable toady or two who could not be got rid of; and
hope for the best. Osbert, and Sacheverell with his Canadian
wife Georgia, were nearly always there acting as stiffeners, to
liven the conversation in those parts of the room geographically
remote from Edith, to encourage the shy and to rescue friends
from bores when they perceived that good manners had reached

snapping point. Poets, from Tom Eliot, Stephen Spender, Louis MacNeice and Dylan Thomas, to some penniless unknown young man whose verses had caught Edith's attention, were always to be found in abundance; publishers, literary agents and editors (except those whose papers had been guilty of printing tepid or slighting notices of the works of herself and her brothers – Alan Pryce-Jones, then editor of *The Times Literary Supplement*, was constantly in hot water and as constantly extricating himself with his usual deft *savoir-faire*); her favourite critics, talkers and wits, especially Maurice Bowra, Kenneth Clark and his wife Jane; her favourite actors, especially John Gielgud and Alec Guinness, and sometimes the leading lights of the ballet world, Fred Ashton, Robert Helpmann and Constant Lambert. Edith's magnetic personality and fame had an extraordinary attraction for near-lunatics, and sometimes one of these managed to get himself, or herself in, causing the utmost confusion, alarm – and comedy.

As I have already related, Edith liked to discuss feuds in the literary world with the greatest zest and most unqualified partizanship, sometimes being very funny indeed in a totally ruthless way. Her own enmities would change into, or back into friendships with extraordinary suddenness, leaving those who weren't entirely up-to-date breathless and bewildered. By nature she was combative – how could she have surmounted the obstacles of her early life if she had not been? – but her capacity for forgiveness was as unlimited as her impulse of kindness towards those she discovered were in trouble or difficulties. But as she once confessed to me, she liked, 'for a lark', to sharpen her wits on wooden heads 'in the way that cats sharpen their claws on the legs of kitchen tables'.

Even when most infuriated she rarely lost her own special brand of wit. Once, in the middle of a row with one of the Sunday papers, she wrote to me: 'I am worn out by my row. . . . One old fool called me a liar – about a poem of my own!! If Philip Frere can find out his address, he is going to be made to apologize to me. A friend of this gentleman's wrote to me, and said I ought not to be "cross" – because he is an ornithologist and kept sheep in Scotland whilst everybody else was being bombed to hell. Really! It is like saying one ought not to object

to being kept awake all night by somebody snoring, because he
once lived in Surrey – or to be surprised at somebody eating
peas off the tip of a knife because a bat once got into his drawing room.'

Exhausted she often was by these feuds, but in a way she
revelled in them too. On one occasion she wrote to me: 'I
quite forgot to tell you. I am writing – – a letter so *insolent* that
even *my* blood turns to ice as I read it. I am telling him I am
compiling a Calendar of great sayings from the Critics. I then
quote to him the most banal, and the most ungrammatical
passages I can find in his work, and ask for permission to include
these and, also, rights of translation into the English language.
. . .'

One of the most remarkable traits of Edith Sitwell, I have
always thought, was her capacity for making comedy out of
things that happened to herself, occurrences that must, at the
time, have been embarrassing, exhausting and even dangerous.
She wrote to me from San Francisco, on one of the major triumphal tours that she and Osbert carried out in America after
the war, that 'as a result of fatigue, I got bronchitis, for the
second time in three months. I had to give three readings here,
coughing my head off. However, the reading in Hollywood
was a great success, I do think. Lots of film stars, including
Harpo Marx came. And during my reading of the *Macbeth*
sleep-walking scene, I was just announcing that Hell is murky,
when a poor gentleman in the audience uttered the most piercing shrieks, and was carried out by four men, foaming at the
mouth. As one of the spectators said to me "you ought to be
awfully pleased. It was one of the most flattering things I have
ever seen. . . ."[1] We also met Miss Ethel Barrymore, who was
delightful, although Osbert ascribes my bronchitis to her, as
she was breathing heavily. I must say I couldn't have enjoyed
Hollywood more. We think all the waiters at the hotel there
were suffering from the effects of smoking marijuana, their
conduct was so strange. They would shriek with laughter, suddenly join in conversations, and lean on the sofa on which we
sat for our meals, putting their heads between ours.'

[1] In *Taken Care Of*, Edith Sitwell ascribes this remark, or something
similar, to Ethel Barrymore.

At that time Edith was preparing an anthology of American poetry to be published by my firm. She had, from the outset, shown the greatest interest in and enthusiasm for our venture, and hearing no doubt that we were not without our difficulties, she wrote, with great generosity: 'I am very distressed to hear about the proofs and the expense of the American anthology. Now look here. I have for very long wanted to make a present to the firm of Messrs Lehmann. Please allow me to make a present of this book. By which I mean, with the exception of David Higham's fee, I don't want a penny from the book. In fact I won't take one.'

One's memory selects episodes, moments, glimpses to retain with an unusual intensity, according to some mysterious law of its own. I have a vivid recollection of Edith coming to tea at my house one summer's day about this time, while I was writing my British Council booklet about her work. She answered a number of questions I put to her about her early life and how she started writing poetry, and told me what a horribly dark and painful time she had had while nursing Helen Rootham through her last illness before the war. She sat on the sofa in the green and gold light of my library, the green deepened to a darker glow by the tall spreading plane trees outside in the Crescent gardens, and the light from the western window caught in the prisms of the chandeliers and reflected off the plum red, orange and gold of the books in the shelves on either side of the fireplace, like a sombre priestess of prophecy and poetry. Her wide, dark, floppy hat overshadowed her strangely luminous, pale, oval face, the greenish eyes narrowed in their huge rings, the noble nose reminding me of the profiles of Roman emperors set in their marble medallions along the chimneypiece. As she talked very quietly of bitter experiences in the past the ends of her lips turned slightly down in a mask of suffering and sorrow. Then Carlotta came galloping into the room, and Edith's expression changed at once to delight and amusement as she greeted her and demanded an aria.

I shall always see Edith as I saw her that afternoon, a vivid image I put beside the dramatic memory of her reciting 'Still Falls the Rain' at the Churchill Club during a doodlebug raid.

2

When she was made an Honorary Doctor of Letters at Oxford, Edith celebrated by giving a large luncheon party to her friends. I found myself nearly opposite Tom Eliot, and became entirely absorbed towards the end in contemplation of his face: the rather grey lava-like landscape it presented, the furrowed brows, the deep-set eyes behind the spectacles that associated so well with the deep, slow voice. Most striking of all, I thought, was the large mouth with its kindly humorous 'set'; a reminder that this impressive tall figure, with the slightly bowed shoulders that added to the distinctly venerable general look, was the author not only of some of the greatest religious poetry of our time, but also of *Old Possum's Book of Practical Cats*.

As poet and editor and publisher himself, Tom Eliot had constantly shown the friendliest interest in my career and various ventures. From time to time we used to discuss professional matters together, as well as gossip about our friends. At that time he was President of the Alliance Française in Great Britain – a post in which I was to succeed him a few years later – and I remember that I was sitting beside him one afternoon during a long and exhausting meeting at the French Institute. In the intervals we talked about the state of literary magazines. He revealed that at its best his well-known quarterly, *The Criterion*, sold under 1,000 copies and lost its publishers about £500 a year. When he packed it up at the outbreak of war, the circulation had dropped to a couple of hundred – an ironic fact when one considers the historic fame it has since acquired on both sides of the Atlantic. He told me that he had enjoyed the experience very much, all the seventeen years of it, but added regretfully that he had never been satisfied: he should have spent more time on it, and he should have travelled more abroad to study what was going on there. He criticized various contemporary survivors for making what he considered the fatal mistake of trying to combine a 'popular' appeal with a 'highbrow' appeal. But he agreed with me when I said that I found authors often made a similar mistake, in trying to write popular pot-boilers when their talents were really for difficult books that could not appeal to more than a minority audience. It was only later that it occurred to me with dismay that he might have thought I was indirectly referring to his first essay in popular play-writing: *The Cocktail Party* appeared in London very soon after. I certainly did not intend that; and yet for all Tom's skill in evolving a medium to carry both social conversation and high poetry, I am not sure that his plays are not flawed, funda-mentally, by exactly that contradiction.

Tom had a ruthless streak in him, which came out some-times in his judgments of his contemporaries. When I had finally agreed to succeed him at the Alliance, we lunched together at the Athenaeum, and he gave me some useful hints on the prob-lems and personalities of the organization. I particularly re-member him saying to me: 'You will, of course, have to deal with the President of the Alliance in Paris, Monsieur Emile Henriot, a charming man who has written a great many books that will soon be forgotten.'

A couple of years later, on Tom's sixty-fifth birthday, *The New York Times* asked me if I could persuade him to give me a special interview. In the course of our conversation, I reminded him that some years before he had written to me to say he felt he would never write poetry again. 'Well, I was right,' he said, chuckling, 'because I haven't.' When I asked him how, in that case, he accounted for the plays, he immediately replied: 'That doesn't count, it's quite different. It's what you might call *applied* poetry, and if real poetry happens to get into it by the way, that's just something to be thankful for!'

He went on to give the information, which I found quite ex-traordinary, that he had felt as if he was never going to write poetry again several times before in his life. The first time was after writing *The Hollow Men*. By chance Faber's had just started the little series of separately published Ariel poems, and per-suaded him to contribute. 'Writing those Ariel poems released the stream again, and led to *Ash Wednesday*. Then I remember feeling I'd written myself out just before *The Rock* was commis-sioned. I had to write it – I had a deadline – and working on it began to make me interested in writing drama, and led directly to *Murder in the Cathedral.*'

Again, he told me, he felt pure poetry had dried up in him for good; but – most extraordinary of all – there were some lines and fragments that were discarded while *Murder in the Cathedral* was being rehearsed, and out of these fragments he gradually saw a poem shaping itself. 'That was how *Burnt Norton* came to be written. But it might have remained by itself, if it hadn't been for the war. I was very much absorbed in the problems of writing for the stage, and might have gone straight on from *The Family Reunion* to another play; but the war destroyed that impulse for a time, the conditions of one's life changed, and one was thrown in on oneself. So I wrote *East Coker* to follow *Burnt Norton*. And in writing *East Coker* I began to see the poems as the first two in a set of four.'

Such was the series of chances that led to the writing of a masterpiece.

When I said to him: 'But if such random chances have led so often to new poetic creation for you, isn't it possible it might happen again? If someone, for instance, made you promise a poem – for a special occasion?' He laughed and said: 'I'd like to think that . . . but I don't want to repeat what I've already done. It has always struck me as very curious the way certain poets, Browning for instance, have gone on writing in their old age without taking any step forward, making any new discovery. Why go on and on doing what you've already done well? I myself want each poem, or group of poems to be different, a separate creation. Even Milton seems to me to have made a mistake in writing *Paradise Regained*. *Samson Agonistes* is different, it's something new, a new victory.'

I have a vivid recollection of him, a year or so later, after the end of my publishing, at the ceremony which was held to unveil the 'blue plaque' on Oscar Wilde's house in Tite Street. Just before Compton Mackenzie started his moving speech he arrived in an old slouch hat and raincoat, pushing the bath-chair of his friend John Hayward. He became a close friend of Nora Wydenbruck, one of his German translators and author of an excellent book on Rilke which I had the pleasure of publishing. One evening I met him at her house in his gayest form, and I reminded him of the Oscar Wilde ceremony. We talked about Wilde as a writer, and he said that in his opinion the poems were, of course, hopeless, though *The Importance* was a masterpiece; but he remembered being very much excited and stimulated as a young man by reading *Intentions*, and still thought it was a good book for young people to read who intended to be writers. When I drove him back to Cheyne Walk after the party had broken up, he said to me suddenly how much he wished I was still a publisher and could relieve him of part of the responsibility he felt of publishing the work of new poets.

All that was before his sensational elopement with his attractive secretary Valerie Fletcher. To be capable of slipping off in a taxi with a new bride one morning, as one is approaching the age of seventy, and just leaving a note on one's desk to astound one's employer, gives every sensible author hope. Browning, after all, was only in his thirties when he eloped with Elizabeth Barrett.

3

There was a third guardian angel among my elders and betters, to whom I looked for advice and whose interest in and approbation of my doings was extremely important to me. I have described elsewhere[1] the sympathetic encouragement I got from E. M. Forster over *New Writing*, and the tireless battles he waged, in his devastating, impish way, against the philistines and power-maniacs to whom the war was such a golden opportunity.

He used sometimes to come to tea at No. 31, and we would exchange gossip about our mutual friends, Christopher Isherwood, William Plomer, Joe Ackerley and John Morris in particular. He always thought it very funny that William, to whom he is devoted, had a habit of being extremely secretive about his telephone number. He told me that when he was laid up

[1] See *I Am My Brother*, 101–2, 178.

with a broken ankle in London in the autumn of 1951, William had at last relented and offered it to him; but he had refused to use it because he felt it was taking unfair advantage. As he told me this, he became incoherent with laughter over his tea cup.

He had broken his ankle in the tower of Aldeburgh church, and had it in plaster for some weeks. It gave him an opportunity, he said, to do some reading for me if I wanted. I immediately seized the opportunity to ask him to read and advise on Denton Welch's *Journal*, which had just been sent me. I had only to write to him, he told me, and he would do more if he could. Sometimes, however, like every other distinguished literary figure, the importunities of others, especially strangers, overwhelmed him. In the summer of 1952, in reply to a cautious feeler I put out, he replied: 'Yes, it's long since I sat on your nice, low soft sofas and chairs, and I should much like to do it again soon. Will ring in hopes. I'm afraid I can't undertake any little job though yet awhile. I'm snowed up as it is with others' MSS, and no nice big St Bernard to dig me out. There are: a novel by a friend's daughter-in-law, a study on Czechoslovakia by another lady, a translation by a Bengali scientist of Tagore, a short story about child-birth, and a thesis on myself by a Copt. And there is my own work on a Mahratta prince, with which I must say I manage to proceed, despite all. . . .'

When he came to visit me, he often used to ask me to read him some of my poems, among which he had one or two special favourites. I shall never forget that at a moment when the blows of fate seemed to be raining particularly cruelly upon me, he wrote me a marvellous letter of comfort out of the blue. I cannot refrain from quoting it here, because it seems to me an example of the true aristocracy of friendship; 'I have long been minded to write you a line of esteem and affection, and if there ever was a special moment for such a letter perhaps this is it. I do so appreciate what you have done for literature through publishing and the way you have done it. And also – though this you already know – I appreciate your own work, and I was re-reading only the other day your Dark Lieutenant from the Sea. . . .'

4

One of the advantages of being an editor and publisher, if one's friends happen to be mostly in the world of literature and the arts, is that it gives one a reason to work with them and see them intensively from time to time. The longer I live, the more it appears to me that life is disagreeably devised in such a way that friends can hardly fail to drift away from one another, unless special ties of work or contiguity bind them together. The circle of one's intimates in one decade imperceptibly changes, until one realizes in the next decade, with a shock of sadness, that half – perhaps nearly all – of those one loved and enjoyed to be with so much have slipped out of the circle; others have taken their place.

The point of London clubs, of course, is to prevent, or at least to mitigate this – at the cost of throwing one together with a great many bores as well. Even so, there are *several* clubs that cater for writers and their fellow intellectuals of the para-literary world, and one can't be a member of them all. Worse still, they are rarely those that cater for painters, musicians or actors as well. I have been a member of the Athenaeum since the middle 'thirties, but hoping to find a creative writer there is like looking for a pen in a haystack of civil servants, surgeons and bishops. (There *are* some.) A great relief to my condition came when I was elected a member of the Garrick (at least twenty-five years later), but even there I have been conscious, as I feasted on the excellent food and wine, of delectable literary friends lunching far away, in the Travellers', the Savile, the Reform, White's.

Pleasant, then, have been the opportunities that arose from my calling as editor and publisher to grapple a friend closer to my soul for a while. Such an opportunity was my publication (which I have already described) of Billy Chappell's *Studies in Ballet*. Another, one of the most pleasant, arose from the scheme of Hallam Fordham to compile a picture book on the subject of John Gielgud. Hallam put it up to me in the autumn of 1951, and the three of us had a first luncheon to discuss the project, which appealed to me very much, almost immediately after. This gave John an opportunity to talk about his life, his ancestry, his favourite roles, in an extremely fascinating and amusing way, speaking at high speed and scarcely drawing breath. He is one of the most delightful talkers in the world; not so good, however, as a listener. He can be extremely witty in talking about his colleagues, but seldom malicious, a rare gift among actors. I have admired him ever since I saw him as Richard II in 1929, and every time I have heard him in Shakespeare my conviction has deepened that no one can equal him in the speaking of verse on the stage. Though Macbeth cannot, perhaps, be counted as one of his greatest parts, I do not myself think anyone will excel him in giving tragic conviction to the transition of Macbeth from the proud and triumphant warrior to the guilt-ridden murderer haunted by his own imagination. Equally, there will never, for me, be any other Jack Worthing in *The Importance of Being Earnest.*

During the 'forties, I had, nevertheless, felt that certain mannerisms, or affectations, were growing on him, particularly in his playing of romantic parts. I was therefore thrilled when, at this very time when the book was being prepared, I went to see his production of *Much Ado About Nothing* and discovered that he had transformed himself. No doubt the change had been taking place gradually but it hit me with especial force on that night. All the old mannerisms had dropped away in his playing of Benedick: the skill, the wit, the human charm of his acting were dazzling. Some new quality had, it seemed to me, been added to the admirable qualities one already knew, which made it apparent at last without any clouding of doubt that he is one of the greatest actors of our time.

When the book was all but ready for the press, he came to lunch at my house to discuss the final touches. Though rattling away with great vigour, sitting at the table with an Edwardian straightness of back, he was in more reflective mood, and began to talk about the future of his career. Emlyn Williams had recently had a notable success with his recreation of Dickens readings: a bold and brilliant venture that delighted the public in spite of many gloomy prophecies. I suggested that he should do something of the same sort with readings from among his great Shakespearean roles. John seemed at first very reluctant, taking the line that it was the kind of thing one only did at the end of one's career (I did not say that the case of Emlyn Williams seemed to contradict his view). What he really liked, he said, what satisfied his deepest desires as a man of the theatre, was the *whole thing*, a whole play, the entirety of a production through which he could express his creative spirit adequately. After some further discussions, he yielded as far as to say that he might one day do such a series, perhaps for television in the USA. Many years were to pass before he did in fact adopt this idea, with overwhelming success.

I have already described how much pleasure it gave me to be able to include Laurie Lee's *A Bloom of Candles* among my first books. Later on, I published his radio play in verse *The Voyage of Magellan* with illustrations by Edward Burra. I saw a good deal of Laurie in these years, with and without his guitar, but always with his countryman's fund of comic stories. Alan Ross, whose first volume of poems, *The Derelict Day*, I published as well as sending him to Corsica to write *Time was Away* with John Minton, was also a frequent visitor to my home. He and his newly married wife Jennifer Fry took a house in South Terrace, and so were close neighbours of mine. He was an addict of *Penguin New Writing*, and never ceased to lament its death. Many years later, when he was negotiating with me to take over the *London Magazine*, he told me that he thought the formula I had evolved for *PNW* was still the perfect model for such a magazine in our time.

With Roy and Kate Fuller now began to come their startlingly good-looking son John, who was soon to follow his father's footsteps as poet. I have often thought it must need a certain stoic spirit to be the mother as well as the wife of an intellectual poet. This suspicion became conviction when, one day, some years later, during a family holiday in the Lakes, John wrote me on a post card: 'Roy and I are discussing Auden, while Kate watches the sheep.'

I have already written[1] of my great admiration and affection

[1] *I Am My Brother, passim.*

for David Gascoyne, who, eccentric, inhibited and absolutely without the gift for popular success as he is, seems to me the purest and in some ways the most impressive philosophic poet of our time. Compared with Wystan Auden's production, David's is tiny, spasmodic, incomplete. Nevertheless there is no attempt in his poetry to play a role, or to inflate his intellectual conclusions: everything he writes comes with an utter sincerity out of the deep, anguished searchings of a philosopher who expresses himself naturally in poetry, about the nature of the world we live in and the problems of the individual's existence in the nightmare of the twentieth century.

One day, at the beginning of 1950, he suddenly rang the doorbell of my house. I had not been in touch with him for some time. The figure I saw when I opened the door shocked me: his unshaven, quivering, grey-green face looked ravaged by nervous tension, perhaps by waking dreams of persecution and prophetic alarms. All the worst forebodings of the sick age in which we live seemed to writhe like snakes in his ever changing expression. He came in, and poured out a fevered story of his recent life, a Cassandra-like cry into the void. I calmed him down as best I could, and suggested he should collect the poems he had written since the appearance of his wartime, Sutherland-illustrated, volume, and let me publish them. The idea appealed to him, and resulted in the publication of *A Vagrant* at the end of the year, one of the rare books I feel it was a deep privilege for me to have brought to the light. Of the many beautiful poems in the volume, so unlike the fashionable poetry of the time in every way, the one that has come most often to my mind in subsequent years has, I think, been 'Rex Mundi':

> He drove past in a carriage that was drawn by a white goat:
> King of the world to come when all that shall be now is new,
> Calmly he gazed on our pretentious present that is not
> Of morals, classes, business, war, this child
> Knew nothing. We were pardoned when he smiled. . . .

Some time after the book came out, I arranged a luncheon party for him and the American novelist, Carson McCullers, to which I invited Henry Yorke, William Sansom and Moura Budberg. It was one of the most extraordinary parties I have ever given. Sometimes a party coalesces at once, all the guests join in general conversation and strike sparks off one another. On other occasions, often not so satisfactorily, guests talk to their neighbours and no general discussion emerges. On this occasion, however, everyone seemed to be having his own party, with the exception of Bill Sansom and Henry, who cracked esoteric jokes at one another, roaring with laughter, while Carson McCullers watched and listened with a look of rather puzzled misery on her face. Every now and then she would interpolate an astonishing remark about her private life in America, which held up the flow of wise-cracks between Henry and Bill for a moment, then off they went again. Meanwhile David, completely detached from all this, would suddenly make some mysterious, rapid, low-toned observations, addressed to no one in particular, which seemed, as far as one could understand them, to be about existentialism or the state of French poetry. At the other end of the table dear, warm-hearted Moura Budberg did her best to establish, among these disparate performances, what I had already abandoned, a sense of social unity.

Somehow or other, the party was a success, but not really for the host, who can never enjoy himself when all his guests, like wild horses, are pulling frantically in different directions. When Bill is in good form, his remarks have a grotesque humour all their own. I remember one occasion when he came to my house with some other friends, and having recently returned from a tour of South America I enlarged on the horror of flying over tropical jungle in an unsteady aircraft, in a thunderstorm, with the thought ever present in one's mind of what would happen if one had an accident. 'The most loathsome part,' I said, 'would be the tarantulas.' Bill immediately replied: 'Nonsense, John. You'd be frying them on toast and eating them as a delicacy in no time.'

At that time Henry was in his most sparkling form, his unique gifts as a novelist having at last found general recognition, and a special cult for his work having arisen in America. One of his new transatlantic admirers was the southern short-story writer Eudora Welty, and I remember an occasion at my house when they met for the first time and flung themselves at one another. Henry could not have been more recklessly ebullient, and swept

Eudora Welty off her feet. She asked him eagerly: 'I suppose no
new book yet?' Gravely and nonchalantly savouring his opportunity, Henry replied: 'Today.' It was in fact the English publication day of *Nothing*; which he maintained was the first entirely funny book he had ever tried to write, and found very
difficult to bring off.

Not long after that evening, at the invitation of the BBC, I
gave a talk on the Home Service about Henry's novels: a script
that caused me much anxiety, and about the adequacy of which
I had grave doubts. Henry, however, appeared to be delighted.
He wrote to me afterwards: 'I thought your broadcast most
beautifully done. The way you kept to *Party Going*, made sorties
from it so to speak, and then returned to it, was lovely and I
could embrace you for so insisting on the humour. The latter
is all part of a theory of writing I have and which I develop in
July's *Contact*. They offered me such a large fee I couldn't for
the sake of wife and child refuse. When you rang up I thought
to send you a copy, then I considered you must have finished
the script. Anyway there was not a word you said that night
which conflicted with my theory of how novels should be done.'
It is a matter of perpetual and painful regret to me that after
Doting, published two years later, Henry's creative flow dried
up.

To return to David Gascoyne. A few days after the luncheon
party he brought Carson McCullers to dinner again. Tennessee
Williams, who had just arrived in London, joined us. As usual,
Carson and David talked across one another, and at one moment I rather rudely told him to shut up as I wanted so much
to hear what she was saying. He jumped up and made off, and
I had to wheedle him back from the front door and ask his forgiveness. I was particularly struck by the tender and affectionate consideration Tennessee showed Carson. He knew exactly
how to handle his erratic and brilliant friend, and revealed an
impressive side to his character of which I had, I confess, not
been fully aware before. Afterwards, we all jumped into the
car, and drove round and over the river bridges to see the
lights of the Festival of Britain and the Fun Fair in Battersea
Park.

Tennessee expressed regret that the Fun Fair sported no

ferris-wheel. We had published *The Roman Spring of Mrs Stone* the year before, and he had written to me from Rome: 'Rome is now the hottest it has been for 100 years, so Mrs Stone and I are leaving Tuesday night for Vienna. Mrs Stone says she wants to find "the Fourth Man", and I want to take a ride in that big ferris-wheel. . . . If we sail from a northern port this time, I will make every effort, but no promise to get over to London. I want to see you and your sisters, and the Christopher Fry plays I have heard so much about. Peter Ustinov is here doing Nero in the great new MGM spectacle *Quo Vadis* which has already cost 8 million dollars and given employment to almost every street-walker in Rome. . . . They have a pack of lions, about 30 of them, a herd of fighting bulls, a brace of cheetas. The *poveri ragazzi* are quaking with terror of the scenes they have to act with this menagerie. Ustinov did not look so happy when the pair of cheetas walked on, supposedly pets of Octavia's, but perhaps he was only afraid they would steal the scene. A *Vogue* photographer wanted to take our picture together on Nero's throne and Ustinov said, "I don't share my throne with any-body! . . ." '

Tennessee informed me that evening that he had seen some-thing of Paul Bowles's new novel *Let It Come Down*, and was very much excited by it. It arrived by air from Tangier about ten days later: a descent into hell by a master of infernal landscape, with a dry macabre humour running through it that seemed to me an important gain over his first novel *The Sheltering Sky*; a book not to be put down till the very end.

Paul had first appeared in England in the late autumn of 1949, just as *The Sheltering Sky* was being published. In his early middle-age, with his shock of gold hair, slightly curled and as stiff as if made of nylon bristles, he still looked like a slim Greek athlete who might have had a nervous breakdown and taken to an intellectual, bohemian life after just failing to win the *discus* championship. Neatly dressed, with imaginative eyes, over which he wore a shade in the early morning, he was much more reserved than most of the Americans of his generation I had met. In fact the long years he had spent away from his country, in Europe, Central America, and North Africa, had, I thought, left a deep impress not only on his behaviour but also on his writing: he seemed to me far more like an European writer, in thought as well as in style, than an American writer of his generation. He struck me at once by his quiet charm and intelligence, his shrewdness about the ways of the world, and – when the reserve melted – a sharp wit that did not spare his contemporaries, of some of whom he could give very funny imitations.

He seemed at first a little at sea in the literary world of London, and was a listener rather than a talker. He was puzzled, he said, when Cyril Connolly told him he had decided *The Sheltering Sky* was too good to review, and asked me if I did not think a person who spoke like that to an author a very extraordinary chap? He was amazed and fascinated to see someone wearing a kilt at an evening party I gave for him. He listened with an astonishment, in which delight gradually took over, to the conversation at a dinner party during which Henry Yorke, for whose books he had a deep admiration, talked almost without stop at the top of his form, developing fantastic theories (which do not seem quite so fantastic today) about the coming invasion of Britain by coloured peoples from former colonies, culminating in a negro prime minister in 1984, and questioning Elizabeth Bowen about the Royal Commission on Capital Punishment (on which she was serving at the time) in a way that managed to make even that macabre subject grotesquely amusing.

Paul Bowles's books reveal a highly developed gift for descriptive writing, especially in exotic scenes, and also an intuitive understanding of abnormal minds and abnormal states of mind bordering on madness. The same gifts appear in his letters. From England he went on to India and Ceylon, where he had plans for buying an island. In April I had a letter from Trivandrum, in southern India, in which he wrote: 'Madura temple I thought completely wonderful; I've never seen anything remotely like it. As if a madman had conceived a meeting-place for people who automatically went mad on entering it. And of course one does. After you've been in the temple for a couple of hours you begin to feel people tinkering with the inside of your mind, and that leaves you feeling strangely empty afterwards. They literally sit there in their rags, looking straight at you for twenty minutes or half-an-hour at a stretch, and scratch around inside your head; I suppose it is one of their daily exercises. And the bells ring and the flutes and drums play and the priests look and act exactly like bouncers in a low bar, and the people jiggle wildly in front of Sri Ganesh, the elephant god, which in this case is spotted with obscene white patches and wears an enormous dirty sarong of ordinary cotton over its loins, and the "water" in the tank is brilliant green and thick as paste and bubbling with putrefaction, and the place is as big as Grand Central Station, with huge courts where loud-speakers blare and two or three thousand people sit around on the ground under the trees listening, and there is an entire section full of shops which sell everything from sandalwood statues to lollipops, from kitchenware to artificial flowers, from Japanese dolls to postcards. . . . My address continues the same; they will forward things here, once I find a place to settle down for a while. But the whole place is so like a furnace that I can't make up my mind to settle anywhere. It seems the monsoons failed, so everything is parched. People don't seem to be in a very good humour, and they keep wrecking the trains. I wish I had come twenty years ago.'

On his way back from Ceylon, in late May, Paul came to stay with us again, burnt the colour of tanned leather, and with his batteries evidently re-charged by his winter in sunny climes. In a letter which reached me only just before his own arrival, he described an extraordinary episode involving his wife Jane, a dramatist whose plays have still not met their due. 'It seems Connolly went to Paris, and while there looked up Jane, to whom, through the concierge, he announced himself as "a friend of Bowles". In general she is not interested in my friends, so she went downstairs without any make-up and in her bed clothes, whatever they may have been. She is also very near-sighted and has a foul memory besides, so when she saw him she had no idea who he was; the conversation dragged somewhat, from her account. She ended by asking him what instrument he played. . . . She was sure he was a musician of some sort, come to pay his respects while he was on tour in Europe.'

In some ways Paul Bowles's short stories, a collection of which

we published under the title of *A Little Stone*, are, I am inclined
to think, more remarkable than his novels, enlarging the imagination with strange images of primitive vision and belief, of
passion and horror entirely beyond the Christian categories of
good and evil; stories that have no parallel in modern literature
as far as my knowledge goes. I cannot speak of his talents as a
musician, but I am certain that he has the capacity to be one
of the greatest modern writers; a gift that general opinion is
likely to fight against to the last, because he has the quality that
geniuses, great and small, so often display, of being profoundly
disturbing to the deeper conventional assumptions and patterns
of value – and not merely shocking (which he also is) to established codes of behaviour already more or less abandoned by
free-thinking people.

For the jacket designs, I gave each of Paul Bowles's three
books to a different artist. *The Sheltering Sky* to Fred Uhlman
(because he had just been to North Africa), *Let It Come Down*
to John Minton, and *A Little Stone* to Keith Vaughan. If I
valued the opportunities my publishing activities gave me to
be in closer touch with author friends, I was just as happy when
the same thing happened with my artist friends. Keith Vaughan,
as I have already related, was regularly employed by my firm
in its early days, and continued to design spines and jackets and
illustrate various books long after. It was exciting to see him
gradually developing assurance as an artist and attracting the
notice of the serious critics; as I had felt from the very first
sight of his war drawings that he must surely do one day. By the
time the Festival of Britain was put on he had already become
absorbed in the problems which he has been exploring ever
since. His mural in the Dome of Discovery showed huge for-
malized male naked figures in a mysterious state of exaltation,
arriving on strange barren territory. As I was studying it, a
dumpy little woman passed in front of it for a moment, and
exclaimed to her companion, with a giggle: 'Look, we're on the
moon now!'

Though the staunchest of friends, I have never found Keith
the easiest of persons to deal with. Beneath the charm, he has a
very strong streak of tough, unhurried stubbornness. He does
not easily yield an opinion once he has formed it, and he is cool

and wary in his dealings even with intimates. He sees his friends' faults and weaknesses as clearly as he sees their good qualities, and is not afraid to speak of either – with candour but not with malice. But this stubbornness, this quiet certainty of opinion and direction have, I believe, been the great strength in his artistic career. Ignoring fashion, but not the deeper trends of his time, he has been able to work steadily away at the refinement and intensification of his peculiar vision. Visiting a large exhibition of his pictures in London more than twenty years after my first publication of his drawings in *Penguin New Writing*, I was struck by a wonderful purity and strength, an almost Miltonic quality they revealed.

Very different in temperament was his friend John Minton, whose death so early in his career, and in the way it happened, was one of the most saddening things I have known since the war. As mercurial as Keith is level-headed, even in his most extravagant moods of gaiety he could not conceal the melancholy that lay, a dark unstirring pool in the depths of his nature. I had met him through Keith towards the end of the war,[1] and was captivated at once by his warmth, sensitivity and sense of fun; perhaps too, and more intuitively, by the melancholy that I know lies not far below the sanguine and practical surface of my nature also. I can remember gatherings of friends, evenings when his tearing high spirits and absurd clowning infected all the rest of us and made us far wittier and merrier than our normal selves. I can also remember tête-à-tête meetings with him when he would express some of the restless dissatisfaction he felt with his own work, with the way painting was going in our time, and his need to get away from Europe for long periods, to refresh the springs of his creative activity and to sort out the problems of his personal life. It was inevitable, with his temperament, that he should feel strongly that art needed, in our age above all, a close relationship to and meaning in human life as it is lived. The danger of the world, the despair that must at times overcome even the most cheerful people when they stopped to think, were too pressing, he used to say, for any enclosed, cerebral or mathematical art. And it was, I think, because he saw art all over the western world moving towards

[1] See *I Am My Brother*, 312.

abstraction, and knew that he could not sincerely follow it himself, that his despair increased as the years went by and his gaiety became more forced and frenetical.

I remember one extreme example of his behaviour when in manic mood. We had arranged to dine together, and he arrived with a bunch of carnations which he insisted on presenting to me. He was in uproarious form, flinging his arms about like a marionette controlled by a dancing dervish, shouting extremely wild and risqué remarks at the top of his voice (which always became very shrill on such occasions) to the confusion of our fellow-diners at the 'White Tower', even scaring Tennessee Williams who passed our table in an hallucinatory appearance. At one moment he was pouring out almost embarrassingly affectionate sentiments, the next he was mocking and crowing again. He confessed that he had been on a jag already for three nights, and insisted on continuing. My attempts to restrain his mounting ebullience were spoilt by the state of helpless laughter to which he kept on reducing me. Finally I left him when he was buying champagne for everyone (for the second time) in an unidentified night-club. But in later years these demonstrations became painful rather than exhilarating to take part in.

He not only designed a large number of beautiful book-jackets for my publications, and illustrated in his own richly imaginative way a handful of books that would by themselves have made my publishing work worth while, but also gave me, in spontaneous bursts of generosity, what added up to a small portfolio of watercolours and pen drawings. Sometimes they were given as peace (or guilt) offerings, because he had been late with a book-jacket, or a batch of black-and-white decorations; but the need to turn away my wrath existed only in his own mind. What I most treasure are three tables he painted for me, one large round dining table and two small occasional tables. Each had a different dominant theme: one of the small tables seaside and fishing activities, the other classical motifs, while the large table represented the four seasons, with four youthful figures surrounded by his or her appropriate natural symbols. All are ravishing to look at, but the large table is undoubtedly the *chef d'œuvre*, due to the fresh lyrical feeling that pervades it and the marvellous vibrant colour harmonies such as only John could create. I feel sure that John, if he had wanted, could have designed the most exciting décor and costumes for ballet and opera, and it remains a mystery to me why no one in that world spotted this potential gift awaiting encouragement and exploitation.

My publishing life has been full of unexpected ironies. No one could have persuaded me when I started that one of my most successful and famous publications would be a cookery book. One day such a manuscript came in, ill-typed on poor paper. It appeared to be a treatise on continental and Mediterranean cuisine, by someone who signed herself Elizabeth David. At that time Julia Strachey was working for me as a reader: she told me she knew something of the author and something of the subject. I gave her the unprepossessing bundle of grubby typescript rather as a matter of routine than with any idea that I would be able to do anything about it. Julia, however, came back a few days later with the report that it was clearly the work of an expert, and was extremely well written. If I felt like taking a chance, she assured me that this wouldn't be a bad gamble. The cheerless age of austerity was still with us at the time, and I had a hunch that if I were to publish this book it must be done as attractively and unausterely as possible, even if many of the dishes had to remain for some time, for the English cook, mouth-watering dreams rather than realities. So I gave the typescript to John Minton, practically with *carte blanche*, and he came back with the exquisitely pretty decorations that everyone is acquainted with. As far as I know, it was the very first of such books to be published after the war; in any case it was an instant success, and in fact set a fashion. I became devoted to the author, with a devotion in which there was only one snag: I found it almost impossible to bring myself to invite her to a meal from my own kitchen.

I have always maintained that one of the lesser reasons for its success was a misprint. At one point Elizabeth wrote: 'Take 2/3 eggs. . . .' She did not, however, notice when correcting the proofs that the compositor had printed: 'Take 23 eggs.' Visions of delicious plenty – for 1950!

With another young author-artist I much admired my relations were, unfortunately, posthumous in this period. Denton

Welch came into my editorial life in the middle of the war,[1] when he sent me a short story, 'The Barn', for *New Writing*, and I encouraged him to design some tail-pieces for the Penguin. I shall always regret that I never went down to see him in his Kentish home, and how a series of mischances kept us from meeting on his rare visits to London. He was killed, as everyone knows, by the lingering illness that afflicted him after he had been knocked down by a car. Soon after his death in 1948, I was surprised to find that his previous publisher did not appear to want the novel he had left in an all but completed state. I read the MS and was deeply moved: scarcely veiled autobiography, it seemed to me a marvellous piece of work, not merely as a story but as literature, and I immediately accepted it. I gave it the title of *A Voice Through a Cloud*.

I began to see a good deal of his close friend Eric Oliver, who had been looking after him at the time of his death. Together we sifted through his drawings, eventually finding some appropriate enough to use as decorations in the text, and as endpapers and jacket.

I remember an occasion, about a year after Denton's death, when Eric came to lunch at No. 31, with Christopher Kininmonth. Eric arrived, looking very sunburnt, in a flaming orange shirt. He was always awkward in company strange to him: he twisted himself like a corkscrew about the room, would suddenly stop in the middle of an incoherent sentence, and then smile in an embarrassed way. Christopher was speechless with amazement, the party nevertheless turned out a great success. Eric insisted on cutting bread and dishing out for everyone, and told us many stories of Denton, revealing that there were a dozen or so short stories still to come out of his literary remains, also a sheaf of poems. At the end he took Christopher off in the most extraordinary tumble-down contraption to go by the name of car I have ever seen. They vanished into the Fulham Road in a cloud of blue smoke, and I uttered a silent prayer.

A year later, I published a volume of these still uncollected short stories and poems, together with reproductions of the best of his very small, but immensely engaging and rather mysterious work as a painter, as *A Last Sheaf*.

[1] See *I Am My Brother*, 239-42.

Eric Oliver asked me to house some of Denton Welch's rare pieces of furniture, silver and paintings for a time in my cottage in the country. The cottage had only just been bought, and was still rather bare. Denton's possessions transformed it, particularly his baroque wooden angels, an Etruscan head on a snake pedestal, and an exquisite fantasy painting, by a sixteenth century minor Flemish master, of the Colossus of Rhodes, showing the Colossus as a wistful Eros. Later, when Eric Oliver had found a place in which he could keep them himself, he left with me as a precious gift one of Denton's most characteristic and mysterious small paintings: *A Cat Brooding*.

The reviews for *A Voice Through a Cloud* were among the most enthusiastic I had for any book. They spoke of 'writer born', 'a work of genius', 'a tragic and unforgettable book', of 'sunshine blazing through a leaf, showing up every vein,' 'a triumph'. And Stephen Spender wrote to me from Cornwall: 'It's one of the most wonderful and terrifying books I've ever read. Certainly the first three-quarters of it make a masterpiece. Poor Denton Welch. How dreadfully sorry I am. I feel it will be impossible to think of anything else for days. I am very shaken by it.' I agreed with him; but I have now to reflect sadly on the chances of so small a literary output, and in a way so specialized, surviving the importunate and ever thickening crowd of new names and new reputations urgent for lasting recognition.

From time to time Stephen and I used to meet for a lunch or an evening together, though not so frequently as before, as he was travelling abroad a great deal, lecturing in America, and involving himself ever deeper in the politics of the Committee for Cultural Freedom which had just been formed after the Congress of Writers in Berlin, and which was eventually to be the power behind *Encounter*. In spite of the impression he was apt to make of boyish fluster in public debates, Stephen was really very good at these congresses, showing a strength of will and a political flair that was obviously in his blood. He would sail into a congress like a demolition expert arriving to inspect a row of old cottages that had outlived their usefulness. Before the inhabitants had grasped the significance of his presence, bricks would be thudding to the ground and lorries roaring away with the rubbish. It is always good to see an expert at work, but personally I regretted this particular expert was not at work building poems, a skill which came to occupy less and less of his time.

He was beginning to be more and more dissatisfied with London intellectual life in comparison with what he found abroad, particularly in America. One evening, I remember, we went to see *The Old Ladies* at the Lyric Theatre, Hammersmith, together. Afterwards, in a pub in the Broadway, we began to talk of new writers who were appearing on the English literary scene. I said that I found it strange, and rather disturbing, that no one of the younger generation seemed to take that 'moral' attitude, and not only in literature, that our generation had felt was so vital. He replied bitterly: 'Yes, London is frightful now, it's become like Dublin.' I noticed a large bulge in his coat pocket, and looked at it pointedly: he fished out the proofs of his autobiography, *World Within World*, which he was just correcting, and proffered them to me.

I have already written of the close ties I had at this time with a number of writers, apart from Stephen Spender, who were not published by my firm; especially William Sansom, Henry Yorke (Green), and Elizabeth Bowen. Among my friends in the literary world, Elizabeth was one of the most consistently sympathetic with what I was trying to do, urging me at one moment not to neglect my own poetry, and at another to see that *Penguin New Writing* filled the gap that was growing ominously larger among English literary magazines. She was, I think, beginning to feel increasingly restless in England, and wanted to settle in her ancestral home at Bowen's Court in County Cork, whither she invited me to stay at any time when I happened to be passing, by air, to or from the United States. When her husband, Alan Cameron, died in 1952, even that plan proved too ambitious for her, and to the vast regret of her circle she decided to sell Bowen's Court and live in Oxford. A sad part of one's life since 1945 has been to see so many of one's friends leave estates and houses they loved and settle for small apartments and flats that inevitably lack much of the atmosphere that had seemed so much part of them. This change, as everyone knows, has come about largely owing to the gradual disappearance of what used to be known as the servant class.

Butler and housemaids, head gardeners and grooms have gone to the factories (though I remember Emerald Cunard saying to me: 'It's a great mistake, John, to think you cannot get servants today, you can get *very good* servants – but you have to *pay* for them.) This is, of course, an evolution whole-heartedly to be applauded for the sake of social justice; but something of value has been lost in the process, as probably in every major social change, something that Yeats was thinking of when he wrote of the 'dance-like glory that those walls begot' in 'Coole Park'.

Elizabeth's anxiety about the state of English literary magazines was certainly timely. In the autumn of 1949 Cyril Connolly let it be known that he was thinking of retiring from *Horizon* for a year. 'Cyril must have a rest' was the theme of his helpers. I knew, however, that one cannot 'retire' a magazine for a period and start again where one has left off. This was clearly the end of a great and memorable venture, though Cyril Connolly found it difficult to admit it. A few months later he offered me *Horizon*, over a bottle of champagne at the Athenaeum, at a reduced price. Though I was aware that the magazine was as completely *his* as *New Writing* was mine, I was tempted owing to the difficulties I was encountering at that time in my negotiations with Penguin Books. I suggested to my backers in Purnell that it would be well worth while buying for the small sum involved; but nothing came of it.

After this, Cyril, newly married to Barbara Skelton, was eager to devote himself to writing, and also, it seemed, to the planting of shrubs in his Sussex home. I had recently been planting my garden at the cottage I had just bought near Three Bridges, and one day he challenged me to a contest of Latin names of the most desirable rhododendrons, magnolias and camellias. I had delved as deeply into the catalogues as he had, and I think I held my own fairly well, perhaps to his surprise. He already had plans to write a novel, a successor to *The Rock Pool*, and he told me that he had invented a new 'internal daydream' technique. He confessed, however, to a snag: his imagination conjured up the scenes he intended to create so vividly, and they appeared so funny to him, that he just lay on his sofa and chuckled at the brilliant show his fancy was putting on for him.

It was difficult, in these circumstances, to put anything down on paper.

His faithful assistants on *Horizon*, Lys Lubbock and Sonia Brownell, were dismayed at the end of *Horizon*. Sonia at least had hoped that it could be salvaged, though she knew it had suffered a severe setback in circulation just as *Penguin New Writing* had. We used to meet for tête-à-têtes and at parties from time to time, but not as often as in the old days. She had surprised us all by marrying George Orwell, who was deeply in love with her, and she was inevitably involved in the care of him in his last illness. *Nineteen Eighty Four* had just come out, and I remember finishing it on my visit to New England, with loathing, revolt, but immense admiration for its intellectual brilliance. I wrote in my diary that night: 'It is a sick nightmare. It could not be anything else as it is written without hope. And yet how uncomfortably near the knuckle, and if one can oneself supply the hope how salutary. And the hope is just precisely the hope there always was with the Nazis: *controlled* insanity is impossible, wrong thinking must finally issue in fatal action. Not really a novel; but another of Orwell's brilliant fictionalized pamphlets.'

A new broom had appeared at the august offices of *The Times Literary Supplement*, in Printing House Square. Alan Pryce-Jones, whom I remembered as a slightly younger fellow Etonian, a boy of great physical charm and popularity, had captured the seat of influence. During the war, he had risen to the rank of lieutenant-colonel, and had been with the first western troops to enter Vienna, where his wife Poppy had many relations and family interests. He had been assistant editor to Sir John Squire at the *London Mercury* in the early 'thirties, about which episode he wrote amusingly and affectionately in *Coming to London* some years later. A versatile writer, often under a pseudonym, he had never quite succeeded before the war in making his mark. His wide reading in many literatures, however, his quick sense of the contemporary situation, and his many friendships at all levels of the social hierarchy, made him a good choice for the tricky job of editing a paper profoundly revered in American universities but the subject of constant mocking sallies in the London salons. He determined to modernize it. The mysterious thing about Alan was that he was almost totally elusive. He was rarely to be found in his office when you telephoned. It was touch and go whether he appeared at a gathering to which one had invited him – an invitation he had warmly accepted. It soon became clear to me that Alan was one of those persons who take on far more than they can cope with because they are incapable of saying no. He would pile up social engagements without reference to his diary. A story once circulated (which may well be apocryphal) that a gathering of notabilities he had invited to dinner arrived at his house one night – to have the door opened to them by Alan in full fig and about to dine elsewhere.

As many found out, however, it was a mistake to underrate his capacities. There is another story to balance the one I have just recorded. *The Times Literary Supplement* had planned a special supplement which was to cover the contemporary literature of the South American continent. As the dead line for copy approached, the assistant editor realized with dismay that one of the experts had failed to produce his article. He managed at last to run Alan to ground very late in the evening, and before dawn broke Alan had produced a long, authoritative essay on the modern writers of the country in question.

I have reason to be grateful to Alan for his consistent interest in what I was trying to do as a publisher, and the quickness with which he would almost always spot the point of some new author I was launching.

5

My life in London during those years was very busy indeed. Not only did I have the work of directing my publishing firm and myself reading the manuscripts that Rosamond or Barbara or Julia Strachey recommended to me, of keeping up as far as I could with what was going on in literature in America and across the Channel, of keeping going and then winding up *New Writing*, but I also had other commissions and responsibilities.

I broadcast from time to time on various services of the BBC, Home, European and Overseas. I edited (and published) a series of anthologies of contributions from *New Writing*, apart from *Poems from New Writing* with which I had started, including *French Stories*; *Pleasures of New Writing* (which combined fiction, poetry and articles) and *English Stories*. When the last-named came out, the *Evening Standard*, which chose it as their Book of the Month, gave their review an amusing banner headline: LEHMANN STOPS THE FUNERAL, and George Malcolm Thomson wrote: 'I cannot remember seeing crowded into one volume so many good short stories as are gathered here.... [They] answer conclusively those who not so long ago were celebrating the funeral of English fiction. The corpse has kicked its way out of the coffin.' From time to time I was invited by the British Council to lecture for them abroad, and edited for them, in 1949 and 1950 their pamphlet guides to *The Year's Work in Literature*. At the same time I was invited to join the Council's advisory panel on publications, and later became its chairman. I was a member of the General Committee of the Royal Literary Fund, which hands out thousands of pounds every year to authors in need (after a pretty severe scrutiny), and fought there the battle to permit *young* authors in need to apply and not merely those in their bathchairs or on the point of receiving a telegram from the sovereign on their 100th birthday; a contest which the supporters of the young won (on points).

At the same time I lived a full social life. I entertained my friends and authors in my own house. I tried to arrange luncheons or evening gatherings whenever any interesting author came from abroad in order to introduce them to the English literary world, and parties to celebrate the publication of any special book. And I remember a party to celebrate the appearance of my hundredth book (this was *The Dark Peninsula* by Ernest Frost), in September of 1949, with fourscore guests packing my library and study on the *piano nobile*, champagne corks popping, my housekeeper Ivy (who always rose splendidly to such an occasion) and her friend Blondie from Leamington Spa working down below like Trojans (if Trojans can be imagined inspired by champagne) with the assistance of John Dolan,

loyal ex-Irish guardsman of inexhaustible high spirits, dealing
with hats, coats, empties and the impulses released in the overflowing hearts of Ivy and Blondie, amid the last roaring flights
of the Battle of Britain commemoration and the deepening
violet light of evening.

I won't pretend that I didn't enjoy all this social life, in spite
of the effort it cost me and in spite of the feeling that it post-
poned even further into the future the time I could spend on my
own writing. I try to look at it objectively, and I think I can say
that the fact that the fortunes of my publishing house depended
more than those of other publishing houses on myself and my
own assumed flair for finding and fostering new talent, made it
almost obligatory for me to create such a social centre, where
new acquaintances and friends could be made among authors,
painters and exponents of the other arts. I wanted all those
with whose work I was dealing to feel that they were as much
part of a band of friends inspired by common ideals as involved
in a commercial venture (which in any case would never make
my fortune.) Of course, such an attempt has its dangers: those
who are not invited on every occasion feel jealous at having
been excluded – a jealousy that one only discovers long after,
at first to one's amazed incomprehension. And now, when I
look at the invitation lists of those days, I see to my sorrow that
many, all too many of my guests have faded out of my life, that
some have died, and that others have removed themselves to
the uttermost corners of the earth.

My interests were by no means confined to the literary world.
I have always had a special interest in painting and painters,
and have tried, whenever my means allowed me, to add to a
small collection of contemporary paintings and drawings, which
now includes works by Duncan Grant, Graham Sutherland,
John Piper, Keith Vaughan, John Minton, Michael Ayrton,
Len Rosoman, Leslie Hurry, Denton Welch and John Craxton.
Curiously enough, considering my musical and music-loving
ancestors, Henri Lehmann, the friend and devotee of Liszt, my
grandmother Nina with her marvellous gift for the piano and
my grandfather Frederick for the violin, and my cousin Liza
Lehmann the singer and composer, I have never had any true
understanding of music. It is rare, I think, for a writer, poet or

novelist to have an equal sympathy for all the arts. Nevertheless coloratura singing, whether of Tetrazzini, Galli-Curci, Callas or Tebaldi, has always deeply fascinated me; the theatre, not merely because my sister Beatrix is one of the great tragic and character actresses of her time, has always evoked in me a thrilled and expectant response; and during the war I began to find a deep artistic satisfaction in the art of ballet. I was an early spectator when any new ballet, by Fred Ashton or Robert Helpmann or Ninette de Valois herself was put on by the Sadlers Wells Company at the New or Prince's Theatre, and was in the audience on that exciting evening when they graduated at last to the re-opened Royal Opera House, in their performance of *The Sleeping Beauty* with Oliver Messel's dreamlike décor and costumes.

How sad it is to reflect on the brief summer of a ballet-dancer's glory. Among the solo dancers of those early post-war years, rapturously received whenever they came on, Moira Shearer, Violette Elvin, Beryl Gray, Pamela May, Robert Helpmann, Michael Somes and Alexis Rassine have all left the company, and none of them at an age which would be considered old in any other sphere of artistic activity.

Their greatest post-war triumph was, I suppose, their first tour as a company of the United States, in the autumn of 1949. This triumph came at a good moment for national morale, when we, the victors in the recent war, felt poor and humiliated, floundering in a bog of misfortune out of which it seemed we might never be able to struggle. It was especially satisfying, as many American ballet folk, who had come over after the end of the war, had been rather lukewarm and patronizing – or so we thought. My friend Alexis Rassine, who accompanied them as one of the chief male soloists, kept me regularly posted with accounts of the rapturous critics and audiences, and their almost royal progress across the continent in their special trains. One of his first letters described his personal triumph in the Blue Bird variations of *The Sleeping Beauty*, He was thunderously clapped all through and surrounded by admirers afterwards. So successful was the tour, that a second, and perhaps even more furiously fêted tour followed a year later. The great moment for Alexis, passionate movie fan since early childhood, was his arrival in Los Angeles and Hollywood and meeting many of the top filmstars, including Charlie Chaplin, at the reception organized for them. Christopher Isherwood took charge of him, and reported to me how his New York success in *Sleeping Beauty* was repeated on the west coast. 'I do wish you could have been there on the opening night, when he found himself confronted by a practically inexperienced dancer for his Blue Bird dance. Not one instant did he hesitate but, gripping her firmly by the ears, whirled her away. Applause began to break out immediately and went right through the variations. All Alexis said later was "It was a lovely audience" – that's so typical of him.'

The members of the company loaded themselves up on both occasions with gifts for their (in comparison with the austerity-free Yankees) underprivileged friends in Britain, food, shirts, nylons, sweaters, ties, scent and anything else their dazzled eyes lit upon in the great department stores of the American cities. As far as I could make out, the British customs, on their return home like a flock of twittering swallows with the spring, gave one look at their toppling luggage, despaired, and chalked them through without a word.

6

It was just about this time that an event occurred which acted like a small but violent earthquake in the fairly closely knit intellectual world of our generation, reminding us that the past could suddenly strike out at us and that under the surface a subsidence of earth could have taken place without anyone realizing it.

In the first week in June (1951) the Foreign Office suddenly announced that two members of the service had been missing since May 25th, and had been 'suspended with effect from June 1st'. Their names were Donald Maclean and Guy Burgess.

The shock was terrific, because it became clear almost immediately that the two young officials had not merely gone off on an unauthorized holiday but were in flight, and heading pretty certainly for Moscow. The *Daily Express*, which was on the scent at once and soon had the whole pack of its top reporters in full cry, announced simply: 'there is a possibility that they may have important papers with them.'

Guy Burgess was an Etonian, several years my junior, whom I had got to know through mutual friends some time in the late 'thirties. He was an extremely intelligent, sanguine character, with a boisterous sense of fun and a malicious edge to his tongue. Not creative himself, he nevertheless had an immense interest in the writers who were my contemporaries, particularly Wystan Auden and Stephen Spender, and in his own way had tagged along with the pre-war anti-fascist movement of which they were the leading literary lights. He was an old friend and devoted admirer of Rosamond.

Donald Maclean was not known to me personally, though I may have been introduced to him at some party during the 'forties. He was, however, well-known to many of my friends, including Cyril Connolly, Goronwy Rees, and Philip Toynbee, and also to my cousin Sir Ronald Campbell. Ronald had been the British Ambassador at Cairo when Donald, who had been appointed Head of Chancery at the Embassy in 1948, had what was euphemistically known as a 'breakdown', the culmination of a long series of drinking bouts. Ronald, it seems to me, treated him with great tolerance and consideration, and had had him quietly sent home a year before the dramatic flight.

During those early post-war years it so happened that I saw very little of Guy, and I knew neither of his close association with Donald Maclean, nor of his crazy behaviour in America which had led to his recall by the Foreign Office.

At a French Embassy reception the day after the news broke, nobody seemed able or willing to believe in the full implications. The theory was even canvassed that the story was a double bluff on the part of the Foreign Office.

As far as my own particular part in the story is concerned, the first thing that happened was that, by pure chance, very soon after the French reception, I happened to ring up Humphrey Slater about something to do with his writing. He told me, to my amazement, that he'd been almost certain for a long time that Donald had been a secret member of the Communist Party, and had wondered whether he ought to turn him in. The second thing was that, the same day, Rosamond told me, over the telephone, an extraordinary story. She said that ever since the news of Guy's flight had come out, she had been trying to recall everything that Guy had said and done in the years before 1945 when they had seen much of one another. She had been uneasy for a long time; now she was completely convinced not only that Guy, originally out of pure idealism, *had* become a communist agent, but also that even if he had wanted to he had been unable later to get out of the one-way lobster-pot, and that his flight – she felt sure – was due to the fact that the security net was closing round him. She further told me that she had already got in touch with the security authorities, and though she had been mystified by the lack of urgency with which an eminent military figure had appeared to treat the whole affair, she had managed to obtain an appointment and was going to tell them all she knew – and all her deductions.

On June 10th the *Observer* carried an interview with Stephen Spender, who was at that time holidaying in Italy. In it he said that he found it very difficult to believe that Guy was a communist sympathizer, because only very shortly before he disappeared Guy had rung him up to praise his autobiography *World Within World*, which had many disillusioned things to say about Soviet communism.

The same day, by coincidence, I wrote to Stephen about something entirely different. Here is my letter in full:

'I wonder whether you can help me. I wrote to Wystan (c/o your address) before I went to Paris, asking him to help me land the British rights for *The King and the Corpse*. Do you remember if he ever got the letter?

'I am rather anxious to take action about the book as soon as possible. What is Wystan's address?

'Just a word, after reading what you said in this morning's *Observer* about Guy's disappearance. I was in touch yesterday with someone whom you know very well, who told me she'd worried for *years* about Guy, owing to a piece of information that came her way during the war; and now that all the pieces fitted together, she was absolutely sure.

'And exactly the same information about D.M. – from someone else we both know; who had seriously thought during the last few months of denouncing him.

'Assuming what these two people said is correct, it can't be long before the news breaks.

'Hope you and Natasha and the children are having a lovely time.'

On the evening of Friday June 15th there was a ring at my doorbell. Two reporters from the *Daily Express* were on the steps. They asked if they could interview me about the Burgess and Maclean affair. I told them I didn't think I could help them very much, but if they wished they could come in and talk for a few minutes. I was not at all alarmed; if anything I was slightly amused, as it had become a joke in our circle to say: 'Poor so-and-so hasn't been interviewed yet about Guy and Donald.' I was still very green about the methods some of the popular newspapers were prepared to employ in order to get their story.

They asked a few routine questions about my acquaintance with the two missing men, and then suddenly said that they understood I had written to Stephen Spender with some important information. Startled by this, I began to say that there was nothing of any great importance in the letter except to urge caution on Stephen in his public pronouncements, when one of them cut in: 'Mr Lehmann, we have been talking to Spender on Lake Garda, and we have a copy here of your letter to him. May we read it to you?'

I listened in speechless amazement as my letter was read out verbatim. It seemed to me almost incredible that Stephen could have let them have my letter to copy. I had to think quickly, as it seemed to me essential that Rosamond's name should not come out, not only because she was now in contact with our counter-espionage people, but also to save her from being plagued by telephone calls, requests for interviews, and photographers.

The two reporters tried to press home their advantage, but I refused to be drawn about the identity of the woman I had referred to in my letter. They told me it was in the national interest that I should reveal her name. I replied to this extra-

I

ordinary observation that she was already in touch with MI5, and that seemed to me to be that. After a little more nagging and needling they left, one of them remarking casually and charmingly 'If I were you, Mr Lehmann, I would leave my telephone off the hook tomorrow morning.'

The reason for this menacing piece of advice became clear next day. Splashed across the front page of the *Daily Express* was the headline: DIPLOMATS – THE SECRET. 'Known to two people in England.' MYSTERY WOMAN 'PHONES MI5. . . . As I began to read the story that followed I was suddenly horrified to see that the third paragraph of my letter to Stephen had been photographed and reproduced in the middle. So Stephen had actually *given* them my letter. My bewilderment and anger were now boundless. I sat down at once and wrote what is generally known as 'a stinker' to Stephen. And I arranged an interview with my lawyer for the Monday morning, for it seemed to me that at the very least the *Daily Express* had committed a gross breach of copyright in publishing extracts from my letter without getting my permission.

My letter to Lake Garda crossed one from Stephen. He was coming to from the anaesthetic of his excitement, and beginning to have qualms. If he could have known what persecution from the press my sisters were already undergoing when he wrote, his letter would have had a very different tone. No, he had trustingly given my letter to the *Daily Express* and was only just beginning to grasp what use they might make of it. Already, before my 'stinker' arrived, however, he had seen the full reports in the Italian press of the repercussions of his indiscretion, and was 'appalled and frightfully sorry'. At the same time he believed that 'fortunately these agitating things are soon forgotten'.

Over in England the *Express* was doing its best to prevent that happy conclusion. My lawyer had already succeeded in getting them to admit breach of copyright. After some haggling they agreed to pay token compensation (a cheque for 100 guineas which I handed over to the Royal Literary Fund), and insert an apology. Perhaps this swift action prevented further exploitation of the episode in the paper, but the damage had been done. For days the only women the press could think of as likely to be known intimately to myself and Stephen, i.e., my sisters, had been pursued by reporters in an inhuman and intolerable fashion. They sat on their doorsteps, they rang their telephones without cease, they even besieged Beatrix in the theatre where she was appearing at the time.

Meanwhile Stephen's letters from Lake Garda grew more and and more agitated, as he became fully and distressedly aware of the chain reaction he had set off. I did not write to him again; but my lawyer did, informing him that I still held him firmly responsible for what had happened. Stephen was certainly all penitence and anxious to present himself publicly in sackcloth and ashes. Unfortunately none of the schemes he proposed nor letters he drafted for publication could satisfactorily explain, to any averagely shrewd person following the case – or indeed to anyone who had not got the necessary key to Stephen's so often child-like psychology – one simple fact: why he had casually handed over my private letter to a reporter he had never seen before and of whom he had no knowledge. (It is only fair to say that, as he told me later, he expected my letter to be given back to him the same day.) He was advised by sage mutual friends to drop it, for fear of making matters worse. A year later, at my request, he got the *Express* to return the letters to me, thus setting at rest many unfair rumours that had for a time been rife.

Everyone, of course, is capable of insane-seeming actions in situations that knock them temporarily off their perch; people of highly strung artistic temperament perhaps more than others. Stephen's aberration, which I am now absolutely convinced had no malice about it, set back our friendship for a long while.

The hullabaloo that the *Daily Express*, as self-appointed substitute for the security services they considered incapable, made about the letter did not advance their desperate chase in search of the truth about Burgess and Maclean in the slightest. It only caused a great deal of pain to several totally innocent people who were trying to keep their heads and do their duty.

Friends rallied round with exemplary loyalty, deeply shaken though most of them were by what already looked like a deliberate act of treachery on the part of Guy and Donald. Edith and Osbert Sitwell rang up as soon as they saw the *Daily Express*. They were almost incoherent with horror. At a party organized at the French Institute by my friends Roger Senhouse and Fred Warburg, the publishers of Colette, friend after friend came up to express sympathy, curiosity, disgust and finally difficulty in believing what had happened. And a few days later, at the 'monster' luncheon party given by Edith to celebrate the Honorary Doctorate of Letters that Oxford had just given her (and which I have already mentioned), attended by Tom Eliot, John Hayward, Christabel Aberconway, Alan and Poppy Pryce-Jones and a host of others, I had to tell the whole story again and again to choruses of outraged indignation against the behaviour of that section of the press which had been hounding me and my sisters.

I remember with especial gratitude a letter expressing bewilderment and sympathy from Harold Nicolson, one of Guy's friends in an older generation who was most deeply upset by the flight. When, some years later, the Soviet authorities eventually allowed Guy and Donald to admit to the world press that they were living and working in Moscow, Harold, loyal to his friends above all things, did get in touch with Guy. But I myself never saw him nor spoke with him again. When I visited Leningrad and Moscow in 1963 for a congress of European writers he was already seriously ill, and the tragedy – for tragedy I continue to think it – was nearly over.

The 'someone else' I mentioned in my letter in connection with Donald Maclean was, of course, Humphrey Slater, whose novel *The Conspirator* I had published two or three years before. The whole affair was as if the story of *The Conspirator* had taken on actual life among his friends.

7

One of the pleasures of living in London during these years was that I had friends and relations in country houses not too far away, and could make visits to them at week-ends, and during occasional longer spells of absence from my office. Manuscripts submitted by authors, known and unknown, were always in my suitcase. Sometimes I would devote almost the whole of a week-end to them; sometimes the hours passed away in pleasant discussion, walks and festivity.

From 1947 my mother lived in her new home outside Beaconsfield, where the most precious possessions from the old family home at Fieldhead, and all books, pictures and other objects, from statuettes and rowing trophies to Chinese candlesticks and walking sticks, most of them loaded with associations of the past had, somehow or other, been re-arranged in a far smaller space. The house was dark on the road side, but sunny and attractive on the other, garden side, looking out over the fields, copses and orchards to the south-west. It was also easy to run, but I don't think my mother was ever entirely happy there, as she was constantly exploring other houses, especially on the high ground near Penn and down in the valley by the river. Nevertheless, she always prepared a most comforting and relaxing welcome for her children. I would often motor down with my eldest sister, Helen, who was at that time putting all her astonishing energy, enthusiasm and single-minded pertinacity in overcoming tricky obstacles, into her work for the Society of Authors: and we would shout stories of the eccentricities of the literary world at each other all the way. As the years went by, my mother's lameness (from her accident) increased, and she gradually gave up many of the extraordinarily varied public interests she had had. Thus, she settled into an ever more detached calm, viewing us, I think, with occasional amusement as well as love: her ship seemed to sail into serene waters as she approached harbour, and people would remark not only on a freshness of complexion remarkable in an old lady of eighty, but also on the spiritual incandescence that underlay it.

She followed my publishing career with intense interest, reading all the books as they came out, and finding especial delight in the series of Henry James reprints in The Chiltern Library. We would sit for long hours of a Saturday or Sunday evening in her drawing room, I with a pile of typescript on my lap, she with a copy of *Roderick Hudson* or *The Bostonians*, reading quietly together.

In the Isle of Wight, that still drew us all irresistibly as it had drawn us in our childhood, and our grandfather and grandmother a hundred years before, my beloved godmother, Violet Hammersley, still had her exquisite little early Victorian house at Totland Bay, only a few yards from the crumbling cliffs, with a glimpse of blue sea between the fuchsia bushes and the Spanish gorse. Between the wars, she had lopped off the top floor, converting it more or less into a bungalow, and enlarged the verandah on one side to make of it a delightful semi-circular loggia, where she would lie on the *chaise-longue* during the summer days. Outside, a huge and ancient magnolia, whose roots threatened to split the wall, grew over the verandah roof. With its white walls, the vivid and aromatic flowers in the garden, and its sheltered position, on a warm and sunny day it reminded me of a villa in balmier climes, far further south.

To this abode she would invite me each year for bathing and (for she was a determined and almost indefatigable walker even in her seventies) climbs over the heather downs, past the abandoned forts of Napoleonic times, to the coloured cliffs of Alum Bay and the Tennyson Memorial above Freshwater. I remember introducing Lottie to sea-bathing there. Nothing daunted by the mysterious motion of the waves, she gallantly, but with a certain desperation, launched herself into the salt water as soon as she saw me swimming out beyond the seaweed-slippery rocks. And from Totland Bay we used to make expeditions to General Oglander (whose publisher I became during the war) and his wife at their historic manor house, Nunwell, on the other side of the island; and, for the short space of years they settled there, to Jack Priestley and Jacquetta at Brooke.

Even after my mother's death, some years later, it was impossible to think of Violet as old, except for her deafness and the sudden illnesses which overwhelmed her – and from which she seemed to arise so swiftly with indomitable vitality restored. With her dark hair that never turned white, and her voice as musical and vibrant as ever; with her enormous curiosity about people, politics, art and literature, her sense of humour, her dramatic retelling of stories from past and present, her habit of asking for immediate answers to the most profound and anxious problems, she still appeared to me as I had always known her.

She had never been very democratic in outlook, and the rapid egalitarian changes that took place in English social life after the war were not at all to her liking. At the same time, she could always be made to laugh at herself if teased about this trait. She used to go every year to France to stay with one of her oldest friends, the Comtesse Costa de Beauregard, at her château at Fontaines-les-Nonnes; and the contrast between the large, almost feudal staff and the luxurious living there and pinched conditions in similar homes in England used to fill her with baffled rage and at the same time evoked some of her most hilarious stories and comic imitations.

Beyond Beaconsfield, on the road westwards, Rosamond was living in her beautiful, rambling Georgian house at Little Wittenham, under the shadow of the Clumps, with the upper reaches of the river only a few minutes away across the meadows. Beatrix had also installed herself in the large, picturesque barn in the same grounds, so a visit to one was always pleasantly a visit to both. From there it was easy to make sallies upon Oxford, and friends further north; in particular Rex Warner (after his return from abroad) and his second wife Barbara, daughter of Mary Hutchinson and previously married to Victor Rothschild, who occupied first of all a small but elegant country seat (there is no other word for it) in the village of Tackley, and then took a smaller house, with a long narrow flower-garden behind, in the little town of Woodstock, just outside the park precincts of Blenheim.

Some of my happiest memories are of those westward expeditions – which often turned into evening visits to the theatre at Stratford – between 1949 and 1952. I find in my diary the following extracts. First for February 1950: 'Yesterday down to Oxford by car, to talk to the Oxford University Poetry Society, one of the usual, ineluctable duty visits promised long ahead. In this case the gloom was much relieved by combining it with a visit to Rex and Barbara at Tackley. After a rather spark-less dinner and a rather unanimated (though closely attentive) meeting, I drove back through the rainy night to Tackley. We had a late supper of turkey and Alsatian wine, and discussed Rex's book *Views of Attica* which he is writing for me, and the failure of modern English novelists (the three star ones) to deal adequately with the subject of love. As usual, we got very up-roarious, and went to bed very late.'

And this, nearly eighteen months later, at the end of July 1951: 'Yesterday I motored from Beaconsfield where I had spent two nights with Mother, down to Woodstock to see Rex and Barbara. Behind the unassuming but very attractive Georgian grey stone façade of this house, only a few yards from the gates of Blenheim Palace, I found tremendous preparations afoot: hammerings, sawings, paintings, a large house with handsome rooms already with beautiful wallpaper laid on the walls and beautiful furniture stacked everywhere; Barbara in the midst of it all, looking pretty and desirable as ever, but a little more matronly, slipping out from time to time to keep an eye on her new baby Lucy, who has the brightest blue eyes and the most remarkable society smile, in a pram in the long finger of garden behind; Rex returning from the pub, as rugged, jolly, imperturbable-seeming and delightful in conversation as ever. We had lunch at the 'Bear', talked a great deal about the Burgess-Maclean business and cracked jokes at one another for a solid two hours. I persuaded Rex to join my 'reading panel', and then under the apple-tree he read me passages from his new translation (for the Penguin Classics) of Thucydides.

'After that I left for Banbury, Sulgrave and Weston, to stay with Sachie and Georgia Sitwell, through the silvery-green rolling landscape (I had almost forgotten how beautiful) into the very heart of rural England – green-golden fields of corn, starred with poppies and cow parsley and vistas criss-crossed with hazy dark-green hedgerows and blobs of elms. When I arrived, I found Sachie and Georgia out in the garden. We sat there and talked, again about the Burgess-Maclean affair, and then about the Sadler's Wells and the Oliviers. Sachie showed me his old-fashioned roses, an enormous collection in bed after bed, intensely perfumed but looking rather in need of dead-heading. In the morning I took some colour-pictures of the old house and the two of them, and then set off for Stratford, while the earth slowly turned to its iron-red Warwickshire colour; lunch at the 'Falcon', a deep inhaling of the air of beloved Stratford; and then back to Oxford and Little Wittenham to stay at the Barn with Beatrix.

The visits to Stratford were by no means always for 'a deep inhaling of the air'. Some weeks later I find the following entry: 'Beatrix and I set off for Stratford, picking up Rex and Barbara at Woodstock. We went on in Rex's car, and on the way Barbara, and Rex too, spoke with a contempt that surprised me of the "clique" behind the scenes in the literary world. . . . Also many compliments on my books and their get-up, and talk of the difficulties of young publishing firms. The talk was continued when we returned late after the theatre and stopped at Woodstock again for wine and ham sandwiches.

'*The Tempest* was an enchantment, Loudon Sainthill's décor and costumes magical in their spiky, rock-pool dream shapes, and soft, aqueous colours. The lighting and movement were admirably conceived by Michael Benthall; but as so often happens with a M.B. production the words came last instead of first, and there was altogether too much ballet technique, which seemed to me to spoil an otherwise excellent performance by Michael Redgrave. Caliban was deeply moving, making Prospero seem a cruel tyrant; Ariel also wonderfully effective and moving. On the way home, we all talked of the mystery of Ariel's relationship to Prospero, and the under-meanings of the play.'

During the years while Rosamond was reading for the firm, our editorial discussions took place, of course mainly in London. Sometimes, however, we continued them at Little Wittenham, on walks up to the Clumps and down along the river. Her daughter Sally and her son Hugo were often there. There had been talk of my nephew coming into publishing with me, but when he discussed it with his grandfather, Lord Milford, the idea had not found great favour. His clinching remark was, according to Hugo: 'Your Uncle John's got a good business head, I've always known that – but publishing is a spiv's game.'

It was not only to Lord Milford that publishing sometimes seemed a spiv's, or at least a mug's game. I find in my diary at about the same time the following entry: 'Who would be a publisher? I sometimes wonder how much longer I can stick it, second nature though it had become after all these years. It's not merely the endless MSS to be read, translations to be vetted, drafts about which advice must be given; the administrative and financial job that comes on top of the literary and artistic job; but the endless anxiety about each book, the letters and telephone calls to critics and editors that go with proofs and advance copies; and, following that, the strain of disappointment and worry if certain books are not reviewed soon enough in the right places, a feeling as if the result of a crucial lottery was about to be declared when one opens the *Sunday Times* or the *Observer* each week. And then the problems of other publicity continually going with it: there is never a moment when one of the current books, one's children, is not giving anxiety in one way or another. . . . Far too much of the last three weeks, afternoons and evenings, I would gladly have devoted to reading the multitude of books I long to get my teeth into – let alone preparation for my autobiographical book and the poems that begin to swim again into my mind – instead has had to be devoted to reading, with that word-for-word care they demand, the translations of Stendhal's *Aux Ames Sensibles,* Malraux's *Les Noyers d'Altenbourg* and Pavese's *La Luna e i Falo* which have just come in. Proud to have them, yes indeed, but when shall I find someone I can trust (and pay) to do just this special kind of work for me?'

In the autumn of 1951 Rosamond, deeply troubled in her personal life, decided to leave Wittenham and live in London. I felt extremely sad about it, as I had always thought of her house as a dream fulfilment of my ideal of Thames valley manor, with its purity of design, its warmly mellowing brickwork, and ancient history embedded in every field around. As bad, it meant that Beatrix would be leaving the barn. The last Sunday night I spent there, at the end of November, Hugo and his new wife Margaret were there, and Rosamond was working at her novel *The Echoing Grove* until Rex and Barbara arrived for dinner: the party then went with a roar, and we shouted and laughed till long after midnight.

I took Rosamond back to London with me, and we discussed – what we had touched on the evening before with the Warners – the comparative failure of new writers to materialize on this side of the Atlantic, the continuing sense of war exhaustion, the empty despair that seemed to characterize (at that moment) the war generation, and the need of our generation, who had stronger roots, to hold on against all in the coming years. Rosamond then said something that touched me deeply: 'all our friends think the work you are doing is almost superhuman, but I think you ought to be editing *the* literary magazine . . . of course you can't, with all the problems of publishing on your shoulders.'

Meanwhile, as I have already mentioned, I had bought a cottage in the country, on the northern borders of Sussex, not far from Three Bridges. It had once been part of the Montefiore estate, which began to be broken up and built over in the twenties. Originally a farm building, or forge, it had been converted soon after the war into a habitable house by an architect for his own use. No sooner had he finished it, however, than he decided to leave for South Africa – perhaps appalled by the restrictions and generally black outlook of the winter of 1947. I was therefore the first to live in it.

What immediately appealed to me and made me feel that I must acquire it was not so much the house itself, which was attractively painted white and as unlike as possible the usual modern bungalow of the Home Counties, but the situation. The two acres or so of its grounds were filled with huge trees, nearly a score of great spreading oaks at least two hundred years old, beeches with mighty trunks and conifers as well, and a host of willows, aspens, silver birches, sycamores, poplars, yews, hollies, cypresses, portugal laurels, old twisted hawthorns and crab-apple trees. This zoo of trees was mainly grouped, except on the side of the cottage, round a large pond or miniature lake which had originally served as a hammer pond in the far-off days when all that part of the country had been almost continuous forest. We soon discovered that it was chock-full of fish, though unfortunately not of a very interesting sort. It was also full of the most grotesque junk, relics of its wartime use as a dump by a Canadian regiment stationed nearby. This was also true of parts of the garden – if one could have given the name of garden to the overgrown wilderness out of which the cottage rose like a miniature version of the castle in which the Sleeping Beauty was discovered by Prince Florimond.

I have always had a deep need to live near water, whether

river or sea or lake, and I had a vision at once of a smooth lawn made from the cottage to the banks of the lake, planted here and there with flowering shrubs and crowded on the edge of the water with bulbs to flower from early spring to late summer, crocuses, jonquils, irises, day lilies and montbretias. When my friend Alexis Rassine saw it, he also fell in love with it and was eager to become part-owner, envisaging it as a place in which to repose and enjoy garden pursuits in the intervals of the long tours which stretched ahead of the now world-famous Sadler's Wells Ballet. Carlotta approved, to judge by the excitement of her furiously wagging tail sticking out of the undergrowth and the reckless plunges she made into the water in pursuit of moor-hens. I decided to buy.

The immediate tasks were to remove the junk, cut down dead trees, hack away undergrowth and sprawling laurels, and create lawns, orchard, rock garden and pathways out of the waste. The work went on all during autumn and spring. Lorry after lorry was loaded with broken bricks, rusted coils of barbed wire, huge oil-containers that had been wallowing in the water like hippopotami, shoals of old cans and soggy, discarded army boots, and were driven away to return with good earth to moderate the heavy clay, paving stones, gravel, and young bushes of every sort, aucubas, rhododendrons, azaleas, magnolias, camellias, hydrangeas, cotoneaster, veronica, berberis – and roses. Gradually the vision took shape: it was an intoxicating time, and I have rarely enjoyed myself so much.

Now that I have owned Lake Cottage for fifteen years or more, I still look on it as a source of inexhaustible interest and pleasure: a refuge for work, a place to entertain friends and relations and refreshing one's own petrol-filled lungs with country air and garden scents, and a centre for expeditions. There is never a time, except in the brief depths of winter, when some flower or ornamental leaves or sprays from a blossoming shrub cannot be gathered from the grounds. As much as anything I have enjoyed observing wild life there. At the beginning, we were surrounded, in the fields and copses just outside our limits, by rabbits and hares, and had to buy fences to protect our tender young fruit trees from them; now that myxamatosis has wiped them out, I would gladly sacrifice a row or two of lettuces to have them back. Hedgehogs and moles hide themselves in the woodland, squirrels spring from branch to branch, and steal stealthily across the lawns thinking to evade canine pursuit on their way to raid the peach and pear-trees. There are old inhabitants, a vole and a pair of grass-snakes who can sometimes in summer be seen swimming across the water. For years a large toad lived behind some flower-pots in the greenhouse I built to house a vine, feasting on the insects that would have feasted on the plants, and became almost a friend. Charlie, an exceptionally large tortoise of outstandingly independent and misanthropic nature, did not, alas, survive more than a couple of English winters. He must have been already very old when he reached us. It would have been kinder if he had been left on his Aegean shores to end his days.

Above all, as the housing estates of the new town of Crawley have crept ever nearer, the place has become a bird sanctuary. Year after year, moorhens have never failed to build their nests under the trees on the opposite side of the lake. From time to time mallard duck settle in the evening on the water, and are gone at the first opening of a window in the morning. Until recent years herons used regularly to come and fish under the branches: once in the woodland I managed to catch one that had been wounded in some way, and dumped it, hissing, over the fence which it was unable to climb or fly over. Now I think they have gone, frightened by houses pressing ever closer to their old nesting places on the lower lake beyond my boundary. Kingfishers still haunt, however, flashing in sudden sapphire from branch to branch. Owls hoot almost nightly among the tree-tops, and once I found one dead, inexplicably, under a magnolia tree on the lawn. Robins have divided up their territory and sing with piercing sweetness to defend it. The dawn chorus in early summer is deafening, and in winter crumbs thrown on the hard ground bring, beside the robins, hedge sparrows and house sparrows, cole-tits and blue-tits, blackbirds, thrushes, chaffinches (and sometimes even a bullfinch), woodpeckers, nuthatches, tree creepers and wrens, and swooping down for sudden forays, jays and magpies, rooks and jackdaws and pigeons.

In the first spring I spent there I noticed to my delight that clumps of aconites and wild anemones appeared at the foot of some of the trees in the woodland. Later, the whole untamed area was carpeted with violets, interspersed with primroses and bluebells. Nearer the house, at the foot of some of the tallest oaks, I planted dog-tooth violets, wild cyclamens and autumn crocuses, which now have a hard time to survive against the pouncing and rolling of Carlotta's successor, my golden retriever Rudy, who has chosen this particular corner to amuse himself with his ball.

Out of notes in my diary, I will make a series of pictures of the changing year at Lake Cottage, ignoring the sequence of years. . . .

February/March: 'Yesterday I took Christopher [Isherwood] down to the cottage in the car, where we found Alexis installed. The day started foggy, but the afternoon was deliciously fresh, still and sunny. A. and I did a lot of potting and planting of bulbs, primulas, and so on, while Christopher dozed off indoors by the fire. While we were on our way in the car, C. talked of his friends in England having become a sort of mythology for him, so that even if they died while he was away they would still be there for him, talking in his mind. . . . A perfect mild Saturday in the garden at Lake, spring so balmy on its arrival. The almond tree is showing its pale-pink buds for the first time, the crocuses are leaping up in tight masses everywhere, the tiny irises (reticulata) with their deep plum-purple sheen have suddenly opened in the border by the greenhouse, the wild tulips, the Christmas roses and at last the daphne mezereum in the rockery. All the evening I have struggled to prepare my lecture for Cambridge tomorrow (the Shirley Society), to be repeated on Monday at London University.'

April: 'William [Plomer] and his friend Charles arrived after lunch. William was bubbling with talk and in his best form, pouring out anecdotes about literary personalities – the Scawen Blunts in particular – and their haunts in the neighbourhood, and the history of hammerponds. He seemed increasingly enchanted, as he walked around, with the romantic attractions and poetical advantages of the cottage. When William and Alexis launched themselves on the lake in the canoe, his friend Charles danced on the shore in transports of gleeful hope that they'd capsize. Before going, they walked through the woods collecting early wildflowers, and admired the golden late afternoon light falling on the opposite bank from the house. . . . As William observed yesterday, in such a place as this one could become entirely absorbed in bird-watching. Today I saw for the first time a thrush on the lawn feeding its chosen mate. She stood rather shyly in one corner, while he hopped around, cocking his head for worms, plunging his beak in and dragging one out. Then he would flutter across to her and she would open her beak and flutter her wings coyly and accept the titbit from him. It was the most touching and comical sight.'

May/June (on the way to Milan): 'Every since leaving England I have been haunted by Sunday evening at the cottage. Johnnie Minton was sketching under the trees by the lake, Rickie had wandered over to watch the horses on the far side, Beatrix was helping A. in the kitchen. An extraordinary orange storm light fell over everything, making the white hawthorn just across the lake and the yellow and golden azaleas on this side glow with a mysterious intensity as if the light were actually coming out of them.'

July: 'Two hot, blissfully sunny days. Watering is now problem No. 1 and vast lengths of hosepipe have been purchased and at sundown are attached to the cold tap in the kitchen. The rhododendrons are my chief anxiety, though perhaps the least danger. The white and purple veronicas are both coming out, and the lovely arch-sprayed cotoneaster with its scented nutmeg white blossom. The climbing roses are hanging their last blooms, but the hybrid teas on the lawn are still budding in fine display. The evergreen honeysuckle is out, the golden cups of the St John's wort on the bank just beginning to reveal all their delicate red stamens; the astilbes and moneywort adding their colour to the lakeside. Dramas of wild life continue. A baby mole with incredibly soft fur was found dead in the woodland and buried under a tree. The moorhens have hatched a brood of four little scurrying black balls of fluff, the squirrels leap about the garden lawn when they imagine we aren't looking. The grey heron, having fished almost invisibly for hours, takes off into the trees.'

August/September: 'The golden days of this late summer,

after the rains and the thunderstorms that followed the drought, have gone on all through the long week-end of the beginning of my holiday. The dead-still skies, the misty veil over the sun and the distant prospects at morning and evening; the pallor of the skies, blue losing its colour after June's intensity; a fresh chill in the air at twilight, though not sharp; and the first real crop of peaches, small but delicious, plucked from the wall, with the ripening figs next to them, and the grapes – our first grapes – at last turning purple in the greenhouse among the leaves as if among the wings of scenery in a theatre. The plucking of blackberries has begun, and our own apples to go with them into the stewing pan. The new 'royal red' buddleia is beginning to burn with its deep purple flame, and the butterflies are fluttering round, peacocks, red admirals, fritillaries, cabbage whites, and even a painted lady. The michaelmas daisies are beginning to show the colour of their buds as the phlox fade.'

And so into the falling of the leaves, the aromatic smoke of bonfires, and the bare branches of winter.

8

I used to slip over from time to time to Paris, to keep in touch with what was going on in the literary world there, and to see my growing number of friends among the writers and publishers. I would make a date first of all with Jennie Bradley, then with Dionys Mascolo of Gallimard. At Jennie's I would hear above all the latest gossip of the town, what new authors were the rage, which publishers were going up, and which struggling to keep abreast, and at the same time as often as not be given a delicious lunch cooked by Jennie's *bonne-à-tout-faire*. I would also hear the latest gossip from New York, for Jennie kept in very close contact with American publishers, and Blanche Knopf was one of her most devoted friends.

At Gallimard Mascolo would greet me as ever with his boyish smile, and then settle behind his mountain of books and papers to discuss the various contracts we were engaged upon, the new books I had asked about and other books he wanted to suggest to me. He was a tough bargainer, or rather the Gallimard brothers were tough bargainers, but he was an admirer of my firm, and I'm inclined to think I got away with things that would have been impossible for another publisher. He was always eager to know the latest of Sonia Orwell and other mutual friends of the Paris-London intellectual commuting world. I used to see No. 5 rue Sebastien-Bottin as a kind of writers' zoo, for a remarkable proportion of the interesting French novelists and critics seemed to be working for Gallimard, each with a little office down a long corridor on one floor or another, like script-writers in Hollywood. So a confabulation with Mascolo would be followed by a visit to Jacques Lemarchand, whose *Geneviève* Rosamond had translated, and to Raymond Queneau, with his friendly cheshire cat grin behind his glasses, one of the few truly original French writers of our time, whose wit, interest in experiment and unflagging curiosity about language made him extremely sympathetic to me. Some of his books are surely impossible to translate, depending as they do on the most uncompromising *argot* and a firework display of verbal invention of his own; but during the short life of John Lehmann Ltd we managed, nevertheless, to publish a translation of *Un Rude Hiver* (A Hard Winter) by Betty Askwith and of *Pierrot Mon Ami* (Pierrot) by Julian Maclaren-Ross.

Dates would follow with Marie-Laure de Noailles, with André Chamson, and if I could locate them, with some of the younger writers who had not been corralled by Gallimard. Marie-Laure maintained, in her grand house in the place des Etats-Unis, almost as lively a salon as before the war. Writers, artists, dancers, actors, many of them of the latest avant-garde were always to be met there, though her friendships were highly selective. After lunch, coffee and cognac were served in the huge room upstairs where gigantic modern paintings were permanently on display. Marie-Laure could at times be moody and sharp-tongued, but she could also invariably turn on great charm when she wished, and her luncheon parties never failed to be entertaining. Raymond Queneau was her particular lion in the 'middle' generation at this time, but she never lost her zeal to take trouble about young writers and artists, among

K

whom she was constantly making new, delighted discoveries. The elegant and wittily grotesque drawings and paintings of Philippe Jullian, who executed an exquisite series of book-jackets for my Henry James reprints in The Chiltern Library, had immensely attracted her; he was often to be found at her table, chattering away with sparkling abandon. Another young writer I met there at this time was Guy Dumur, a fair-haired and good-looking boy of medium height, with a sensitive face in which frail health was all too clearly marked. Marie-Laure's husband, Charles de Noailles, who speaks impeccable English, was seldom to be seen; but I remember on one occasion he was present when I presented Marie-Laure with an early copy of Nora Wydenbruck's book on Rilke. The gift immediately provoked an immense commotion and a flood of reminiscences between the vicomte and Marie-Laure, about '*le pauvre René*', and '*La princesse qui l'aimait tant – quoiqu'il était si difficile.*'

Perhaps the most interesting of all the encounters I had in Paris during those years, was my interview with Ivan Bunin, which was arranged by a friend and agent, Dr H. I felt not a little emotion at the thought of meeting this remarkable genius, whose work I had admired for so long, the last living representative of the great line of pre-revolutionary Russian novelists. I saw before me a little goblin king of a man, with skin yellow as creased parchment, blowing his toothless cheeks out as he talked – a little in French to me, and a great deal in Russian to Dr H. He was in his eightieth year at the time, but he could, I felt, have been a hundred and fifty years old. His eyes, his whole face – that reminded me at moments of Leonard Woolf, though more elfin – gave an impression of fatigue and illness. And then suddenly a smile of great fascination would flash across it, and his eyes be lit by a wicked spark of lightning, especially when speaking of the misdeeds of editors and publishers, and the inhumanity of the tax laws. Only shortly before, I had arranged to publish an English translation by David Magarshack of Lydia Avilov's story of her relationship with Chekhov in the 'nineties, *Chekhov in My Life*. I mentioned this to him, and he immediately said that I should not read too much into this romantic story. He had known Lydia Avilov well, and he was fairly certain that she had been more in love with Chekhov than he with her. In any case, their affair had never been intimate in the true sense of the word.

I have described in my two earlier volumes my long discussion with André Malraux when he was *chef de cabinet* of General de Gaulle directly after the war, and my first encounter with him during the Spanish Civil War. I had always been haunted by the slightly bulging greenish eyes in the pale unsmiling face, the long French nose and the finely sculptured hands, and the strange *other* sound (due to an old wound), as if from a second person, that accompanied his voice as he poured out his theories on politics, war, literature and art. Humourless, obsessively romantic about danger and daring, a mythopaeic believer in destiny to the point of absurdity – Malraux seemed to me the same twenty years later on as when I first knew him. I have nevertheless always thought of him as one of the key writers of our time, and brilliant though the coruscation of ideas may be in the great works of aesthetics he devoted himself to before he rejoined his hero general when he came to political power again in the 'fifties, I have never ceased to regret his abandonment of the novel. I now had designs on him. I knew he had refused to allow the first volume of his unfinished trilogy, *Les Noyers d'Altenbourg*, to be translated, on the grounds that it was but a fragment and would not properly be understood without the other two, unwritten volumes of what was to have been called *La Lutte Avec l'Ange*. He had told me that if the Gestapo had not taken away the notes he had made, he would have completed the work and revised *Les Noyers d'Altenbourg* in the process. Nevertheless, it seemed to me a work of such profound interest and power, that it ought without question to appear in an English translation.

I went to see him in his home in Boulogne-sur-Seine, in the hope of persuading him. He received me in a study leading off a large, modern, white-painted music-room studio, looking I thought rather iller than usual, though in the intervals of the hoarse spasms which as usual punctuated his conversation, I seemed to detect – for the first time – an occasional faint ghost of a smile. He talked a great deal of his *Saturne*, which he seemed very keen that I should have; but I gradually worked him round to the subject of *Les Noyers*, and at last extracted a half-promise that I should have the English rights. At the same time, to my great surprise, he told me that another project that was waiting for the completion of his great series on the Psychology of Art was a sequel to *l'Espoir*, and suggested that I should agree to take that too. Nothing could have suited me better, but though I did very soon succeed in publishing *Les Noyers*, in a translation by Xan Fielding, as *The Walnut Trees of Altenburg*, the sequel to *l'Espoir* is still alas, to be written.

Many years later, when he was already Minister of Fine Arts, we had a long discussion one evening in his office after all his officials had left. I reproached him for neglecting *his* destiny as a novelist, more important than politics, or even theories about art. He then told me that he considered it essential for a man if he was to remain truly alive, to be where the central stream of his time was running. Nevertheless, he said, in some part of his mind all that he was witnessing and all the drama he was taking part in, as one of the general's closest collaborators, was being quietly and secretly digested into the cud of art. The rest of our talk – which was, indeed, mainly a monologue with promptings from me – about the future of France and the world, though of the utmost fascination, cannot be revealed here. André Malraux has a rooted objection to being reported, and would certainly not have spoken as freely as he did if I had not made a promise to keep silence.

André Malraux has suffered so many abrupt unbelievably unkind blows of fate in his private and family life, that it would not be surprising if he treated political ambitions as a way of deadening the pain. Nevertheless I feel fairly certain that his close association with De Gaulle arises from a deeper, anterior need in his nature. Viewed from a certain angle, what one can perhaps admire most about him is his refusal to play in with the inbred Parisian world of inflated intellectuals, of *cher maître* this and *hommages* that. During one of our discussions in the 'thirties, I asked him what he thought of Gide's *Au Retour de l'Urss*. He immediately replied that the trouble with Gide was that during his Russian trip he had only met the boring Soviet intellectuals. Now if he had only met some of the glorious Soviet airmen. ...

One day, on one of these visits, I persuaded André Gide to let me bring young Gore Vidal to be introduced to him. This

was an event that Gore had dreamed of for years, and he was in
a high state of excitement as we rang the door bell in the rue
Vaneau. The master was in his most cordial mood, and questioned Gore closely about the restraints on frankness about sex
in American writing. At the end Gore rather nervously mentioned that he had sent Gide a copy of his *The City and the Pillar*,
though he had received no acknowledgment. Gide replied
that he remembered perfectly well; and then immediately
switched the conversation to the stranger perversions that were
prevalent, he was told, among rich spinsters and widows in
New York. Afterwards, Gore sighed and said he supposed that
just meant that Gide had not read his book. I was not so sure.
Roger Martin du Gard has told the story how Gide came to
visit him once at the seaside, and appeared delighted when he
suggested he should read him his latest play. While the reading
was in progress, Gide took up a pair of fieldglasses and studied
two young men, who were bathing naked on a distant part of
the beach, with minute attention. Roger Martin du Gard,
furious, finally stopped reading. The same evening Gide, pre-
tending not to have noticed the painful impression he had
made, launched into a detailed critique of the work – which
showed that he had followed everything.

In the winter of 1949–50 I was again in Paris, and rang Gide
up. He was not at all well, he said, but he would make a special
exception and see me. When I entered his room, I was horrified
and wished I had not taken advantage of his kindness: his face
was grey, his cheeks were sunken, he was unshaven and gasping
for breath. Nevertheless, rather miraculously, he showed his
usual animated curiosity about friends and events in the literary
world of England. He was particularly interested in the new, un-
bowdlerized version of *De Profundis* which had just then been
published. He told me that he remembered once witnessing, in
Algiers, a terrible quarrel between Oscar Wilde and Bosie which
left Wilde white and shaking. Afterwards, Wilde turned to him
and said: 'Everyone imagines I am in the midst of joy and carefree happiness – and you see what has just happened – it
happens all the time.'

Two years later, I went to see Dorothy Bussy, Lytton Strachey's sister, whose translation of Valéry's *Dance and the Soul* I

had just published, in her home in Nice. She told me the saga of Gide's funeral: how infuriated Mme Lambert and Roger Martin du Gard were to discover, on arrival in the little village, not only a deputation of '*anciens combattants*' but also a Protestant pastor who actually read out some passages from the *Journal* and followed the recitation by prayers at the grave-side. Roger Martin du Gard kept silence until it was all over, then could contain his indignation no longer and made a terrible *esclandre* about this insult to an immovable atheist. 'It seems destined,' said Janie, Dorothy's daughter, 'that funerals should always be either unendurable or comic.' Gide, I believe, would have found it comic, as he kept his sense of humour and his defiance of the Churches to the end, as his remarks on his death-bed about Cardinal Mindzenty show.

I would generally finish my Paris trips with a visit to André Chamson, oldest and most faithful of friends. At this time, he was curator of the museum of the Petit Palais, and inhabited a flat right at the top of the building. I remember a particularly delightful evening, when I dined *en famille* with André, his wife, his pretty dark-haired daughter (who had also started to write novels) and her new, young, romantically attractive husband who had determined to devote his life to the theatre.

I was especially interested to find how keenly the two young people followed English films (and, whenever possible, English plays) that came to Paris, and how strongly the feeling of admiration and affection for the British people prevailed. I cannot repress a certain feeling of sadness in looking back on this epoch of Anglo-French relations, when the enthusiasm for many aspects of our civilization was as strong on the other side of the Channel as our enthusiasm for France, and when so many intelligent Frenchmen believed that 'one must look to the English' – for a counterpoise to the Americans as much as for a defence against Stalin. Alas, the General – great admirer though I have been of De Gaulle's genius, I must say alas – has changed all that.

After dinner, André read us some passages from the new novel he was at work on, surrounded by the eager, loving circle of his family. In my opinion, he is underestimated as a writer in France today, largely, I think, because his lacerated humanism, and his special gift for recreating the world of his boyhood in the Cevennes, does not awake any particular responsive chord in a younger generation nourished on the immensely powerful negative existentialism of Jean-Paul Sartre and his disciples. His early autobiography, published in England as *A Time to Keep*, seems to me one of the very best books of its kind ever written, and I am still haunted by many extraordinary and gruesome passages in his book about France during the German occupation, *Le Puits des Miracles*.

He was already conscious, I think, of a distance growing between himself and the younger generation, and when I told him how struck I had been by the fact that so many of the French novels submitted to me for possible publication in England during the previous two years had drawn crude pictures of a youth without scruples or morals, he immediately nodded agreement and said that his new novel was meant to be a kind of counterblast to make it impossible to write such books any more. 'The trouble,' he said, with a melancholy look of frustration, 'is the utter absence of any *heritage* for the young now.'

9

One of the most exciting things, for my generation, after the war, was the rediscovery of Italy. Englishmen have, I believe, a natural affinity for that country which goes a long way back into history. The stupid interlude of fascism did not kill that affinity, but made intelligent islanders, particularly those of artistic leanings, miserable that a place they had loved, and continued to love, had been as it were requisitioned and scrawled over by a gang of interlopers who were using it for evil purposes. When fascism had at last been brought to its absurd and bloody end, I think that most of us were only too eager to resume a relationship that had brought so much happiness, and had been so fruitful in the past; to revel again in the idyllic nature of that country, to make friends again with a naturally friendly people whose temperament seems so precisely complementary to our own, and to revisit the inestimable masterpieces of art of which Italy is the treasure-house and cornucopia.

In addition to this deep-welling readiness to forgive the wrongs and forget the bitterness, we had a new interest, full of surprise and pleasure, in the post-fascist Italy that began to emerge from the ruins. I am not speaking of politics, but of the vigorous ferment of creative ideas that we increasingly discovered as the natural genius of the people reasserted itself: new artists, new poets and novelists, new movements of thought and feeling that appeared not merely in Rome but in all the other great centres, Milan, Venice, Florence and Naples. In those early post-war years, Italians had not yet had the chance to show that they could compete with the cleverest and most inventive brains in the world in engineering and design, particularly in cars and men's as well as women's fashions, but there was already a sparkle in the intellectual air that made one feel that anything was possible. While some millenial quality or virtue seemed to remain almost untouched, the process of change was accelerating. Not merely the grotesque Italy of Mussolini, but also the other Italy of E. M. Forster and D. H. Lawrence was whirling away into the past.

For myself, who had scarcely visited the country at all since my teens, to the pleasure of discovering the new Italy was added the pleasure of getting to know, with immensely increased understanding and appreciation, the ancient Italy that I had neglected for so long. My ignorance was not so great as in the case of Greece, but I found that even when I had become acquainted with classical ruins, architectural splendours, frescoes, sculptures and dazzling landscapes all those years before, I was seeing them with new eyes and with as great an intensity of aesthetic response as I saw what was hitherto entirely unknown to me except through photographs and descriptions.

The circumstances were particularly favourable. Not only did I now have a large number of friends who had settled or were making long sojourns in Italy, but also in all the main centres those who were working for the British Council, or other English cultural services, were eager to show me around and to introduce me to writers and painters and editors who might be able to provide fodder for *New Writing* or for the list of my own publishing firm.

The first post-war encounter with Rome was perhaps the supreme moment for me. It was the beginning of June, the oleanders were out, the flower-sellers' stalls at the bottom of the Spanish Steps were piled high with spring blossoms, and the late spring light was making the characteristic rose pink and golden-orange tints of the city glow with what seemed to be a soft internal illumination, so that one was surprised to see it fade with the fading of the day. I wandered about, exploring Roman ruins and baroque churches, feeling that to walk among the pines of the Borghese Gardens and the mazy walls and tessellated floors of the Baths of Caracalla, or through beckoning side streets where palm branches curled luxuriantly over high walls topped with white statues against a deep blue sky, was like awakening into a new kind of happiness. Ever since, Rome has retained for me something of that first shock of delight. In spite of not particularly caring for Italian food, I feel better there, more alert and impressionable than anywhere else. Each time I visit it, I find new beauty, a church façade or interior, a vista, or corner of ancient ruins incorporated in later building, an Egyptian obelisk sticking up improbably in the middle of a sun-drenched piazza, a flight of steps or a curiously carved fountain I had not noticed before.

About eighteen months earlier, Rosamond and I had been very much struck by a novel by a new Italian author called Ennio Flaiano. The title of the novel was *Tempo di Uccidere*, the story of an Italian officer in Abyssinia whose brief affair with a native woman entangles him in a web of guilt and fear that seems to become more intricate the more he struggles to free himself from it. What impressed me was not only the extra-ordinary dramatic power of the telling, but the psychological insight, the compassion and irony. We published the novel as *Mariam*, in a translation by Stuart Hood. It was made an alternative fiction choice by the Book Society, and the critics were enthusiastic.

As I was extremely keen to find out more about this remarkable author, I got in touch with him as soon as I arrived in Rome. It was a lucky throw: he turned up at my hotel in a little

Fiat, and offered himself at once as a guide round Rome. He proved a delightful, witty, intelligent friend, and a tremendous asset in my sight-seeing. Without those hair-raising sallies, by day and by night, into the infinite confusion of Rome's geographical lay-out, I do not think I should ever have approached an intimate understanding of the city and its treasures. It was due to him that I realized the immensely important part that fountains play in the life and history of Rome. While we walked, with heads thrown back, through the Sistine Chapel (which was miraculously and inexplicably empty) he kept up the most fascinating disquisition on the greatness of Michelangelo and the tragic complexity of his character. In the Vatican galleries he pointed out detail after detail that I might otherwise have missed, and opened my eyes to the beauty of the antique paintings of the nuptials of Imeneus and the adventures of Odysseus, that appeared as if they had the light of the morning of the world upon them. In the Etruscan museum he explained to me how D. H. Lawrence was really responsible for the revived Italian interest in Etruscan remains, and quoted with approbation Lawrence's remark that all that was good in Italian character and history, the delight above all in life as it is, came from the Etruscans, and all that was bad – the rhetoric, the shabby imperial dreams – from the Romans.

One evening, he introduced me to the Trastevere district, a world in itself that I had not been even aware of during my visit as a young Etonian more than two decades before. We bounced through its winding cobbled streets, passing as if in a fairy-tale (to me) in and out of little piazzas with bubbling fountains and silver baroque church fronts and crumbling palaces. Everywhere the inhabitants were sitting out in the streets, round tables and lights, arguing and drinking wine, sometimes, as Flaiano pointed out, between two broken Roman pillars, or under an old Roman carved shop sign. When I asked my guide whether they would be discussing politics or family affairs, he replied: 'No, no, just football – nothing but football.'

I had had many absorbing talks with Edwin Muir when I visited Prague two or three years before. I now had the good fortune to find him in charge of the British Institute in Rome. Every encounter with him made me admire him more: his gentleness, his sensitive intellectual and artistic perceptions, the quality of imagination that ran through his conversation, his absolute independence of cliques and the rather silly boostings of some of my contemporaries. Looking at his wrists one evening as we were talking and drinking round a table, I suddenly saw that he was as old as his years, something I had found it hard to believe before. During our talks he spoke with constant bitterness of the folly of closing the Institute in Rome, a move already planned by the high-ups of the British Council, and of the great work it had done and the place it had in the affections of the Romans. He observed with gloom that he saw the Council developing more and more as an inferior Foreign Office bureaucracy.

Soon after the war, I had made the acquaintance of the redoubtable Marguerite Caetani, who became Princess Bassiano and then Ducesa di Sermoneta. An American heiress, born Marguerite Chapin in Connecticut in 1880 (and therefore only a few years younger than my own mother), a true-life Princess Casamassima married to an Italian aristocrat of extremely ancient lineage, with inflexible will-power and a passion for the arts, she had before the war – between 1924 and 1932 – run a literary and artistic magazine in Paris called *Commerce*. In this she had the help of some of the most notable French intellectuals of the day, including Valery Larbaud and Leon-Paul Fargue. St Jean Perse translated T. S. Eliot (who was related to her) for *Commerce* and Valery Larbaud some early passages of *Ulysses*. It was a most distinguished venture.

Since the war, she had started in Italy a multi-lingual literary magazine to which she gave the picturesque name of the street in Rome where the ancestral Caetani palazzo stood, *Botteghe Oscure*. Every number of this bulky occasional magazine had an Italian, a French, and an Anglo-American section, each under a different editor or rather sub-editor. She wanted to enlist my help in finding young British contributors, and I was able to suggest to her various names of poets to some of whom she afterwards became a most generous patron. *Botteghe Oscure* never made anything but a large loss, and was heavily subsidized by her own private fortune. She ran it on the admirable system of paying her contributors – who included Dylan Thomas, Vernon

Watkins, Theodor Roethke, Robert Lowell, Tennessee Williams and Burns Singer for the Anglo-American section – what she thought, or found out that they needed; and when she became particularly interested in a young poet she would give him additional support by providing him with free accommodation somewhere on her family properties. In some curious way Marguerite managed to retain the puritan New England prejudices of her upbringing, while publishing avant-garde authors who flouted them all.

She was at her country estate of Ninfa, south of Rome in the hills, on the occasion of my visit, and invited me out for luncheon there one Sunday. Sylvia Sprigge motored me out, and I remember a large party of mixed Americans, English and Italians, at which everything under the sun was discussed over delicious food. I remember in particular how she told me that, during the war when rumours came that the Germans were approaching, the entire population of Ninfa, with their household goods and beasts, with Marguerite and her husband at their head, removed themselves to the mountain fastnesses of Sermoneta – which we could see in the blue distance as we drank our coffee – and locked themselves in, in true mediaeval, feudal fashion.

A little later I was able to publish for her in England an anthology of the best Italian short stories which had appeared in *Botteghe Oscure*, an arrangement through which I made the acquaintance and friendship of the novelist and film-director, Mario Soldati, one of the most original figures on the Italian scene. He looked rather like Groucho Marx, I remember thinking when I first met him, and had a passionate interest in English literature, in particular the works of Graham Greene. I brought out his collection of linked long-short stories, *The Commander Comes to Dine* in the last year of my publishing.

On my way to Rome, I had stopped off in Florence to visit my old friend Harold Acton at his magnificent family villa La Pietra on the Via Bolognese, and a number of other friends including Humphrey Slater and his wife Moira, and Tony Bower, who were living in the surroundings of the city at that time. My memory of Florence, at this ideal moment of spring, was indeed of cool villas perched on the hills at one point or another of the compass outside the city, the Villa Natalia where Harold put me up on his family estate, La Pietra itself, and perhaps most idyllic of all the villa which Tony Bower had taken. The corn and the poppies in their midst, the olive trees and the cypresses climbed up the slopes to the very edge of the garden, in which fig-trees and huge magnolias, pink espalier roses and oleander bushes in flower lay basking in the hot golden air, until sundown brought the fireflies out and the frogs began their croaking, while all the lights of Florence in the distant hollow burned like taper points.

I spent a great deal of time with Harold, for whom, ever since Eton days, I had had a deep affection. I had come to know him in my teens through David Hammersley, the second son of my godmother Violet, but during the 'thirties our ways had parted. While much of my time was spent in central Europe, he had settled in Peking, to enjoy the happiest period of his life, in the last days of a society to which his own extraordinary sense of oriental courtesy, his erudite and mischievous wit, and his devotion to the ancient Chinese way of life instinctively drew him. In his autobiography, *Memoirs of an Aesthete*, he has described how, after the London house he shared with his brother had been sold, he decided that fascist Italy was too stifling for him, and set out on his travels. As Odysseus was ensnared by the spells of Circe, so Harold in these travels fell under the spell of China. He did not return till 1939, when I began to see him again. I have described in *I Am My Brother* how we wrote to one another continually as he was moved about the world in his RAF postings, until he finished up in liberated Paris. Fond and loyal, with a clairvoyant understanding of my deepest impulses, he would say to me, in moments when I was discouraged or ruffled by passing setbacks: 'Don't be defeated by things of no importance. Believe in your star, my dear John, believe in your star.'

I remember my first evening with him in the city, as one of especial delight and illumination. Florence, absurd though it sounds to say it, was still strange to me – in my early forties. Engrossed in conversation, we suddenly came upon the flood-lit façades of baptistry, campanile and duomo, and I caught my breath at the unexpected splendour of chequerboard marble in that dramatic light.

La Pietra, of which I had had a romantic mental image ever since I had read Harold's autobiography, was no disappointment: in fact the reality appeared more beautiful than the dream. His father had filled the spacious rooms with priceless, often ravishingly beautiful quattrocento works of art – he had begun collecting in the far-off days when masterpieces were to be had for a (comparative) song. Outside, terrace after descending terrace of formal garden overhung the distant view of the city. Among these bosky terraces one continually came across weather-worn garden statues, mostly Venetian in style and very much to my taste. But the features that perhaps struck me most powerfully on this first visit were the lemon garden at the back of the house, and the great, narrow dipping avenue of cypresses that led from the front to the park gates.

As Harold showed me round, he talked with a sad gravity, all too seldom illuminated by his impish Chinese mandarin's smile, of his problems, the difficulties of life with his possessive parents, and his new plan to take an apartment in Naples and live there with some of the freedom with which he had lived in China. He had not yet started on his *magnum opus*, the history of the Bourbons of Naples.

It was not till two or three years later that I met Bernard Berenson, the sage of I Tatti, the magnificent villa further up in the hills. Rosamond had become a close and much admired friend; and I was invited up one day in spring. I saw him sitting on the sofa in his drawing-room, a frail little man with a small head and a neat white beard. I found him very genial and charming and welcoming, though his conversation on this occasion was not very witty or very profound. He was surrounded by adoring American, English and Italian women, who treated him as a mixture of the Oracle of Delphi and God the Father. I must confess that this atmosphere dismayed me (though I should have been prepared for it), and I could not entirely resist the question rising in my mind, whether all this reverence and adoration would have been lavished on him if he had not made a great fortune by his transactions in the picture markets of the world. The next day I confessed these doubts to Harold. He calmed them by saying that he himself found that the cult sometimes reached nauseating heights (or depths), but there was no doubt in his mind that B.B. was a great intellectual figure of our time, especially in his far-reaching, continuous work of art-attribution; though he had certain reservations about the whole Duveen phase.

I must add that B.B. himself started off by mocking his *raison d'être*, observing to me that 'art is a vast department in the empire of humbug'. And he followed this by some very uncomplimentary references to Duveen.

The main object, or rather the starting point of my visit to Italy that spring, was to attend a meeting in Venice of the Société Européenne de Culture, to which I had been invited as an English delegate. This society was the brain-child of a young Italian professor of Padua University, Umberto Campagnola, full of demonic energy and slightly inchoate dreams (which I found characteristic of post-war Italy) of creating a cultural society where intellectuals of the European nations of the west could sit down at the same table with their dittos of the eastern iron-curtain nations, and engage in a prolonged *dialogue*. This *dialogue* was supposed to resolve differences of outlook, contribute to peace and international amity, and make of the intellectual world an effective force independent of politics – or rather *influencing* politics by its independent harmony – but unfortunately, at this stage of the cold war, took no account of the fact that iron-curtain intellectuals permitted to attend such gatherings were bound to be Marxist propagandists incapable (on the surface at any rate) of being influenced or deflected in any way at all. One either played their game or remained glaring as before. Another difficulty was the incapacity of the post-war Italians (and to a lesser degree of the French) to understand the English mind, our unshakeable preference for pragmatic rather than dogmatic solutions, and our deep suspicion of rhetoric. This failure in understanding was made worse by the fact that we had gone through no experience of German occupation and largely communist-led resistance movements, and had not been landed with large communist parties in our body politic. The result was that distinguished Latin intellectuals would release torrents of rhetoric couched in Marxist or pseudo-Marxist jargon, while the Anglo-Saxons looked more and more uncomfortable, bewildered and bored; sometimes (I am afraid) sniggering at one another behind their hands. Nor could French or Italians understand the absolute lack of status of writers in Britain. They were inclined to regard our diffident apologies on this subject, our attempt to explain that high-sounding declarations and denunciations of this or that (which we all signed) would cut no ice at home, as further examples of Anglo-Saxon duplicity.

Nevertheless, I must admit that in spite of the stifling and largely useless *séances de travail*, these congresses and assemblies attracted me, not merely because one received free and generous hospitality abroad, but also because it gave one the opportunity to meet many interesting writers from many countries *outside* the conference room. And what more entrancing city to hold a congress in than Venice?

After a few days, I wrote in my diary: 'I find it almost impossible to define and capture the effect Venice has on me. The multiplicity of impressions confuse and stimulate me beyond measure, the beauty of the buildings, the history within the buildings, the beauty of sudden passing youthful features – surely the young are more beautiful here than anywhere else in Italy except Rome. And always there is the appeal of the sea beyond anything one is doing or saying, beyond anywhere one is, the invitation to the light, the colour, the freedom of the lagoon – and then the open sea. What is wonderful in this city at night, as one crosses the silent bridges over the side-street canals, is to see the *sleeping* gondolas, perhaps very gently rocking on a water into which a little moonlight has been shaken. And at dusk, as I go down the Grand Canal, I keep my eyes open in tense anticipation on the *piano nobile* of the palaces, for most probably someone inside will just be switching on the lights, and chandelier after chandelier will begin to sparkle and dance, with all their exquisite fantasy of silvery and coloured glass leaves and sea beasts and stars. The little, shadowy creeper-festooned *calle* seemed more mysterious and inviting than I remembered them, the ringing, clanging, chiming, booming of the bells more enveloping, the mood – with an English destroyer in and Italian sailors everywhere as well, tourists beginning to pour in – more recklessly festive than ever; the pagan gods winking behind every pillar. But *not* a city for serious conferences, because nothing can be serious here, nothing has been serious for generations, the atmosphere of fantasy and frivolous merry-making is far too strong. Perhaps one should write something to examine the demoralization caused by water if brought into the very veins of our daily life. . . .' As I listened to the sonorously intoned platitudes of the speakers at our inaugural session, I was aware all the time of the louder voice of the dazzling golden surroundings, the glittering reaches of the lagoon outside the windows.

One of the most interesting people I met during this congress – or rather, met again after many years – was Louis Guilloux, novelist of Brittany, author of an excellent book before the war, *Le Sang Noir*, and a leading figure with Malraux, Sartre, Nizan, Cassou and Chamson in the intellectual antifascist movement of the 'thirties.

One evening he hauled me off to the piazza to '*boire une coupe*' with him, and discuss what had happened to us in the twelve years since we had last met. Looking rather like a miniature Lloyd George, with many rhetorical gestures and smoothings back of his disordered greying locks, he told me about his war experiences: the German terror in Brittany, the dangerous chance encounters, heart in mouth, with German soldiers late at night. He also told me for the first time of some remarkable episodes during the famous tour of the USSR on which he and Jef Last had accompanied André Gide. In particular, he described, with humour but not without a certain touch of horror in his detachment, how Gide used to prepare 'little games' to amuse and entice the adolescent boys he met in the various cities where they stayed. One evening in Tiflis, in the Park (of Culture and Rest) Gide had started cuddling an especially attractive young Georgian in his teens, when the Ogpu arrived. They asked Gide for his papers, let him go, but hauled the boy off. When Guilloux asked Gide whether he didn't feel guilt, and a certain distress for the boy's misadventure, he thought for a moment and then said: '*Presque. . . .*'

I was also especially glad to make the acquaintance at this congress of Mario Praz, the distinguished anglophile Italian professor, author of that seminal book of criticism *The Romantic Agony*. At the official banquet in the Biennale, we discussed the pathology of Swinburne's *Lesbia Brandon*, about which I found him immensely learned and illuminating, as well as witty. It was clear to me that he kept a sharp watch on literary developments in England, and in spite of the close questioning to which he subjected me, was remarkably well informed. He has a curious way of seeming not to look at you during a conversation, while in fact he is studying you carefully; a trait that makes him seem shyer and more self-defensive than I soon discovered that he was. It was only some years later that he invited me to his famous apartment in the Via Giulia in Rome, more like a museum than a home, in which every object, whether of furniture, *objets d'art*, painting or statuary, belongs to the Empire or Regency period: the treasure-house of a lifetime ruled by a collector's single-minded passion.

Among the English delegation, I made a particular friend of Michael Goodwin, whom I remembered meeting as a rather shy, good-looking and innocent young man with John Lepper before the war. He was no longer shy, but full of intelligent ambitions which he pursued with quiet pertinacity (and, in the event, all too little success). He had become editor of the *Nineteenth Century and After*, which Freddie Voigt had run during the war with the most laudably immovable contempt for the political promptings of the authorities. Nothing could persuade Voigt that the masters of the Soviet empire had turned into angels when they became our allies in the struggle against Hitler, nor that their control over the greater part of the partisan resistance in the Balkans was not a long-term menace to our interests. Michael's ambition was to turn the magazine into a much more cultural paper, a scheme in which he endeavoured to enlist my help, with all the charm and banter at his command.

He had also conceived the idea of writing a history of 'Bloomsbury'. He was intensely absorbed by this plan at that moment: to my amazement, because he had never had any contact with it in its heyday. He had already managed to persuade several of the surviving figures to talk freely with him, and he drew me out to discuss my own experiences. The more I talked to him, the more I wanted to say to him: 'You're quite crazy – you can't do this – no one can understand it who wasn't of it – and how on earth are you going to tackle the immensely complicated web of personal relations within it?' Michael Goodwin never wrote the history; but since then many others have been fired with the same ambition. I remain of the opinion that no true picture can be given for another fifty years – if ever.

We made many entrancing expeditions to Padua, to Torcello and elsewhere in the lagoon in the intervals of our official re-unions. Among the delegates was an elderly Swedish professor, of clearly exceptional erudition about Venice and the Veneto. Whenever we came to an outstanding *sehenswürdigkeit*, whether church or palace or piazza, he would plant himself in the middle and deliver himself of a learned lecture – in French. He was ignored by the Italians, not without reason, and by the French out of their usual bad manners; but I was pleased to note that some of the English felt it incumbent on them to hang around, even if sheepishly; thus reinforcing my view that in international gatherings our countrymen, though often lamentably ignorant and tongue-tied, nearly always display the greatest sense of human decency.

Once upon a time Venice was filled with Englishmen, lovers of Italy, who rented dilapidated palaces for a song and lived a life enclosed within a dream of eighteenth and nineteenth century cultivated indolence. By 1950 this dream was coming at last to an end. England no longer commanded the world. More Americans than ever Henry James imagined were competing for the palaces and Englishmen encountered difficulty in finding the foreign exchange for rapidly rising prices. I was privileged to visit on this trip two of the survivors of the Venice-loving English settlers: Leslie Hartley in the Palazzo Boulini and Victor Cunard in the Palazzo Foscarini. In spite of the gaiety of our meetings, and my enthusiasm for Leslie's works, a profound melancholy seemed to emanate from them, the last representatives of a dying princely race who had lived surrounded by their gondolieri, their books and pictures, their fading painted ceilings that one could almost see in the exterior views of Canaletto and Guardi.

I O

Meanwhile things were changing in England. The end of the misery of austerity seemed suddenly in sight, and the end of an era of repressive bureaucracy as well, even if still in the distance.

While I was in Venice, Barbara Cooper wrote to me regretfully about the death of Robert Herring's *Life and Letters*, which I had followed ever since its earliest days under Desmond MacCarthy and added at the end: 'I expect you have heard that points (food) have come to an end, also petrol rationing.' Even when all the ration schemes had been abolished, I knew people who held on to their grubby little official books with a kind of superstitious reverence, not quite believing that they could prosper without this talisman they had clutched for so long, nor be safe against sudden starvation and denunciation if caught without them. I threw mine into the fire with a sigh of relief.

More important still, for those – even radicals among whom I liked to count myself – who believed that it was time the natural gift of the British for individual enterprise was let out of its prison cell, and who had been dismayed by the class venom that so often seemed to inspire the attitude of its spokesmen and supporters, the Labour administration was clearly falling out of popular favour at last.

A few months before, in the February general election when Attlee only narrowly held on to power, I had written in my diary:

'The election days and nights were among the most extraordinary I can remember. It seemed to begin soberly enough with the actual business of voting at the Oratory Hall in the morning, and talking with my neighbour Susan Ertz at the entrance about how all of us were really liberal and yet to vote Liberal seemed pretty hopeless. When I lunched with Alan Pryce-Jones at the Ivy our talk was almost not of politics at all, but of books and gossip about our literary friends, and the pitfalls when they married rich women. Even at night, when I

went to change for the *Daily Telegraph* party at the Savoy, I
said to Beatrix I felt nothing so much as that I wanted to go to
bed. And even when I got to that vast beano, that seemed without beginning or end or centre, and, with its mixture of so many
people one knew with so many more one didn't know, all under
some restless compulsion of expectation, their minds unfocussed,
was like a gathering after death, an ante-hall where one awaited
God's decision whether one was to go to Heaven or Hell, I
began by feeling only half attached to the results. The first
counts seemed to follow too closely the pattern of what had
been to rouse one out of one's habitual self. And yet by 1.30 a.m.
when I left the party (perhaps it was partly the champagne) a
sense came over me of dramatic possibilities in the air, so that in
my bedroom I stayed up until the battery began to fail at 3.20
a.m. suddenly realizing that the county results had not come in
and the counties would almost certainly narrow the gap. When
I turned on the radio again at 8 a.m. there was still a large gap,
but getting no larger. All day the fever mounted with everyone,
so that Friday's lunch with William [Plomer] was much more
under the shadow of the excitement of uncertainty, though we
both lamented the greater likelihood of the same dreary old
gang getting back. After lunch as the gap narrowed, work became almost impossible in the office, and at No. 31 quite impossible. I was shouting all the time upstairs and downstairs.
When at 6.45 p.m. I had to leave for the BBC and the rehearsal
of the discussion on the novel with Rose Macaulay (risen ghastly
from the bed of bronchitis) and Leslie Hartley, with Howard
Newby attending, I was not only, like everyone else, extremely
worn with the fever but almost incapable of concentrating on
anything else, least of all on the novel, as we sat at the dinner-
table in the studio with ear-phones beside us on a chair. Then,
at last, one saw that, though the gap had narrowed and widened
again, the *others* were not after all going to succeed, and the
fever died down again.'

And yet, I thought, a change in our lives had taken place, a
new era was at hand, and the future was once more full of in-
scrutable possibilities.

Part Three

I

My publishing career lasted until the end of 1952. I had therefore – though I did not know it – only four years to accomplish
the best I could from the moment when, in 1948, the printers
who had taken over my firm, gave me the green light to go
ahead without thinking (for the time being) about capital problems. As I have already mentioned, my state of mind was
extremely ambivalent about this development. I felt that great
opportunities, of a rarely lucky kind, stretched before me. At
the same time, I had my doubts about the freedom I had been
promised. Did my new backers realize the difficulties of building up a list, which would be successful financially, on a mainly
literary basis? I believed I could do it, but not at once. Again,
if the administrative pressure and the effort involved in keeping
up with competition increased – as it seemed almost certain
they would as free supply conditions returned – was I prepared
to make sufficient sacrifice of the other, creative side of myself,
the self that wanted to write poetry?

I remember a long, late evening discussion with Blanche
Knopf, who remained all through one of the most intimately
sympathetic of my many well-wishers on the other side of the
Atlantic. She objected that I was taking too much upon myself; that the load would break me; and that I ought in reality
to be chief literary adviser to a big and established firm, and not
to have to bother with the rest. In my heart, I half agreed with
her; but my New England and Scottish blood urged me on to
dangerous adventures, where the prizes – not of money but of
reputation – still beckoned almost irresistibly in the distance. I
thought not only of the success I might have as personal to my
own career; but also of what I could do – so it presented itself
to me – for English literature.

So it was, that when Donald Klopfer of Random House came

to see me (in 1951), and said quite simply: 'I was told you were
the best publisher in England today, so I thought I must come
and pay my respects before I go home', I felt a glow of pleasure
and surprise; and simultaneously a kind of guilt and an urge to
say to him what I could not possibly have given utterance to:
'You touch me and flatter me, but if only you knew what doubts
and anxieties I have about being able to keep it up . . .'

By the beginning of 1952, I could look back on six years of
hard, exciting and on the whole surprisingly productive work.
I had an impressive group of the most promising young Americans on my list. I had made a success even beyond my early
hopes of my Modern European Library. One of the last of my
'scoops' had given me especial pleasure: Nikos Kazantzakis'
Alexis Zorba, which I re-christened *Zorba the Greek*. I had always
wanted to build up a top list of contemporary poets, as I had
begun to do at the Hogarth Press with the great reputation in
that field of Leonard and Virginia Woolf behind me. The list
was already very much to my liking, though I wanted to go
much further. I had not the slightest doubt, which my experience with *New Soundings* confirmed, that the new post-war poets
who began to appear at this time, would have come to me.

I have already described the specially commissioned and
illustrated books which gave me particular pleasure, to which
I should add Michael Ayrton's edition of Nashe's *The Unfortunate Traveller* with fifteen of his own lithographs in illustration.
I planned a series of authoritative biographies of great figures
in the background to modern literature, and had begun with
Countess Wydenbruck's *Rilke*, Ernest Simmons's *Tolstoy* and
Dostoevsky, David Magarshack's *Chekhov the Dramatist*, and
Ronald Mason's study of Melville, *The Spirit Above the Dust*. In
addition, in this branch, there were the books on drama and
ballet.

An unexpected opportunity that had come my way was in
stories for boys, on the young adolescent level. It had begun
with the surprise arrival of Roy Fuller's excellent adventure
story, *Savage Gold*, which I had illustrated by Robert Medley.
The success of *Savage Gold* began at once to attract others – by
serious novelists or poets, not simply professional purveyors of
'stories for young readers' – including Jocelyn Brooke's *The*

Wonderful Summer and P. H. Newby's *The Spirit of Jem*, one of
the rare examples of illustration in line by Keith Vaughan. I
felt that this was a field I could develop with both profit and
pleasure. I must confess that I enjoyed the books very much
myself.

Another, and deeply satisfying opportunity that came my
way when the printers offered me very handsome supplies of
paper, was the bringing back into print of English and American classics. As I have already related, when I started The
Chiltern Library, in 1946, the scarcity of editions of the classics
was desperate; but I saw that I ought in general to concentrate
on special authors, just a little apart from the popular stream.
Sooner, probably, rather than later, the Oxford University Press,
Collins and Everyman would bring their most popular classics
back on to the market, using plates that already existed. Rosamond had a particular enthusiasm for Mrs Gaskell, so we
planned a series of her chief books, if possible to include everything if we were successful. The revival in Henry James, one of
our favourite authors, was reaching its height; Graham Greene
at Eyre and Spottiswoode was planning, we heard, to republish
the later novels of 'James the Old Pretender', so we decided
to start on the novels and stories of the early and middle periods
which were, with very rare exceptions, totally unobtainable
and likely to remain so. We began with *Roderick Hudson*, and by
the end had ten volumes in print. I decided to add to this some
of the unobtainable works of Herman Melville, interest in
whom had grown very rapidly during the war. Curiously
enough, they included *Billy Budd*.[1]

These reprints gave me the chance of commissioning new
introductions by leading contemporary writers. I was, for instance, glad to have William Plomer, Peter Quennell, Elizabeth Bowen and V. S. Pritchett on my list in this, however
minor way. When the end came, though the rewards of reprinting the classics had already become far more difficult, I had
many extensions of The Chiltern Library still in mind.

[1] These were only, so to speak, the central block of the building, for we
included single volumes, such as *Tristram Shandy*, some re-translations (by
David Magarshack) of shorter works of Dostoievsky, Disraeli's *Coningsby*,
Byron's *Don Juan*, Smollett's *Travels through France and Italy*, and many
others.

Our plans for bringing, or bringing back, foreign classics into English translation did not stop there. I discovered that *Lucien Leuven*, Stendhal's great unfinished novel had never been brought out in English; we published it in two volumes, *The Green Huntsman* and *The Telegraph*, in H. L. R. Edwards' scholarly version. We followed this by *To the Happy Few*, Norman Cameron's translation of a selection of Stendhal's letters which had recently been a great success in France. Later, I also found that Benjamin Constant's autobiographical novel, *Cecile*, a kind of sequel to *Adolphe*, which had only been discovered a few years earlier, had not yet been taken for translation into English. I published it among my last books, again in Norman Cameron's version. Being a great admirer of Balzac's cycle of Vautrin novels, I managed to get Kathleen Raine to re-translate them, with Philippe Jullian contributing illustrations for which he seemed to me so admirably suited. Alas, we only managed to do the first half, *Lost Illusions*, as a bumper volume; but we planned to follow it by another bumper volume containing *Splendeurs et Misères des Courtisanes* and *La Dernière Incarnation de Vautrin*.

With these flower-beds in the garden, the young American authors, the new Europeans, the poets, the travel books, the books on literature and art, and the reprints, already showing such a fine variety of blooms, I was conscious that the bed devoted to new English novelists looked a little thin. By a curious coincidence, I had been able to do for Denton Welch what I had done in the past, in my Hogarth Press days, for Christopher Isherwood and Henry Green: I had responded with enthusiasm to a second or third book that the original publishers saw little merit in, and revived the author's reputation. With Denton it was, unfortunately, too late. Four other new novelists I had great hopes of: Ernest Frost, because he seemed to be deeply concerned with the inner life at a time when the glorified documentary was in vogue; Roland Camberton because he wrote with such wit and psychological insight of the low life of Soho and the East End long before it became fashionable; Percy Coates, a Yorkshire miner, because of the remarkable warmth and truth of his vision, and Robin Jenkins because he seemed to me a natural writer of great force and imaginative power. These three were, I thought, a good beginning, but I was saddened by the enormous number of novels we were reading in manuscript which were good, which showed gifts of many sorts, and were yet not quite good enough. I felt that more ought to have come out of the great promise of the war years; I believed that, with patience, I would see it arriving; but I was not given the chance.

I should perhaps apologize for devoting so many pages to a recapitulation in detail of what we had achieved before the end; but only so, I feel, can I show what impetus we had managed to attain in those few, hectic, stimulating, pioneering years. A publishing firm is only different from any other business in that it deals with the precious substance of art. But serious publishing, unless in the exceptional periods such as have been produced by war and social upheaval, needs heavy capitalization. And I was to learn that success, and a growing reputation, in normal times, are not enough. What is needed is *great* success, the big best-seller *every* season.

By the middle of 1951 the printers had obtained the lease of a house in Gilbert Street, and offered us accommodation there, together with other associated companies in their group. We moved in during July. I had a comfortable ground-floor office, with room in it for an assistant's desk which Barbara Cooper took over. Higher up were the general offices, presided over by Clive (John) Hall, and a special room at the top where Julia Strachey could devote herself to reading and preparing reports about the MSS which were piled high on tables and shelves. Val Biro, our new production manager, an immovably good-natured, sturdily built, good-looking young Hungarian-born artist, with glossy black hair, a disarming intelligent smile (and a glamorous wife), also had his own room where he prepared lay-out and specimen pages for each accepted MS as it came to him, and also designed spines and jackets.

One day, as we were discussing the work, Julia Strachey exclaimed to me what a happy family we all were in the office. And this was indeed true: we all had our appointed jobs and none felt subordinate to any of the others beyond what smoothly working routine required. I was, I suppose, conductor of the orchestra, but most of us were creative in our own right – Barbara and Julia as prose-writers, Clive as a poet, Val as an artist – and there was absolutely no office 'bull'. We were all friends who met one another outside office hours, and all were there because they were seriously interested in what we were trying to do. I made it clear from the beginning that anyone could come into my room whenever he or she liked, to discuss any problem that had arisen, without the fuss of knocking or asking permission through a secretary. When Ted Sloane, our London traveller, came in with a batch of orders or to pick up advance copies, he behaved in exactly the same way; and after his session with me he would go upstairs to talk with the others and crack a few jokes with them. In fact, we had a great many special office jokes, and my recollection is of continual merriment in the midst of keen work. Perhaps it would have been impossible in a larger office; perhaps it was too good to last; but I remain firmly of the opinion that it was the *right* way to run a literary publishing office.

I must add that our relations with the printing works down in Somerset were also extremely pleasant. They were presided over by Wilfred Harvey's brother, a genial, efficient unassuming character who very rarely let me down over an order, and if he had to do so immediately gave very cogent reasons for the delay. I liked the foremen in the various departments of the huge factory, largely local west-countrymen, and with my passion for printing, always enjoyed walking with them through the sheds and seeing the giant machines at work, especially those that were printing several thousand copies of a four-colour 64-page sheet every hour, with only one man supervising and fiddling around with an oil can.

Of course these four-colour mass production jobs were never ours. Next door to us in the Gilbert Street house was Sampson Low, a distinguished old firm that had been bought up by Harvey and transformed to his own needs, busily engaged on *Jane's Fighting Ships* and Enid Blyton's juveniles.

Every week some young man or woman would come to see me, looking for a job in publishing. I found this part of my duties nearly always engrossing for the human interest of the stories I was told, but also often rather heart-breaking. So many young people saw publishing as a happy compromise between commerce or finance and a highly risky life devoted to writing or painting; so few of them realized how small the number of available jobs was compared with the number of young people like themselves looking for them. So many of them were ready to risk a couple of thousand pounds, all they or their parents could scrape together, to get a junior directorship; so few of them knew how hot the stove of publishing was to make these little drops of capital disappear in steam in the twinkling of an eye. Unless they were clearly well-to-do, I used to advise them against these adventures; but I also used to tell them that if they had a real passion or obsession with publishing, it didn't matter where they were slipped into the tank, how humble the starting job was. If they had the right gifts, they would sooner or later be able to swim over to the sunny side.

One day a young man came to see me who had been sent by Jimmy Stern, and who stood out among the many I had interviewed at that time. His name was Miles Huddleston. I was attracted to him at once, not only for his charm of expression and gentleness of voice, but also for his obviously deep passion for books. He had come from a home where he had been surrounded by books in his childhood. 'I read almost every night, and far into the night.' I took an interest in his reading, and I gave him lists of books, the background to modern literature I thought he ought to know if he was going to become a serious publisher. I couldn't do anything for him in my own firm, but I found a way in which I could help him to get into the tank; and as I judged would certainly happen in his case, he has since gone from strength to strength.

Miles told me that the great blow of his childhood was losing his father at Dunkirk. This had made him very restless, and he had abandoned his schooling at Wellington at the age of seventeen, to go to live and work on his uncle's estate in the Argentine. An unfortunate incident, very much à la Colette, had brought him home again, and he was now living in London with his sister, almost, it seemed, without friends.

Miles proved to be the most sympathetic and undemanding of companions. From the stories he told me I got a glimpse of the passionate and often morbid state of mind of some of his generation. He told me, for instance, of one young man who, whenever he could, wore his dead father's army pullover,

unwashed, with the bloodstains on it. His father had been run
over by a tank.

Later, I was often to entertain him and his young German-
born wife Gerda at Egerton Crescent and Lake Cottage.

Towards the end of 1951 I was invited to give a talk to the
Society of Bookmen. As usual with my talks and lectures at this
period, I did not or could not set aside enough time to plan it
properly, and found myself the evening before with only scattered notes. From 10 p.m. I worked feverishly, through half the
night, to give body and coherence to these notes. I called the
talk 'A post-war publisher in the narrows', and tried in it to
get to the root of the difficulties which beset someone in my
position, caught in the cross-winds and cross-currents of the
book-market in the first seven years after the war. I was over-
whelmingly conscious of its deficiencies. On arrival at Kettner's
restaurant, where the dinners of the Society of Bookmen were
always held, I was astonished to find an enormous gathering,
including most of my friends and acquaintances among the
publishing fraternity. I was told it was the second largest gathering they had ever had. Pure sweating panic seized me, as I sat
down between Ian Parsons of Chatto & Windus and Bertie van
Thal. However, wine was flowing and gaiety abounding, and
in that genial and tolerant atmosphere I was inspired to make
the most of my miserable script, and relieved to find that it
appeared to go down very well. A vigorous discussion followed,
in which my old friend Rupert Hart-Davis rose gloriously to
my defence. When I reached home I was completely exhausted
as well as tipsy.

What surprised me even more was that the repercussions
went on for a long time after. A couple of days later I had a
letter from David Farrar of Secker & Warburg, in which he
said: 'Just a line of congratulations on your brilliant speech at
the Society of Bookmen last night. It combined wit and weight
in altogether admirable proportions, and it is a long time since
any speech has held my attention and admiration so completely.'

I was convinced that it did not deserve these compliments,
and that if it had been a success it was for other more intangible
reasons; perhaps because I had uncovered something that was

A meeting of the Societa Europea di Cultura:
above The author with Michael Goodwin and others at Torcello

below The author signing the roll in Venice

Cyprus: The beach at Salamis

Cyprus: Hussein and his Greek friend at Soli

all too rarely allowed to come to the surface. But the compliments continued to arrive, by telephone and letter and word of mouth, at parties and in the bookshops.

Looking back I am inclined to see this evening at the Society of Bookmen as symbolizing the high water-mark in my career as a publisher. I had reached the moment of deepest understanding of the problems with which I was wrestling. And, in some way or other, I had managed to touch the imagination of my colleagues and friends in the world of books, so that they had the highest hopes of me and were generously willing to wish me well on the dangerous voyage ahead.

Danger indeed was gathering, like ominous little livid clouds on the horizon. The gods may shower one with gifts, but the more abundantly and suddenly they offer them, the more likely it is, it seems to me, that one crucial gift will be left out. The unknown Carabosse who had been forgotten among the invitations to my christening as a publisher, had condemned me to a fatal lack of free access to the materials of my trade. It was for that lack that I had mortgaged my independence. I have often thought that if I had merely lacked capital, the judgment upon me of my great-grandfather, Robert Chambers, would have been severe. He would have told me that one must accumulate capital before one takes to risky business ventures; and that one only accumulates it by caution and patience as well as by unremitting work. Robert Chambers, however, was never stumped for paper to print his books on.

The plain fact was that my relations with the printers, who now controlled the fate of John Lehmann Ltd, were deteriorating. Wilfred Harvey was getting restive about the failure of the firm to show a clear profit. I was charged by the works the normal price which they tendered to any outside firm, which included of course profits at every stage of the operations, composition, supply of paper, printing and binding. It was therefore, after these had been debited, that my success or failure in making a publishing profit was reckoned. It was my contention – it would be better described as my guess, perhaps – that even if I was still in the red on that reckoning, there was almost certainly a concealed profit, apart from the fact that I always endeavoured to supply the works with my jobs when they were

M

comparatively slack, thus keeping the wheels turning. It was even more seriously my contention that the kind of literary publishing house it was my aim to create needed time for the fruits to ripen, far more time than I had yet had for development; and that the unusual proportion of prestige successes I had had were exactly what was needed to bring eventual financial success as well.

The chairman, however, was not impressed, even though some other members of the board were more sympathetic. He was used to quick success and big profits, and the appearance of a laggard in his team, and a laggard obstinately set on going his own way, clearly discomfited him. I do not believe he understood what I was after. There was no very cogent reason why a business genius of his calibre should, though he had given me the impression at the start that he welcomed the addition to his empire of a small highbrow principality.

The geniality of our meetings began to evaporate, the temperature of our exchanges about the accounts to drop to glacial. In a way they were very funny because of the total incomprehension, but I was too anxious most of the time to see the funny side – except in those moments of pure philosophic detachment which have throughout my life saved me from despair and dispersed at last the bile of extreme bitterness. One thing I should make clear: I never, until the final showdown, pleaded that the loss my accounts showed on their reckoning was a trifle in their huge profit-making operations, though in my opinion it was a fact. It was for them to say that it was worth it; not for me.

I should not give the impression that Wilfred Harvey found no merit at all in the endeavours of John Lehmann Ltd. No doubt he realized that the leading press reviews, the praise and the controversy, the Book Society Recommendations, the *Evening Standard* choices, the public acclaim for production and design, were marks of some kind of achievement; but they were strange to him. When he praised a book we had taken on, it was generally one that was a little outside our usual range, such as *Miracle at Carville*, or *Victory in my Hands*. In spite of this, until nearly the end he did not try to control our editorial judgment. It was when he began to show signs, as I thought, of wanting to interfere in that department that I knew the game was – all but – up.

In April 1951, after a very brief discussion he said drily that he'd carry on for another year and then see how things had shaped. I had never before had to do with the head of a complex business empire, who could only spare ten minutes for small fry like myself. I felt rather like Alice, when she found herself asked to show a ticket in the railway carriage in the Third Square, and the voices all said together, 'Don't keep him waiting, child! Why his time is worth a thousand pounds a minute!' Leonard Woolf was not a tycoon. He belonged to the same intellectual world as myself, and I had a great respect for him, even when I differed strongly from him in judgment or thought he was being unreasonable. Leonard liked long, wrangling arguments, and could always find time for them. When he greeted some remark of mine with: 'But, John, it's *grotesque* . . .' I knew that the bell had gone for the next round. Allen Lane was nearer to tycoon status, and always had too much to do; but he would listen and be swayed by arguments I put up. I always felt that Harvey had made up his mind before the five minutes had started.

The pressure increased in the early part of 1952. Before a crucial interview in February I determined not to yield any ground. I had decided that figures were the only thing that interested the chairman, and had prepared a string of clear and exact calculations to prove that our results for the previous year weren't so bad after all. This was the only occasion I can remember on which Harvey listened with attention, but I rather doubt whether his attention was in fact due to my demonstration. I had found a new ally. Eric Harvey, his son, who directed Macdonald's, had obviously put in a plea for me; and when Gibbs, who was as usual present, started on his well-worn theme of the need for economies – in what I considered essentials – he was sharply opposed by Eric. I went away feeling astonishingly calm; but the calm came not so much from having gained a reprieve, but from the sudden realization that in my long previous broodings I had crossed the Rubicon and was prepared for the worst.

When I told Christopher Isherwood about this interview, he

remarked: 'In Hollywood one starts by saying yes, but gets to the top by saying no.'

Though I told Christopher, and of course Rosamond, what the situation was, I knew that it was extremely important not to let anyone else have an inkling. I was already beginning to cast about in my mind for drastic solutions. Assuming I found one, I realized I should only be worse off if a whisper of disaster had got around before.

Rosamond was very divided in her attitude. She saw how much the publishing of good books and the building and fostering of promising authors meant to me. She saw that I had put myself in pawn to some extent by the sanguine gesture of giving my own name to the firm. She knew that its reputation was riding higher than ever, and had a golden opportunity of carrying everything before it. At the same time, she was convinced that if I had to go on with the kind of struggle that building the first storey had involved me in, I would cripple myself as a creative artist. She would have liked me to be relieved of most of the administration and financial care. If only a substitute could be found for Purnell, a group with equal resources but run by people who understood and sympathized with my aims. Perhaps then I could write poetry again. Perhaps I might even be able to start a literary magazine in the place of *Penguin New Writing*.

At this juncture, it occurred to me to go and see a new man in the book world. His name was Robert Maxwell. He had the keenest ambition, immense energy and drive, resourcefulness, and a brilliant organizational mind. I had taken a liking to him, because of the audacity and pluck he showed in challenging the conservative British book world with his new ideas. I also found his story romantic: born of the poorest parents in a remote part of Europe (which I had travelled in myself just before the war), he had escaped from the Nazis as a youngster, joined the Czech army in France and on the collapse of France had managed to get away to England. He acquired a new name, a commission in His Majesty's forces, and very soon after an MC. We had met and discussed publishing on a number of occasions. I found that my liking for him was returned.

The publishers and booksellers of London, however, were

cagey. They thought that his pluck was cheek, and found his methods too unorthodox. He had begun by building up a technical publishing firm on the basis of his Control Commission contacts in Berlin directly after the war. With a mind that worked about twice as fast as the ordinary man's, and a flair for persuading bankers and others who had money to lend it to him, added to a total disbelief in sparing himself, he managed to make a dizzy success of this venture in an astonishingly short time. By then he had got to know quite a lot about British publishing, and saw that it had a central weakness: the inadequacy of its wholesaling organization. He bought up Simpkin Marshall, who had for years been the main wholesalers in London but had fallen on evil days. Scheme after scheme had been tried to put them on their feet again, with little result.[1] Robert Maxwell, being well acquainted with efficient book distribution organizations on the continent, decided to accept the challenge.

All this he told me, bit by bit, during our discussions, and while he showed me over the old brewery warehouse in the Euston Road which he was converting to house the huge stock Simpkin Marshall needed to carry in order to function efficiently. He made it clear to me that he didn't expect to make money out of it. He had as much money as he wanted from his technical publishing operations. He just felt that it ought to be done, and wanted to have a shot. In the event, even his flair failed in this Augean task; but that is another story.

We met several times, and he listened to my story with patience, interest and occasional comments. He knew of my reputation in the literary world, and gradually let me see that he was tempted to help me. By the late summer we had formed a rough plan: I would offer to buy back my firm from Harvey,

[1] Before the war they managed to keep their head above water but in the 1940 blitz were completely wiped out by fire bombs. Realizing the value of the organization to the Book Trade, a small consortium of publishers was formed to maintain the name and the service in a large garage in St Johns Wood. It was a great strain, both financial and physical, on that small band, and as soon as the war was over the firm of Pitman decided to take it under their wing and established Simpkin Marshall in what is now known as the Book Centre. After a few years they, too, found it quite uneconomic and, after offering the business to W. H. Smith & Son and anyone else who might be interested, decided to put the firm into liquidation.

he would supply the finance up to an agreed limit, and we would then reorganize John Lehmann Ltd with more opportunity for me to devote myself to the literary side.

Bob Maxwell's support heartened me immensely. At the same time I had a curious feeling as if I were imprisoned in ice; so numb had the long struggle with Purnell made me.

By the beginning of November we had all agreed on our tactics. I asked for an interview with the chairman, who sent word that he could see me at Paulton on the first Thursday of the month. By chance it so happened that Thursday was the day on which I had arranged to give a party for John Gielgud's book. I had therefore to make all arrangements for the party beforehand. I got my helpers to come in on the Wednesday, explained to my loyal and understanding housekeeper, Mrs Crew, exactly what had to be done, and arranged with my sister Beatrix to start it off if I were to be late. I calculated that, as Harvey was expecting me he would be able to see me before lunch, and I could catch the 3.18 from Bath back to London. Plenty of time if so.

The only person I sounded out in Purnell beforehand was Eric Harvey, to whom I outlined my plans on the Tuesday. On the train down to Bath I let Gibbs into my secret, and managed, I thought, to persuade him that the project was reasonable.

On arrival at Paulton, however, we found to our consternation, that Harvey had retired incommunicado into a close huddle with one of the Woolworth high-ups. No one dared disturb him. Lunch time arrived. During lunch, Harvey, at the head of the table, gave us a lecture on 'the kind of book the public likes'. The rest of the table sat eating their peaches and cream in reverently squashed silence. The lecture, I felt, was aimed obliquely at me. As we broke up Gibbs was able to collar him, and make him promise to come down and talk to me for a few minutes as soon as he could. Time trickled by. . . . I saw that catching the 3.18 was a lost cause, and sent a teleprinter message up to London to warn Beatrix and Barbara Cooper. At last Harvey appeared in the front office, and as succinctly as I could and as politely as I could, I said my say. He appeared to listen with care, and promised to study the figures I had brought down. He would give me an answer within a few days. The interview was over in ten minutes. Ten minutes, I thought, to plead for my life.

The party went with a bang. I have never had a stranger feeling at a party in my life.

A week later the blow fell. Soon after the interview at Paulton, Harvey had sent me a letter, setting out the calculations by which he had arrived at what he considered a fair price for John Lehmann Ltd. I was stunned. It was far above anything I thought he would ask. I failed to understand why, if he considered it worth all that money, he was so hostile to it. I had a series of interviews with Bob Maxwell and my accountant, Maurice Holt, to decide on a counter-offer, and the tone of the letter I should write. When we agreed, I wrote my letter, got Maxwell's 100 per cent approval, and then took it to Eric Harvey. It was couched, I thought, in the most reasonable and courteous terms, and fully recognized the value of what they had allowed me to do. Eric became very agitated, and told me he was personally appalled at the thought of winding up the firm. He feared that his father would sweep my counter-offer aside, but at the week-end he would try to influence him to make a compromise.

At the same time I sent a copy to Gibbs. He hurried into the office next morning, and told me he very much doubted if the 'old man' would bite at all. We argued about the price. At last I said what had been in my mind for so long: 'My new backers, who are hard-headed business men, take the view that your price is several thousand pounds more than what the company is worth at break-up value. They also make the point that whatever the profit and loss account may have shown, they doubt whether you have lost over the operation, because a firm like mine does not occupy more than a fraction of your production capacity, but merely keeps the machines turning in the idle moments between big jobs. Some might even go so far as to say that my books have only cost the materials and the electric current. And if your chairman is a man of generosity and vision as well as of supreme business acumen, he will see that the sums involved over John Lehmann Ltd are as nothing in the big total of his consolidated accounts, whereas my name is of the greatest importance to me.'

For the first time, Gibbs seemed shaken, and appeared ready to admit much of the truth of what I said. On Friday evening, however, (the 14th) he rang me at my house to say that Harvey rejected my counter-offer altogether. He proposed to wind up the company in due course, and gave notice to terminate my service agreement on December 31st.

This seemed to me a most brusque and ruthless gesture, following my appeal, and it made me, of course, very angry. If I had misunderstood the position, Harvey could have taken the trouble to explain it to me. If his claim for a far higher price was well founded, he could have expounded it to me. But no; he rejected the idea of negotiation or discussion altogether. It was this total refusal to negotiate when so much was at stake for me that stuck in my gullet then – and still sticks. I had no intention of keeping my mouth shut, as I might have if more consideration and respect for my feelings and the plight I found myself in had been shown.

I saw that the adventure was over, and my hopes lay in ruins. I must extricate myself as best I could. In that operation my first duty lay towards my staff; my next towards my authors. I must give the former as long notice as possible that they were going to need to find new jobs. And I must see that none of the latter were tied, if I could help it, against their will.

The news was a deep shock to Barbara; but considering the insecurity of her own position it struck me that she took it with great loyalty and sympathy, which moved me very much. Clive Hall was away with measles, but I asked Val Biro, who even Purnell acknowledged to be in the top flight of contemporary book-designers, to come and see me next evening. I told him the full story, and he immediately said he was going to send in his resignation at once, as Barbara had.

The next step was to prepare a brief announcement for the press on December 1st, and let my most intimate friends in the publishing world and in Fleet Street know by telephone or by letter. I made my announcement quite brief and bold: 'Mr John Lehmann announces that on December 31st he will cease to have anything to do with the publishing company of John Lehmann Ltd, which he founded in 1946 and has directed ever since. Owing to differences of opinion over future policy, Messrs

Purnell, who own the controlling interest, have informed him
that they will not require his services beyond the end of the year.'

Val took the announcement to the Press Association in his
car in the morning. By the afternoon it was on the front page
of the *Evening Standard,* and from that moment my telephone
never stopped ringing. Next morning the news was in the
Express, the *Manchester Guardian,* the *Daily Telegraph* and the
News Chronicle. It was at that point that I had agreed to go to
see some of the Purnell directors at Maddox Street to discuss
various technical points about the contracts with authors. I
found them in what seemed to me a state of mingled rage and
confusion. It was wicked of me, apparently, to have told my
staff what had happened; and even more wicked to have let
the press know. Clearly, I was another case of the '*animal
méchant . . . quand on le bat, il se défend*'.

After that, the letters began to pour in; from intimate friends,
from authors, from publishing colleagues, and from a host of
other people I hardly knew at all, all expressing shock, indignation and solidarity. The *Observer* invited me to lunch, in order
to prepare a paragraph about the event. Edmond Segrave of
the *Bookseller* invited me to dinner and promised all support.
Henry Yorke wrote to say that he was going to organize a luncheon party in my honour; and Rose Macaulay that she was
going to get signatures for a letter to *The Times.* I was overwhelmed and deeply moved by the general sympathy my
misfortune evoked. I had never imagined that it could be so
widespread.

In the midst of all this almost embarrassing solidarity, I must
confess to have had an extremely uncertain and ambiguous
feeling about the future. I wrote to all my friends that I felt
myself to be a 'publishing animal', and would sooner or later
reappear, somehow or somewhere, in the publishing world. I
made a final effort to launch myself into a continuous future,
by asking Purnell if I could purchase from them, at cost, the
eight or nine books which were currently in production. This
request was curtly refused. I contemplated, with a kind of
agonized detachment, the column advertisement which appeared in *The Times Literary Supplement* reviewing the year's successes in our publishing programme: Malraux's *The Walnut*

Trees of Altenburg, Paul Bowles's *Let It Come Down*, Nikos Kazant-zakis' *Zorba the Greek*, Jean-Louis Curtis's *Lucifer's Dream*, Ben-jamin Constant's *Cécile*, John Gielgud's biography in pictures, Annette Hopkins' biography of Elizabeth Gaskell and my own anthology *Pleasures of New Writing*. What would it all lead to? Would I ever again, in spite of my brave assurances, be able to make the tremendous effort of building up a new publishing firm? In the almost impenetrable fog that settled on London that week-end, completely exhausted, I settled myself by the fire in my library, with Lottie beside me, and read *David Copperfield*.

The letter which appeared in *The Times* read as follows: 'The news that Mr John Lehmann has severed his connection with John Lehmann Limited will have been received with re-gret, and even with dismay, by writers and readers in many parts of the world. There can be few people of literary inter-ests who, during the last fifteen years, have not often been grateful to Mr Lehmann for the breadth and fervour of his enthusiasms; and there must be very many writers, both in this country and abroad, who can bear witness to Mr Lehmann's qualities as an inspired encourager. In France, Italy, Czecho-slovakia and Greece his patronage has been particularly well-directed; and since he founded in 1946 his own publishing house, he has contrived to give an idiosyncratic flavour not only to the contents or his list but also to the appearance and decoration of the books themselves. Thus it is that many young painters will also have reason to regret the departure of one who has chosen to neglect his own considerable gifts as a writer in order to devote himself, unselfishly, and unsparingly to fur-thering the gifts of others.'

It was signed by Freddie Ayer, Patrick Leigh-Fermor, Henry Green, Graham Greene, John Hayward, Arthur Koestler, Rose Macaulay, Raymond Mortimer, Harold Nicolson, Simon Nowell-Smith, John Russell, Roger Senhouse, Stephen Spender and Angus Wilson.

Thinking of this wonderful tribute, the leader in *The Times Literary Supplement*, and the repeated notices in the *Bookseller*, I began to have a curious feeling that I had died, and was leading a ghost-like posthumous life. And sometimes I felt that all this was about someone else. How could I answer all the letters, except in the terms of a brother or son of the deceased?

I was pulled up to reality again by the final days, before Christmas, at Gilbert Street. We spent them sorting out, packing up and tearing up. There were tears, dramatic demonstrations, and laughter too. We had been asked by Purnell to label everything very carefully before we left. The two typists, Pauline and Janet, determined to carry out this last demand with meticulous care. They completed their work by labelling the office tea-pot as 'tea-pot', the table as 'table', the window as 'window' and finally the floor as 'floor'. By lunch time on Christmas Eve, they had all gone after many affecting farewells, and my car was at the door loaded up with various parcels of books and papers that belonged to me. Barbara, with smiling but tear-stained face, saw me off.

The luncheon that Henry Green organized for me took place at the Trocadero on January 14th. Tom Eliot took a leading part, and there were nearly thirty of my fellow writers there, including, of course, Rosamond, and to my great delight, E. M. Forster. I enjoyed it, although I felt almost unbearably keyed up and nervous about my own speech. Henry muttered to me: 'This is the first occasion authors have given one of their own kind a *meal* since Coleridge organized a dinner for Leigh Hunt on his release from prison.' Cyril Connolly, who was obviously enjoying himself very much, likened us all to Harley Street surgeons and doctors, and suggested as we dispersed that we ought to form ourselves into a monthly luncheon club. Alas, nothing came of this excellent idea. Tom Eliot warmed up as the occasion warmed up, and described to me the technique he himself had developed to deal with stage and film tycoons.

My Mother had written to me: 'I have had you very much in my thoughts since the crisis and I know you have been under a hideous strain. But how splendid to have so great intellectual support: it does prove that true culture in this country is not commercial.'

I did not know at the time that it was the end of my publishing career. Only my sanguine temperament, like a machine that insists on whirling on in spite of sand thrown into the cogs, carried me forward to the next stage, the next events.

Part Four

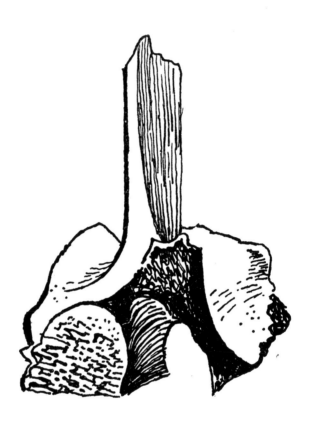

I

In the meantime, another development had taken place which was to give me one of my most exciting opportunities to discover and present new authors and new literary ideas. I had become editor and compère of the first BBC 'literary magazine of the air', *New Soundings*. It was the continuing existence of this programme that softened a little the blow that the extinction of my publishing firm had dealt me; though only for a few months.

One day, a few years before, a very young poet, who happened to be doing his military service in the RAF, came to see me with a sheaf of poems in his hand. His name was David Hughes. Tall and slim, with curly black hair and a cupid's bow of a mouth, he seemed almost improbably the type of the romantic young Shelleyan poet. He was an ardent fan of *New Writing*, and was bitterly disappointed when the Penguin came to an end. I encouraged him in his writing, though his poems did not appear to me ready for publication as yet. At the end of his time in the RAF he went up to Oxford, and we kept in fairly close contact. He touched me by showing an almost greater concern for a successor to the Penguin than I had felt myself. Eventually, he conceived the idea that, in order to achieve as wide an audience as possible, the successor should be a radio programme produced at regular intervals like a quarterly or monthly magazine. I liked the idea, as it came out of our constant repeated discussions, and encouraged him to try and convince the BBC of its worth. I was nevertheless astonished and impressed when he told me that he had managed to interest the novelist P. H. Newby, at that time one of the leading Third Programme producers, to the point when he thought the BBC would definitely buy the idea.

Sure enough, Howard Newby came to see me one day towards the end of September 1951, and told me that the scheme was on. The BBC wanted me to organize and edit it. The terms and facilities they offered seemed to me to provide immense opportunities in what was an entirely new field. I accepted with little hesitation. Even if I had not been personally eager to tackle the experiment, I knew that it had to be done.

One more into battle. When the details were finally fixed, I started contacting all the authors I thought might provide appropriate contributions, particularly the younger poets and novelists whose work had only recently come to my notice. I had been given forty-five minutes once a month on the Third, with a repeat. The arrangement at the beginning was that I should confine myself to British authors; I intended to mix new work by authors already known, more or less of the *Penguin New Writing* generation, with the younger hopefuls, and have occasional comments by older writers. David Hughes, who was already editing *Isis*, was beginning to grumble, not unnaturally, that the BBC was leaving no room for him in a programme that was his brain-child; but his loyalty to me was unshakeable, and he eagerly agreed to arrange an Oxford party for me, at which I could meet all the budding undergraduate writers. At this party, which took place in the second half of November, I met Elizabeth Jennings, John Bowen, Paul West, Simon Broadbent, James Price and Derwent May for the first time. I did not find time to go down to Cambridge before the first broadcast, which was fixed for the beginning of January, but Dadie Rylands put me in touch with Peter Green, who made some suggestions which turned out extremely valuable.

This was an exciting moment of discovery and fermenting dreams. Word began to get around even before January with astonishing speed, and unsolicited typescripts began to arrive almost every day. I saw all sorts of pitfalls looming, especially in the amount of difficult allusive poetry listeners would be ready to take, and the length of the prose literature contributions; but I felt that I must plunge in, make the first two broadcasts as stimulating as possible in spite of whatever technical blunders I might commit, and learn from them as quickly as I could, before the permissive enthusiasm – if I succeeded in generating it – began to evaporate. I knew at least that the dearth of literary magazines since *Horizon* and *Penguin New*

The *London Magazine* launching party:
above E. M. Forster, Rex Warner, William Plomer
below Rosamond Lehmann, Cecil King and profile of the author

The *London Magazine* launching party:
above Louis MacNeice, Rose Macaulay, Edmund Wilson
below Billy Collins, David Carver, Veronica Wedgwood,
Harold Acton and Rosamond Lehmann

Writing had come to an end, put much initial sympathy on my side.

When the evening of the first broadcast came, I felt extremely nervous, though Howard Newby had been encouraging and optimistic about the authors I had chosen and the editorial comment I had woven around them. I always felt keyed up and at my most alive on entering a broadcasting studio; but this time I began to wonder whether I hadn't bitten off more than I could chew.

This sense of dismay was increased as I observed Henry Green on the other side of the microphone table, looking as if he had reached the ultimate point of dislocated world-weariness. Punch in the attack, however, and variety in the material seemed to carry the day. I had chosen poems by three new Oxford poets, Elizabeth Jennings, James Price and Simon Broadbent; a strange and beautiful poem by Lynette Roberts, who, I considered, ought to be known better than she was; a poem by James Michie, who had been editor of *Oxford Poetry* in 1949; and a long ballad by Vernon Watkins. The 'surprise' prose piece was an extraordinarily vivid and naturally written description of a prisoner-of-war escape by a young sailor, Leading Electrical Mechanic Wilde. It was from an autobiography he had written called *My Life from the Age of 18*. This was sandwiched between a piece by Henry Green, which consisted partly of an extract from the novel he was writing and partly of a commentary on prose style which led up to the extract; and a vigorous piece of advice to young writers by Tom Hopkinson. Tom (who became extremely enthusiastic about Wilde's piece) did a brilliant job converting what was in fact a fairly run-of-the mill piece of good journalism into something much better by a first-class performance; and Hallam Fordham impressed us all by his dramatic reading of Vernon Watkins' ballad.

It is perhaps worth quoting my introductory flourish in full, as it reveals all the thoughts that were stirring in my mind at the time:

'In comparatively recent years, a new disease has attacked rhododendrons in this country. It is called "bud blast", and it causes the buds to turn brown and rot during the long period of incubation between their formation and their opening.

N

'Something of the same sort seems to have been happening in the arts, especially in imaginative literature. Most of those who have been concerned, in one way or another, with the fostering of young talent will agree with me, I think, when I say that during the last seven years or so there has been a tragic failure of fulfilment. A young poet has written two or three poems of promise and originality; he has appeared to be just about to find his voice; then two years later he has made no advance, but rather sunk into the clichés of his time and the repetition of the first tricks he learned. A young novelist has excited all the critics with a first novel in which a fresh eye seems to be viewing the world, and the attitudes of a new generation defining themselves. Alas, his second novel tries to recapture in melodrama what his first created from passion; and his third is still going the rounds of the publishers. Worse still – and this is the true "bud blast" – many young would-be writers who have just reached the time, at their universities or in their first explorations of the world, when they should be experimenting with vigour, making slapdash mistakes but fizzing over with something to say – even in a passion of imitation of someone else's style – these young writers show themselves timid, confused and imitative without passion.

'What is wrong? Of course it is not at all as bad as all that – as I hope to show in my programmes; but when you come to think of it, it's not unnatural that those young men and women who celebrated their twenty-first birthdays between 1945 and 1952 should feel that they lacked, in Hopkins's phrase, "the one rapture of an inspiration". The poets of the 'thirties were carried forward on a great wave of belief, or hope, that they could remould the world. The poets of the war years were strengthened by that deep searching of the roots of our spiritual life that was an instinctive reaction in this country from the first shock of the ending of peace. The poets of today have as their inheritance a peace that has never succeeded in becoming real, a ruined economy, and a thick atomic fog of insecurity over the future of Europe, of the world.

'No wonder that they find it difficult to open up a clear path of advance for themselves. No wonder they wrestle almost vainly with the problem of defining an attitude, or discovering the symbols of a philosophy. And yet, even though fallow periods are inevitable in the history of a literature, there never was a time, a challenge to which art, poetry, could not find an answer.

'But the search requires weapons and equipment, and one of the most important items of equipment is a magazine: a place to be published in, a place where reports can be pooled of new soundings that are being made, new ideas stirred into life and old arguments brought up to date. Alas, very few such magazines exist today. Their mortality since the war may partly, of course, be explained by the very failure of fulfilment I have been talking about; but there is no doubt that it has enormously aggravated the sickness.

'In this new series of programmes we are going to try to do something that has never been attempted before. We want to provide in the spoken broadcast word a substitute that may, with luck favouring, turn out to be something very much more. If I were starting a literary magazine now, a magazine that aimed to be the focus of new life in literature, whether written by entirely new talents or those still in the unfolding spring of their creative power, I should want to pay particular attention to questions of style, to experiments or natural discoveries in phrasing, imagery, flow; not only because so much in our modern lives conspires to deaden the vital response to words, but also because a new style, or styles, can crystallize or release the expression of a whole generation. I say "styles" because there never need be only one style. Think how different the style of *To the Lighthouse* is from the style of *Crome Yellow* – and yet in the 'twenties both released vast new energies in the novel.

'The air provides, I think, an excellent medium for this purpose; and a medium whose discipline is to my mind altogether beneficial. It demands a certain clarity and definition, a certain immediacy of impact either by thought or image or rhythm, and will hardly tolerate the intellectual mists and verbiage in which young writers all too often try to escape the searching eye of judgement.

'This may sound rather sternly commanding; and I am reminded that in the battle of literature it is the business of an editor, not to order his troops about, but to follow where the most spirited lead. . . .'

In spite of my panic doubts, the programme went over exactly as I hoped it would, though one or two listeners who had difficulty in getting good reception on the Third confessed to me that towards the end the only words that came out clear and strong were the 'Sodom, Sodom' of the refrain in Vernon Watkins' ballad, causing a certain hilarity round the fireside. The press was good, and a few days later I had a letter from Howard Newby, in which he said: 'I have now been able to gather a few opinions about *New Soundings I*. Everyone here is pleased with it . . . the general summing up is one of warm approval.'

The result was that, while I was collecting material for the second programme, and dealing with the immediately accelerated pouring-in of letters and manuscripts, I was invited to lunch by Harman Grisewood, the director of the Third Programme at that time. He was so pleased with the launching, that he offered me another quarter of an hour for each programme (making sixty minutes in all), gave me permission to use American and other foreign contributions in translation, and extended the run to six months. I told him that, as far as authors went, I had everything my own way, provided I could find the right material. After all, *New Soundings* was not just another highbrow literary magazine come in to fill a vacuum, but a broadcast programme with a national audience running into six figures, well paid, with – for the poets at least – the possibility of reprinting in the *Listener* for another good fee.

And indeed I was getting some first-class recruits. Geoffrey Grigson wrote in to tell me that John Wain, who had contributed the last article to the last number of *Penguin New Writing*, was also a poet, and had a small volume of poems, *Mixed Feelings*, privately printed at Reading University. When I eventually got hold of a copy, I at once liked the clarity, the wit, the pithy concentration with its romantic undertones to the classical manner, and took several of them for *New Soundings*. John became an important contributor who gave me great hope for the future.

About the same time, another contributor appeared who inspired in me almost exactly the same feeling. In the autumn a friend had shown me a small volume of naval short stories,

which had just been published, written by an ex-sailor called
Charles Causley who was now a schoolmaster in Cornwall. I
discovered that he was also the author of a very slim pamphlet
of poems published (with their usual courage) by The Hand
and Flower Press. I liked them so much, that I wrote off to him
at once, and, after some correspondence received from him a
poem or ballad, 'Ou Phrontis', which not only delighted me
but seemed quite admirably suited for broadcasting. This was
the beginning of a long association, friendly and professional,
with Charles Causley, a poet with a style and inspiration that
have remained utterly unlike anything else in his generation.

The second programme, however, ran into a road-block.
The script was ready, the performers all booked, when the news
came through of the death of King George VI. All scheduled
broadcasting programmes were immediately cancelled, even on
the Third. Nevertheless we recorded it at exactly the same time
that evening, just as if it had been going out. Louis MacNeice,
who had scarcely recovered from a chill, pulled himself together
to give a remarkable reading of several sections of a long harrowing poem about a cat which had belonged to him in Athens,
all the more moving for the strange, lazy drawl in which he
spoke. I was always glad when contributors were accomplished
enough to read their own works, and this poem was one of our
outstanding successes. Christopher Isherwood, who happened
to be in England again at this time, also gave a highly characteristic performance in reading a piece he had written for us on
six up-and-coming young American writers: very confidential
in manner, serious and yet subtly managing to give his audience
the impression that he could hardly refrain from chuckling,
that he found some of the information he was giving peculiarly
funny. He chose Ray Bradbury, Truman Capote, William
Goyen, Speed Lamkin, Norman Mailer and Calder Willingham. I can still hear the relish that gradually came into his
voice as he spoke about Truman Capote and the southern
school of writers that seemed then to dominate the American
literary scene: 'There are, in fact, two souths that people write
about. One of them is the real contemporary south; a land
where industrialization is increasing, education is spreading and
considerable progress is being made towards solving the Negro

problem. The other is the gothic-romantic, macabre south of decaying mansions, degenerate families, despair, drink, Spanish moss, sexual atrocities and lynchings. Truman Capote writes about this second kind of south, and makes it just as gothic, funny and macabre as he knows how. I must confess that this second kind of south bores me utterly – its cult can in some respects be compared with the cult of a romantic Ireland which flourished at the beginning of this century – and the greatest tribute I can pay to Capote's talent is to say that nevertheless I sincerely admire his two novels. . . . He can be very funny and very touching. But I can't help feeling that he is often guilty of playing with the reader, as if trying to see just how much weirdness he can get away with. . . .'

After recording this programme, Christopher left to make his first post-war visit to Berlin, with an assignment for the *Observer* to write two articles. He returned about a fortnight later, very eager to hear all details about the King's funeral. I had managed to find standing room at the base of the Achilles statue in Hyde Park, and described to him the overwhelming effect of the pageantry and sorrowful beauty of the procession with the sailors drawing the gun-carriage, followed on foot by other members of the Royal Family including the Duke of Windsor and various crowned heads of Europe.

Christopher was particularly enthralled by the gush some of the newspapers put out, which I had kept for him, especially *The Times* reporter who wrote of a blackbird 'trilling its sweet requiem' in the silence of Hyde Park Corner. He then told us about his sensational return to his friend Heinz and his old landlady Frau Thurau, who had shrieked for joy on seeing him and danced with him in the street. He was in the best of spirits. A day or two later, however, he seemed to be submerged by one of his waves of despair, burned all unanswered letters, told the BBC he couldn't re-write one of his talks and gave them their money back, and got out of the second of his two *Observer* articles.

By the time I had prepared these two programmes, I had a fairly clear idea of the chief difficulties that confronted us. First of all, I saw that the speaking was the supreme priority, especially with poetry. All the poems we included were new, or at

least only known to the readers of magazines with very esoteric
circulations. It was therefore extremely important that the
reader should not only make the sense of the poem as clear as
possible, but also – in particular when dealing with unrhymed
poetry – by his control of the rhythms and the slightest of
pauses at the end of a line that carried no stop, suggest to the
listeners the shape in which the piece was written. With a poem
like 'Ou Phrontis', for instance, or the ballads by Vernon
Watkins which we broadcast, the problem was negligible; but
many of the poems I chose had, inevitably at that time, a
complex imagery and a compression of the steps of argument
which was not at all easy to follow even in the best reading.
Humpty Dumpty introduced Alice to the conception of portmanteau words; much of modern poetry has consisted, since
the publication of Hopkins, of portmanteau or concertina
poems. These are poems that need, after having made their
original imaginative impact (if they are good poems) to be
quietly unriddled with the printed page beside one. This problem dogged us to the end; but later in the series I tried the experiment of having a poem read once, then trying to give a
few words of elucidation myself, then having it read again.
The main objection to this method – apart from the danger of
my missing the point – was the time it took.

The other bedrock limitation was in the length of the prose
contributions. If as much as half my sixty minutes was devoted
to prose, that only meant time for about 4,000 words, to be
divided between two or three writers. Two was the minimum;
but even three prose pieces were all too few to represent new
imaginative writers and new critical thought. In *New Writing*
the most successful prose contributions, whether short stories
or documentary reports or critical essays, had nearly all been
between 3,000 and 6,000 words in length. In fact, in *New
Soundings*, we had to jettison serious criticism almost entirely,
as I took the view that critical themes of any importance could
not be properly elaborated in 1,000 or 1,500 words. We confined ourselves to more general comment, such as Christopher's
examination of young American writers, Cyril Connolly's con-
fession of infatuation with Petronius's *Satyricon*, or a later display of typical French fireworks by the young French novelist

Roger Nimier on being a writer and twenty years old in Paris directly after the war. The only exception, I think, was André Maurois's presentation of the newly discovered early novel by Proust, *Jean Santeuil*, which we sent a van to record in his country home in France.

It may have been a mistake to use extracts from longer works at all, in spite of the success of Wilde's escape piece and some remarkable scenes from novels in progress by Walter Baxter (his second novel), Hugo Charteris (unknown till then), Philip Toynbee and a young American, William Fifield. The listener was nearly always, I think, left saying to himself, 'Well, what next?' or 'But what led up to that situation?' however self-contained the extract appeared. The temptation, however, was great when one had just come across a novel that struck one as original and exciting, by someone little known or not known at all, and one wanted to give a pre-view of it. Particularly as the short stories we used often had to be cut down. When authors at last realized that it was more or less impossible for *New Soundings* to use any story longer than 1,500 words, they would, in many cases, send in slight sketches, quite failing to see that the limitation on length demanded something more, and not less strong in immediacy and impact. The most successful short stories we used were those written deliberately with the programme in mind by such skilful professionals as William Sansom, Angus Wilson, V. S. Pritchett, and the two young novelists I had discovered in my firm, Robin Jenkins and Ernest Frost.

In spite of these limitations, I think we managed very soon to see how to give weight without stodginess in the comments, and dramatic speaking effect without losing lyrical depth in the poems, as well as how to choose the short fiction extracts without appearing too fragmentary. The problem of variety was always in the forefront of my mind. I was immensely helped by an excellent team of BBC readers, among the most constant of whom were Dennis McCarthy, John Glen, Robert Rietty and Mary O'Farrell; also by many of the authors who were reading their own work and practised in it, each, like Christopher, giving his own special flavour to the performance. I think this was particularly important, as the listener to a radio magazine can't browse and pick and choose as the reader of a printed magazine can, but must listen through to the end if he is to hear all. Some of our recordings became pretty hilarious when good performers were round the table. I remember that, during the fourth session, Mary O'Farrell, who was there to read some beautiful poems by E. J. Scovell and Diana Witherby, appeared convulsed with laughter, as many of the rest of us were, all the way through: at William Plomer, who was reading a piece he had written on the tribulations of being a publisher's reader, the grotesque zest in his voice, the gestures and facial expression he used to help his performance; at Laurie Lee's rendering of an extract from a book about Spain he was writing, with no gestures at all but a sly humour suggested all through by the inflexions of his voice; at Dennis McCarthy's performance in a comic story by William Sansom about a homesick Londoner in Rome; and by John Betjeman, whose pre-recording of the now famous 'Song of a Night-Club Proprietor', *Sun and Fun*, came suddenly booming out of the loudspeaker, transfixing us all by its harrowing absurdity:

> There was Kummel on the handle of the door,
> The ashtrays were unemptied,
> The cleaning unattempted,
> And a squashed tomato sandwich on the floor. . . .

The only other writer I saw use the same accompaniment of gestures as William was Dylan Thomas, when he recited his 'Prologue' in No. 8. In his case the gestures were even more pronounced and extraordinary, as if he were trying to wind up a very heavy bucket from a very deep well. No one who heard only the melodious, magical voice that came over the air could possibly have imagined what went on in the studio.

By that time great interest had been aroused in America. Victor Weybright, the genial and successful publisher of the paperback series New American Library, had just started *New World Writing* in frank imitation of *Penguin New Writing* (which he handsomely acknowledged), and wrote to ask if he could see the script of No. 1 and publish it in his country if a scheme could be worked out. I happened just to have prepared a composite programme out of the first three or four programmes

for the North American service of the BBC, and sent a script
over as an alternative. He and his co-editor, Arabella Porter,
received it with acclaim, and it appeared in *New World Writing*
a few months later.

2

Everything seemed to be going even better than I could have
hoped at my most sanguine. The BBC agreed to commission a
further six programmes, making twelve in all. The press as a
whole had turned from encouraging to enthusiastic. By the
time No. 4 had been broadcast, *New Soundings* had even been
called (in the *Observer*) 'the most interesting programme in
British radio'. I was therefore startled (to put it mildly) when
I received a letter from Howard Newby confirming the exten-
sion for a second six months, but at the same time telling me
that the programme had been such a success that they wanted
to go on with it beyond that – but not with me as editor. The
very success of the programme, he told me, was partly the
reason for this decision! They didn't want to give the impression that any one person had a corner in the market.

This reasoning on the part of the BBC baffled me. The more
I thought about it, the more indignant I became. I feel sure
that if they had said they wanted to introduce another editor,
give him a six-months run, then come back to me for another
six months, and so on, I would have seen a good deal of sound
sense in the proposal. But to dismiss an editor completely because the magazine he had created, organized and kept going
had been a resounding success seemed to me, well, out of a
looking-glass world. I knew that Howard who had been a sympathetic ally from the beginning, was only handing on to me
the decision of his committee, in which he had only one voice,
but it was to him that I had to send my reply and my protest.
Because I had made a success of an entirely new venture in
broadcasting, I asked him, must it promptly be given to someone else? 'If Allen Lane had said to me in the old days, "*Penguin*

New Writing is a great success, therefore we're giving it next
year to **** ***** to carry on", where do you think I would
have told him to ——?' I said I saw the point of this monopoly,
but if that worried them, why didn't they start more magazines-
of-the-air? I ended up, a little intemperately, 'To hell with
such cant.'

Howard replied: 'Your rocket has arrived, still giving out
sparks.' He proposed we should let emotion cool, and then
discuss the situation. I agreed, and we did so. But neither then,
nor at any of my subsequent discussion with him, or Harman
Grisewood, or at the very end with John Morris who had succeeded Grisewood, or Mary Somerville, did I succeed in de-
flecting the BBC from their unholy decision. If I had not
continued, quite unreasonably, to hope that they could be
reasoned out of it, those last months of *New Soundings*, containing as they did the blow of the end of John Lehmann Ltd,
would have been dark indeed.

When the first six programmes were over, Gilbert Phelps
took on from Howard. I have often wondered whether I had
shattered his nerve.

My reaction to my dismissal was echoed in the press. The
Sunday Times, which had said in the autumn that I had made
my radio magazine 'compulsory listening for all who care for
creative imaginative writing' now commented tersely that I
had 'exceeded one's hopes for a year. His curious reward is to
be dropped.' While the last programme was being recorded,
I heard that the so-called 'Listener Research coefficient' for the
programme had gone sharply up to 74 per cent. from the 68
per cent. it had been in the autumn.

Looking back on that series of twelve programmes, I am
particularly glad that *New Soundings* gave the first *national* plat-
form to so many poets who were to make names for themselves
in the 'fifties: John Wain, Charles Causley, Elizabeth Jennings,
Norman McCaig (brought to my notice by Louis MacNeice),
Donald Davie, with a beautiful early poem called 'North
Russia in the Fall', John Holloway with his 'Apollonian Poem'
which electrified all who heard it including Edith Sitwell;
Thom Gunn, who was still at Cambridge, with the 'Secret
Sharer' and 'Incident on a Journey', James Merrill a gifted

American poet little known over here at the time, and Paul Roche whom I had first met in Duncan Grant's studio posing for some of Duncan's most beautiful late drawings and gouaches. All these poets came on with me to the *London Magazine*, and I was therefore rather amused when some of the more strident propagandists for 'the Movement', a chimaera which popped up with teeth bared a few years later, and to which many of them were said to belong, claimed that old has-beens like myself couldn't possibly appreciate what it was all about.

If I showed a partiality in these programmes, it was, I readily admit, towards Greek poets and anything generated by the Greek idea. This was due not only to my very deep feeling for the Greek tradition and those who maintained it so splendidly in our own times, but also to the fact that so much that was above the average that was being written seemed to be inspired by Greece. Among the contributions were not only translations of poems by the great Angelos Sikelianos and by Odysseus Elytis, whose work I had published in *New Writing* and *Orpheus*, but also original poems on Greek themes by Lawrence Durrell, John Heath-Stubbs, Francis King and Kenneth Wood. In addition, I selected an extraordinary and characteristic study of Shakespeare's *The Tempest* by my dead friend Demetrios Capetanakis, from a *cache* of his earliest English writings while at Cambridge, which a friend of his had recently brought me. In commenting on the strange interchangeability of the remarks of Caliban and Ariel at certain points, he wrote: 'The whole play, all motion on the island is a unity, perhaps the unity of our consciousness in contact with poetry. In every person, in every line, we recognize an experience we have had from poetry. . . . Great poetry – like the person one loves – is always the language, the sign of the unknown; Democritus spoke of poetry almost in the same way as Miranda of Ferdinand. . . .'

The main problem for me all through was to find an appropriate critical 'envelope' for the contributions I accepted; more difficult than the task I faced later, of writing a foreword to each number of the *London Magazine*, because my introductory remarks to a *New Soundings* programme had to be far more directly related to what was coming than the foreword to a number of a printed magazine; and I had to continue, in between the separate items, to pursue any theme, or let it slide naturally into another. I harped continually on questions of language and style, because they seemed to me far and away the most important at that time; and I am inclined to think they still are. Rosamond echoed my own thoughts when she said, in a contribution she made: 'Why is so little attention paid nowadays to words? What makes some novelists suppose they can get by without caring how words are arranged, what ring is given out by them?' Raymond Queneau spoke in similar vein about changes in the French language that was spoken all around him: 'A new language calls forth new ideas, and fresh thoughts need a fresh language. . . . Contemporary French will not become a real and fruitful language, until it is used by philosophers themselves and, of course, by men of science. Here, therefore, I hail the first mathematicians who shall write a text-book of algebra in this new tongue, which is one of the few good things still left in this country'.

Many other phrases, epigrams and words of wisdom by my contributors still ring in my ears. Cyril Connolly, for instance, on the chance of finding the lost books of Petronius: 'I know that I would sacrifice everything a space-ship could bring us back from Venus or all the minerals on the moon for a sight of those rolls in their charred cases, and a few more episodes of those aesthetes in adventure.' And again: 'In the picture gallery Eumolpus said that in an age that worshipped drink, sex and money there could be no more great art; people would no longer take the trouble to write well and would rather earn a gold ingot than own an old master. Like many whose gaze is fixed on the past, he was apt to find himself looking into the future.' Iain Fletcher, on the intellectual snobbery of little magazines: 'Poetry does provide the peaks of literature, but we can reach them only by the foothills.' And William Plomer, in talking of the decay of regional novelists: 'There are no longer fairies at the bottom of the garden – only a bus route.' From the poetry, there are too many lines and stanzas that I fell in love with to mention here; but George Barker's 'Letter to a Young Poet' has haunted me more continually than any, with its great climax beginning:

But over the known world of things
The great poem folds its wings
And from a bloody breast will give
Even to those who disbelieve. . . .

I have re-read many of the contributions, after nearly fifteen years, and I am struck to find in so many of them, certainly among those that might be described as left-wing as much as the others, a certain national pride, nowhere near chauvinism, but just and even passionate, that has been rare to find in the nihilism that followed in the later 'fifties.

New Soundings, of course, was only a makeshift on the way to new literary magazines, which eventually turned up. Nevertheless, I am pretty certain that, given the existence of those magazines, the BBC could have organized a magazine-of-the-air, a variation from *New Soundings*, which would have been of great value and given great pleasure. I cannot applaud the directing spirits of that great Corporation for having, after two brief experiments that followed my editorship, given up the enterprise entirely.

My successor, I learned eventually, was to be John Wain, one of the new authors I had been happiest to push forward. He wrote me an extremely nice letter about this. I wrote back to him to say how sorry I was I should not be in London to hear the first programme he had put together, as I was going abroad.

I was badly in need of time to lick my wounds.

Part Five

I

I had long promised myself a Mediterranean holiday, on which I could relax and see if the springs of poetry would start flowing again. I decided on Cyprus, with a visit to Rome and Amalfi on the way. I took with me, as far as Amalfi, a young actor friend, Spence Coulter, who had never seen Italy before.

Rome, in the brilliant rose-golden light, seemed more beautiful than ever. Revisiting the famous classical sites of Rome, Michelangelo's capitol, the baths of Caracalla and the Pantheon, was an especially exciting experience with a companion whose youthful ardour and interest burned so intensely as Spence's. For the first time, I was struck by the strangeness of the fact that Trelawney lay beside Shelley in the Protestant Cemetery, as Severn beside Keats. I lunched with Ian Greenlees, the engaging mandarin figure who was at that time in charge of the British Council in the city, in a dining-room crowded with Guttuso paintings of startling vigour and beauty, and directly afterwards bumped into my old friend, the painter Derek Hill, and Elizabeth Bowen in the Piazza Colonna. I I have found that paradoxically enough, one sees more of one's English friends and gets to know them better, when one meets them on holiday abroad. I had to tell Elizabeth and Derek the whole story of the crisis and climax in the fortunes of my publishing firm, and of the honour and comedy of the luncheon organized for me by Henry Green. Elizabeth, who was collecting material for a book on Rome and soaking herself in the atmosphere of the city, suggested that I should go over and stay with her in her family home in Ireland to finish my autobiography, while she finished her book; an invitation I was eventually able to accept, with very happy results.

We reached Amalfi from Salerno, by a coast road of extraordinary beauty, on the mountain side of which the Judas trees

o

were already in full, pale magenta bloom. Osbert and Edith Sitwell had recommended the hotel to me, a converted monastery perched dizzily on the rock face above the sea. As they appeared to be almost the patron saints of the place, we were received with great deference, and given a room that might once have been a superior kind of monk's cell, with views over the great welcoming haze of the blue-grey silky sea from the huge windows looking south and west.

Both Edith and Osbert were in America at the time, on one of their triumphal tours, and before I left I had been delighted by a letter from Edith which showed that she was in the highest spirits, characteristically, in spite of sciatica, arthritis and sprained muscles. She wrote from Hollywood: '*Please* let me know as soon as you have made any plans. I long to hear. The whole thing is really too disgraceful for words. . . . My principal amusement here is reading the lady gossip-writers: "My telephone bell and front door bells never stopped ringing all day yesterday and the day before. All the so-and-so's friends were so anxious to get in first about how they are shaking their heads over the marriage. She spat in his face at Ciro's on Saturday night, and he hit her back. They were both thrown out on their ears, but continued the fight outside. Pity! Pat is such a lovely girl, and a thorough little lady, and Bill is just the kind of boy every woman would want as her son. And they've only been married a fortnight. It is only her seventeenth marriage, and actually Bill has only been married fifteen times, but everyone hoped they had found happiness already. I rang Pat up and said 'What did you feel like spitting in Bill's face?' And she answered 'And so what, you old bitch!' Pity."

'The other day in conference over my film, we were discussing the part where the Papal Legate threatened Henry VIII with eternal damnation. So one of the people working with me on the actual story, said "That is where you have these Cardinal guys threatening the King with eternal damnation. And you have the King say to them 'You boys can go and tell your Boss the Pope that I am King of England.'"

'Aldous Huxley (a very dear frind of O and myself) drove us out to tea with Dr Hubble, the great astronomer and his wife. The drive takes 45 minutes. The whole way back was occupied by Aldous with a diatribe against Wordsworth in his lesser moments. "*Really,* Edith, that *any* man *presumed* to be in his senses should write:

> I need not say, Louisa dear,
> How glad we are to have you here,
> A lovely convalescent.

Incidentally, what wonderful technique. Really like *The Cocktail Party,* only don't say I said so. . . .'[1]

And now I had another letter, commiserating with me on the end of *New Soundings* and breathing fire and slaughter against the BBC. Her high spirits continued, 'There has been a very bad epidemic of rabies here, and a heatwave. I have started the theory, in Hollywood, that the former arose through all the dogs having been bitten by Miss **** ****, a gossip columnist. You will be shocked to hear that a line of mine

This is the wild spring and the time of the mating of the tigers

has "put ideas" into the heads of all the Jewish adolescents in Brooklyn. I have had a most indignant letter from the mother of two of them – and she has been deputed by thirty other mothers to ask me what the hell I mean by it. It seems that Leah, aged fourteen, and Saul, aged twelve (the children of my correspondent) are "just at the age where brook and river meet" – and the phrase about the tigers has thrown them into a violent state of adolescent eroticism. Saul is fairly bad – but Leah is neither to hold nor to bind. I don't know about Solomon – he wasn't mentioned. And do I "think it right to put into the heads of children that their elders are always thinking about that sort of thing – the mating of tigers and what all!"

'I have replied coldly that I do not know what she is talking about. *Who* is always thinking about that sort of thing? And *what* sort of thing? I argued "does your daughter still think, at the age of fourteen, that tigers grow under cabbages? . . . Tigers live in jungles, and cannot be married by Wesleyan

[1] In *Taken Care Of,* Edith Sitwell attributes these lines (correctly) to Coleridge, but adds some lines by Wordsworth that Aldous Huxley also thought ridiculous.

ministers or rabbis, nor can they wear wedding rings. But they
lead most respectable lives, and lives that are far happier than
those of poets who can be badgered by idiotic questions." '

Amalfi plunged us into a world of drama and poetry at
once, because the day after our arrival was, though we had
forgotten it, Good Friday; and a great procession took place,
as it had for centuries. As dusk gradually fell with its orange
and violet light, the whole population of the little place seemed
to be gathered in the area around the cathedral. The lights
came on, and then, in the distance, in the square, we heard
the singing grow louder as the procession approached. First
came the ranks of the white-sheeted, white-cowled and hooded
ministrants, their eyes appearing through the slits in their
hoods, their heads bound with what was surely a symbol of a
crown of thorns: they carried lighted lanterns, and one in the
middle a black crucifix. There followed the pall-bearers of the
golden bier with the image of the dead Christ upon it, flanked
by rows of dark, silent sailors who seemed a reminder of the
far-off greatness of Amalfi's past, when the republic, incredibly
enough, was one of the richest and most powerful of the Mediterranean world. It suddenly came to me what pride of history
was compacted into that great cry from Webster's tragedy:
'I am Duchess of Malfi still!' After the sailors came the boys'
choir, with their haunting high-soaring chant; and as that
faded into the further streets we went up the wide climbing
steps into the huge cathedral, all lit by hundred of candles
which threw their quivering light over the marble-faced pillars
and the great ceiling with its painted and gilded carvings.
Gradually we heard the procession returning, and saw the
white ministrants mounting the steps on the final stage of their
symbolic journey, with the solemn music ringing all around
them. I am easily moved by beautiful ceremonial; but I had
never before been so moved by a religious drama, nor was
again until I saw the same Good Friday procession, many
years later, pass through the darkened streets of Athens.

Amalfi in spring seemed to me exactly what I had longed
for through all the time of struggle. A thirst for the open
Mediterranean world, for living in the sun on a coast where
scarcely any moment of the year was without its beauty of

nature, for sensing around me a rhythm of life that had changed
so little through the centuries, of a people simple and passionate
with direct roots to the ancient world, had grown in me since
the war. I began to rise like a piece of grass long crushed under
a heavy stone: words and phrases of poems did indeed begin
to move in my mind: perhaps the old power, tiny but with its
ever potent spell over my life, was not dead, but merely sleeping.

I revelled in the rose, violet and blue-green tones of sky and
sea, changing all day long under the hot spring sun, the trans-
lucent depths that washed the grey rocks of this volcanic coast,
that we watched from our windows and from the high peaks
of Ravello to which we clambered. And I saw that the steep
declivities on the edges of which Amalfi had been built might
have suggested, if bare and untouched by the civilizing hand
of man, terror and violence; but instead, terrace after terrace
from the sea to the peaks displayed sprouting vines under pro-
tective awnings of dried leaves, lemon groves with their abundant globes of yellow and golden fruit and their intoxicating
scent, cherry blossom and plum blossom and in the gardens of
the white-washed villas, with their contrasting shutters of pale
green and salmon or shell-pink, fuchsias and geraniums and
stock, stonecrop, violets and primroses covered every inch of
ground upon which plants could flourish. So Amalfi, defying
its gloomy origins, appeared like a storm-bird perched on the
danger of the world. After nightfall, as the scent from all the
luxuriance of leaf and blossom grew more intense, fire-flies
darted hither and thither, disappearing like sparks from a
burning as one approached.

At a table down by the beach, Robert Morley, engaged on
a film up at Ravello, wittily and inexhaustibly held forth to a
worshipping circle of acolytes. Beyond, the fishermen were
mending their nets: others inviting loudly, with flashing grins
that only just concealed the urgency of their appeals, to a trip
by combined row-boat and motor-boat to the Emerald Grotto
round the point.

I was charmed by what seemed to me the unhurrying patterns of traditional southern life; but I was to learn, by rude
shock, that modern Italy had another face. As I have said, we

had become a little vague about times and seasons. Startled to find Good Friday taking place on the day after our arrival, we failed to work out that Easter Sunday would be followed by Easter Monday and its holiday. We had booked a car to take us on Monday to Paestum, the Greek temples and half excavated ruins of which had long been one of the goals of my dream voyaging. Nothing could have seemed more promising. The sun freed itself from the white mist early in the morning, very soon the air was as warm as the most perfect June day in England, and the distant villages along the coast became clearer than ever, picked out in all their sun-golden colours. We left in highest spirits.

When we reached Paestum, my dream world of lonely temples quivering in the heat haze of midday, with wildflowers clustering round the bases of the columns, and a shepherd piping to his flock between half-revealed mosaic floors and the sea, fell to pieces. There indeed were the honey-coloured time-chewed pillars of the greatest temple with its perfect Doric proportions, rising still triumphantly on the edge of the lightly-foamed ripples, with fresh green of little tufts of plants sprouting between the coigns, birds singing on the pediments, larks twittering high in the blue sky above, and electric green lizards flashing when a shadow fell on them to their immemorial hiding-places in the stones . . . but one had to detach these elements by a conscious effort of the mind from the uproarious paraphernalia of an Italian bank holiday that surrounded, swamped and dominated them: innumerable charabancs, baby Fiats, motor bikes, vespas, pony traps and bicycles parked everywhere and still arriving, raucously honking, down the coast road to discharge their swarming families and courting couples and gangs of youths, with their picnic baskets, their transistors, their recordplayers bellowing out jazz tunes and Neapolitan songs, their dolls and games for the kiddies and packets of sweets. Why, I asked myself, in a moment of disgust and dismay, do all this at *Paestum*, when you can't appreciate what it means, don't want to appreciate it, and spoil it for those who do? These uncharitable, undemocratic thoughts were not to be suppressed, even though I recognized that the scene might have had its charm for me anywhere else along the coast at all; but equally not to be entirely suppressed or submerged was the voice that rose from the antique ground celebrating, like the larks, these pure memorials of the Other Time, the time of source and vision and beginning with its mystery and its joy.

Some friends and acquaintances I have met during my life, endowed it seems with second sight or some form of what is now called extra-sensory perception, have claimed that in a long ago pre-incarnation I played some important part in the world of ancient Greece. I do not know about this, as I am sceptical and agnostic by habit of mind; but I do know that every time I meet face to face with the sublime monuments or ruins of Greece, I am profoundly shaken, even to the point of having violent dreams.

After a week of waking to hear the sea, like someone's bath-water perpetually overflowing, caressing the rocks below the windows of the Capuccini Hotel, I returned to Rome, to spend a few more days there before taking the aeroplane to Athens and Cyprus. To my regret, Spence left me at this stage, to return to his dramatic studies in London. I thought to myself (remembering my own youth) that young men of quick imagination are like Eno's Fruit Salts: you pour a few drops of water on their minds, a few ideas, and off they go in a tremendous boil and fizz.

Before I took off for Athens, I had another encounter with unexpected English friends whom I had not seen for a long time. I was invited to a party where I found Jennie Graves, Robert's daughter, Benedetto Croce's intelligent Anglophile daughter Elena, who appeared to be much more *au courant* with what was going on in the intellectual and artistic world of London than I was myself, and those two great luminaries of the Oxford firmament, Maurice Bowra and Isaiah Berlin. Both of them being inexhaustible talkers and entertainers of sparkling wit and recondite knowledge, they had as it were divided the company between them, Maurice holding court in one corner of the room and roaring away like a Roman fountain when the wind suddenly blows the noise towards one in a greater roar; Shah in another corner, sufficiently far away from Maurice for the two platforms not to impinge, holding forth on the eccentricities of Bertie Russell and the philosophical fashions of the young men at Oxford with a nervous intensity like a diesel engine ticking over at a station halt.

I had scarcely arrived in Athens when my friends began to gather round me, immersing me in the tonic fountain of their welcome; but this time they were Greek friends, and not long lost English friends. Very early on my first morning I picked up the telephone to hear the jovial voice of George Katzimbalis, immediately proposing a trip out to the country with the new Director of the British Institute, Wilfred Tatham and his wife, a party the next evening for me to meet again all my available Greek friends, and a carousal at a taverna afterwards. The 'country' turned out to be Sunium again, but a Sunium – and the road to it – transformed by innumerable spring flowers, white and yellow marguerites, moon-white and pink rockroses and little magenta moonflowers and purple vetch, then cushions of spurge and tiny virginia stock and clusters of diminutive wild iris, the inner fields covered with red anemones – which small brown-limbed peasant boys held out to us in tight-fisted bunches on our return – and all against the dazzling sea-prospect, blue this afternoon as a Brazilian butterfly's wing, a-glitter with a million sparkles of sun, the 'curly golden head' of the Aegean, with the pale blue-purple silhouettes of islands in the distance. Again I felt the numinous atmosphere surrounding me on that sacred headland, that I had been so powerfully aware of on my first visit, but as it were in a different key to suit the different season.

I climbed down the cliffside, and saw as if in a dream fragments of pillar and pediment among the rocks, quivering white under the water, like Shelley's ruins of Baiae. We lunched on sea-food by the rocky edge of all this pure translucence, under a group of olive trees, while George held us all willing prisoners under the fountain of his talk, pouring out his stories and quips. He was at the top of his form during my whole sojourn. Especially memorable was a visit with him to the National Museum, not yet entirely finished, where the hall in the basement was filled with prostrate archaic *kouroi* awaiting their definitive placing. This sight inspired George to a lyrical outburst in praise of the *kouroi* – 'hundreds and hundreds of these beautiful young men dug up all over Greece' – of eternal Greek youth and Greek sculpture of the great age; at the end of which he confessed to me that when young he had been told he looked exactly like a *kouros* himself, but now, alas, felt old, over-weight, and castrated.

How heart-warming it was for me, in the midst of my reverses, at this foggy cross-roads in my career, to be the object of so much affection and friendly celebration. I had been especially touched and delighted by an incident on the way back from Sunium. We stopped to take wine at a taverna half-way to Athens, where Rex and I and George had taken wine some years before, and the little, limping proprietor revealed that he remembered me perfectly well, and even remembered reading about my lectures in the papers. Among other stimulating reunions was a lunch with Alexi Solomos, the young theatrical producer who had studied in London, and Tsarouchi the painter, after which they took me out to the Theatre of Dionysos below the Acropolis, where Alexi told me he often came of an afternoon to read and drowse. Tsarouchi became very excited and explained with mounting passion and erudite knowledge exactly how it had looked in classical times, how the plays had been performed, how the actors made their entrances and exits, and how it had changed in subsequent centuries: I could almost hear the choruses of the *Bacchae* echoing round me.

I also saw something more of the quiet and gentle poet Odysseus Elytis, some of whose magical earlier work I had published in *New Writing*. I remembered that when he had been on a visit to England two years before, he had come to a poets' party I had arranged at No. 31, with Stephen Spender, Laurie Lee, David Gascoyne, Clive Hall, and also Alan Pryce-Jones and Rose Macaulay. Elytis had brought Nanos Valaoritis with him; and when Rose discovered that Nanos was the owner of a small island next to the island of Lefkas she wanted to visit, I heard her enquire in business-like tones: 'How long would it take to swim across?'

There was only one sad moment for me. The family of Demetrios Capetanakis had been at great pains to conceal the fact of his death from his mother, who was old and had long been in poor health. She had, nevertheless, as I had always felt in my bones that she would, eventually make the discovery. It had been a greater shock to her, it seemed to me, than if she had been told at the time. She had written me a deeply moving letter; I therefore hoped that I would be allowed to meet her and talk to her on this visit. Demetrios's brother John promised to think this request over, and discuss it with the rest of the family. Eventually he rang me up, and suggested I should come to see him in his flat, which was also his consulting room. The ever kindly Odysseus Elytis shepherded me there. As we waited for John, or Yanni as his intimates called him, in his book-lined inner room, I was suddenly startled to discover on one of the walls an enlargement of a photograph of Demetrios, taken before he left for England, his eyes lowered over a book; it was so natural that I imagined for a moment he might lift his eyes and look at me again, speak a word. When John came in, I noted especially clearly how like Demetrios he was: all his brother's gentleness and sensibility showed in his face, but there was no trace of that impish malice that sometimes would illuminate Demetrios's features when he was in his gayest form. He told me that when their mother had found out she had suffered a tremendous shock, almost a stroke, and symptoms of the same kind recurred every year on the anniversary of his death; therefore he could not bring himself to accept the responsibility of letting her see me, or know that I was in Athens. As John had struck me as a most sincere and sensitive person, I had to accept his verdict, though not without much inner doubt and protest. A few years later she died, so I was never able to tell her in person of all that Demetrios had meant to me and to my English friends.

2

I was lucky to visit Cyprus when I did. Only a few years later it was plunged into the terrible *enosis* struggle, that cast such

dark clouds over the traditional Anglo-Greek friendship and
swept away (luckily only for a time) all the special warmth of
sympathy that was immediately aroused between members of
the two nations in their post-war encounters. It was a bitter
time to live through if one had come to love and admire the
Greeks as I had. Extremism in Athens and terror in the island
were so rabid, that one could only feel the deepest admiration
for those among one's Greek friends who kept their heads.
During this visit, I came to realize that, mixed in blood as the
Cypriots are, an amalgam of primitive races and conqueror
after conqueror, Persians, Romans, Byzantines, Franks, Vene-
tians and Turks, those who spoke Greek *felt* themselves to be
Greeks, just as much as the inhabitants of Rhodes or Crete.
It was absurd to imagine that we British could hold in any kind
of subjection any branch of the Greek people, for more than
the briefest interim period of adjustment. Unfortunately, it
seemed to me, those who pleaded this just cause most eloquently
were apt to forget that there was a Turkish side to the question
which had not been manufactured by us. So the wire-pullers
in the international power-game found their opportunity, and
the slide into violence and confusion began. All this has since
been written of with a sorrowing restraint, a love crossed by
despair, by Lawrence Durrell in the best, most real of his
books about the Greek world, *Bitter Lemons*.

Let my diary take over for this visit, lest my account to-day
should be too much strained with the sadness of the emotions
the long crisis evoked, during which my recollections of en-
joyment rose starkly to confront the daily news of ambush
and atrocity. I have only added here and there lines from the
poems various scenes and encounters inspired, which I began
to write before I left the island.

Thursday April 16th: Platres in the mountains.

A rough air crossing in a small aeroplane from Athens to
Nicosia, which I did not care about, with head-winds buffet-
ing the ridiculous little machine high up in the vast blue empty
sky, and children being sick around me. How *does* one keep
up on this invisible element? A most disagreeable sensation of

trapped insecurity. I tried, but failed totally to take any pleasure in the sight of the islands far below, rocky foam-fringed
oases appearing suddenly in the expanse of sea beneath the
wisps of scudding cloud. Ganymede could not have felt more
helpless on his talon-gripped flight to the world of the gods.
The dark mountainous, deep-cliffed coast of Turkey to the
north-east could so easily become a permanent symbol of the
dispossessed stomach.

But the journey from Nicosia to Platres was sheer delight.
We drove first of all across the flat plain between the mountains to north and south, so green with its luxuriantly growing
corn, the earth showing up rust-red between, the mountains
so purple-dark, so ominous in the thundery light. The roads
were utterly lonely, bordered by mimosa trees in flower.
Every so often the car had to slow down to pass or let pass a
flock of sheep with long dragging tails and black heads, sometimes with skipping lambs beside them; or now and then, in
the villages where peasants were leading the paniers of their
donkeys, goat-flocks with golden-brown goat-kids with floppy
ears and intelligent eyes. The shepherds had a timeless look,
as old as Homer and the Bible, and recalling too the England
of King Richard Coeur de Lion's day where also the hills were
swarming with sheep. Then the climb into the mountains began, up twisting roads among deep-eaved, long balconied
villages, passing a roaring torrent or slender forms of ghost
poplars; up into the pine trees and the darkness, the pure
cold of the night air of the peaks gaining upon us. . . . .

Suddenly, at midday, a great throng of house-martins started
circling and twittering outside, almost flying in at my window.
I watched them, fascinated, for some time before I realized
they were building their hard mud nests under the eaves.

My first walk was down on the road to Limassol and Paphos,
past judas trees not so far advanced as at Amalfi or on the road
to Sunium, with a vision in a sweeping semi-circle of azure
blue sea between fold after fold of dryish mountains where
vines will soon be growing. Far-off, I saw little valleys and
villages in them and tiny Byzantine churches in between with
tall, dark cypresses around them and then the brilliant green
again of cornfields. All these settlements looked as if newly

washed and scrubbed in the crystal clear air. As afternoon advanced, I met, at a crossing, two RAF boys in a lorry, almost the only traffic on the roads: they had lost their way to Paphos:

> 'Thanks, chum.' He turns about,
> Revs up the engine, grins and is gone,
> The roar of the lorry fades along the air,
> Leaving the scene idyllic as before;
> A white-haired shepherd on a rock alone,
> The tinkle of goat-bells drifting down once more. . . .

Friday 17th

Maurice Cardiff, now representative of the British Council here, came to me early in a Council car, and we set off for Curium and Old Paphos (Kouklia) under a hot sun and cloudless sky. Maurice I find a delightful companion, much easier to be friends with than when we last met in Athens – we have both moved on – sympathetic, with a sharp and interesting mind, amusing and amused, expressing concern and indignation at the story of my firm, discussing the literary situation with intelligence and acute judgment, surprisingly in accord with me on many points where we differ from the current and fashionable view; expressing too, great enthusiasm for Demetrios's poems. He had before this been in Milan for the Council where he had seen much of [my niece] Sally. He was sour and witty about the well-to-do Italians of the north: he had found them superficial, and quite empty in their depths; hopeless in their attitude towards artists and writers, whom they treated as social ornaments and pets; and suffering from a confused Anglo-phobia under their surface blandishments, which he felt arose from a deep-down, not entirely conscious refusal to forgive us for destroying Mussolini's régime.

Curium, on its hill-side looking out over the intense peacock blue of the sea, now with tones of vivid green in it, gave me an impression of great confusion: it is, of course, a fairly recent excavation, under the devoted care of a brilliant young American archaeologist, and apart from some beautiful mosaic floors with Greek inscriptions and a temple of Apollo, has still to reveal most of its secrets. Nevertheless, there is much evidence of a big and flourishing town. Peasants were digging away for more, up above us, as we wandered round what had been uncovered. Perhaps because the sandstone here is so crumbly, I had a strong feeling of the ruins wanting to hide themselves, of refusing to speak.

Everywhere, between Curium and Old Paphos there was green corn massed in the fields, with scattered red poppies peeping through, and olive and carob trees breaking up their expanse. The roads were bordered with masses of big yellow daisy flowers and mauve-pink convolvulus. Wherever the cultivation stopped, the rocky heaths were a mass of myrtles and rock-rose bushes densely tufted together.

Old Paphos has the same wonderful situation looking out over the sea to Curium, but is far more extraordinary. The ancient site, with its broken, fluted columns and cyclopean walls is almost inextricably entangled with a little village, still lived in, an exquisite miniature Byzantine chapel built of lichen-splashed grey stone, and (most astonishing of all) a mediaeval sugar refinery with characteristic Cypriot arches. And village, chapel, refinery, all built out of the site, which was obviously much greater than its appearance now suggests, and of very great pre-Hellenic antiquity and veneration. The obliteration is profound here, but it still speaks in a faint wind-lost voice. Big dust-coloured lizards scramble over the ruins. There are old olive-presses in the chapel precincts:

> One cannot blame the villagers,
> They needed shelter like the gods;
> And kings must feed their retinues;
> And profits soar, when conscience nods.

Motoring fast along the coast road after leaving Old Paphos, we passed the bay where Aphrodite is supposed to have been born, bathed in the golden light of afternoon. The chauffeur, muddled and obstinate, refused – or failed – to let us stop, but perhaps even because of the speed of our passage it made a deep, in fact thrilling impression on me. On one side, I thought, it might have been Freshwater Bay or Lulworth Cove; on the other the two famous landmarks, the big rock and the little rock, and the full lines of foam creaming around them, gave it a more exotic appearance. . . .

If you mean gladness: on your beach
Where the elect foam creams across
The golden cove, and wavelets play
Round the great rock and the little, teach
The blinded sense to find the way,
Unriddle here our loss. . . .

As we motored back across the mountains, the scenery struck
me as more like the Georgian Military Highway in the Cauca-
sus than anything else, in its loneliness and grandeur, in the
way the road was carved out of the midway rock, a shelf above
the gorges.

Monday 20th April

Yesterday I motored down from Platres to Kyrenia through
the mountains, another cloudless blue morning. The road was
quite sublime: twisting up and down on the edge of the pine-
forests towering above it, while huge gulfs on the other side
gave glimpses of great limestone boulders and red mountains
almost totally bare in the middle ground. From high up, foaming narrow waterfalls plunged into the gulfs, glimpsed through
pine and arbutus. Every now and then we would come to a
station for fruit trees, cultivated on terrace after terrace down
the mountainside, often white-misted cherry trees closely
packed round the long-eaved houses. Then a deep gorge and
a stream eating its way through it, and we had come to the
monastery and church of St John Lampadistra, nestling
among the trees with its lichen-gnawed tiles like a sweet old
barn with white walls.

A peasant hanging around hurried to fetch the priest, who
appeared, a middle-aged hirsute fellow in dark glasses accompanied by a small dark-haired boy with a little nose as beaky
as an owl, who was prepared to interpret in English. They led
me into a miniature interior courtyard, with a vine trellis and
a fruit-laden orange tree in front of the entrance. It seemed,
from the outside, much like any of the rather seedy little
churches in the villages, and I was quite unprepared for the
astonishing spectacle of the interior. There were two churches
in one, without division, an unique phenomenon in my

experience, Latin on the north side and Orthodox on the south. The Orthodox side was filled with crude (and crudely coloured) paintings which nevertheless impressed by some quality of simple strength. The Latin side was much more sophisticated and westernized, with beautiful deep harmonies set vibrating by the icons, the coats of arms and the carved doors. All too little time to investigate: the little owl waved and murmured 'bye-bye' as we hummed off down the mountain road, through the huge stalks of fennel and the wild chrysanthemums to Lefka.

Now we were suddenly in a sub-tropical landscape, it was hot and we both took off our coats, and as we plunged into the luxuriance of palms and lemon and orange groves the air had an indescribable fragrance. To the north, by the copper mines, we caught a glimpse of blue sea with the cargo boats standing off-shore.

We turned left for Soli, and there were the ruins of the theatre on the flowered hillside. Scarcely had we climbed out of the car, when another very small boy popped up from nowhere, with a rather severe and business-like look, who asserted that he was twelve years old and immediately instituted himself our guide. In spite of the introductory severity, he revealed himself to have a voice and smile of such piercing sweetness that I almost cried every time he spoke or looked at us. He was astonishingly intelligent for his age, with all the known facts about Soli at his command, and spoke good English. He told us his name was Hussein, he was a Turk; and as we clambered up the hillside an even smaller boy, a Greek and his friend, appeared as if from a lark's nest in the grasses, but would not speak, only smile rather shyly, As we wandered about the fields round the theatre, I had the strong impression that they were only a thin covering for vast unexplored marvels; but so brittle that if one set to work to clear it all it might crumble away in a landslide of rubble. Hussein pointed to Vouni on the heights – 'big palace, very fine, all on hilltop' – but we turned back to the car, being late on our schedule, and he padded barefoot down beside us to be rewarded with a sixpence.

Tuesday

A letter from Christopher in Los Angeles, regretting that he had not known about the luncheon that was given for me. 'My blood boils to think how you were treated: you who have done more than anybody else for the things we believe in, and who have set an example which is now, I'm happy to say, being followed by several different groups in this country. . . . I have a rough draft of my novel [*The World in the Evening*] finished and now I hope the whole thing will be done by the end of the summer at the very latest. It has been more trouble than anything else I have ever attempted and I'm not at all sure that this means it is any good; but it has been a great discipline.'

The Dome Hotel here at Kyrenia is the most extraordinary study in human wreckage – one might almost say wreckage of a contracting empire – a sort of Buxton-cum-Cheltenham by the Middle Sea. Shaky old jossers in old school ties with arthritic wives, blue-haired widows of incalculable antiquity gallantly keeping up appearances, creeping along on sticks, only just held together (one feels) by pins, booze-sodden ex-military men with aggressively flowering white moustaches under purple noses, nagged by their women folk at every meal, middle-aged suburban couples so nondescript they seem to fade into the furnishings, with the smiling neuter Cypriots hurrying to and fro to attend to their wants and soothe their plaints. Among these a few holiday-makers from London, surprisingly a publisher and his wife known to me, friends of Rosamond's, and an old gent in an OE tie who turns out to have known my father.

This morning I met Lawrence Durrell at a little wine bar, very much bronzed but not so rotund as I remember him at our last meeting in Athens. He introduced me to the artist Sigmund Pollitzer, charming, sensitive-faced, who in the afternoon took us over to his little white-washed cottage by the shore, surrounded by a sea of yellow wild chrysanthemums. It has an exquisite interior patio filled with flowers, a fountain and fluttering white pigeons. Filled me with envy and longing. I was struck by his pottery, which seemed to me full of imagi-

P

nation, and his black-and-white drawings, a strangely austere
(or neurotic?) reaction to this landscape of changing, burning
colours.

Friday 24th

Larry Durrell has been a good friend, a very agreeable companion to find here. We talked endlessly (he is a great talker),
in his place on the beach (where he settles himself in bathing
costume every afternoon, with his 18-months-old little daughter
and Diana, the attractive South African girl who accompanied him from Belgrade), in his favourite wine-shop, and
on the expedition we made on Wednesday to St Hilarion
and Bellapais. Ideas bubble out of him continually, ideas
for books *he* should write, ideas for books *I* should publish,
and every other kind of literary scheme imaginable, some
comic and quite impossible, some tempting, tempting. He appears, poor chap, to be in a pretty bad jam: his wife had a
mental collapse and left him, and he says he can't work because he has to look after the child. All the same he seems in
very good spirits. I would say myself that he's also in a deeper
jam, because he lives too much abroad, too much out of touch
with what people are saying and thinking in London and the
continual sharpening of the edge of the mind that life there
demands. I may be wrong, but I've tried every argument to
make him come home and live, for a time at least, amongst
us, a move that might inspire him or drive him to write the one
book to break the barrier – to persuade others to recognize the
great imaginative and word-making gifts he has – but he's
immoveable. An impulse towards the periphery seems to run
fairly deeply through his psychology now, and even his most
beautiful poems seem to suffer from an element of evasion.

He plans to settle here, and took me to see the little house
he has bought in the village above Bellapais honey-coloured
abbey, a bargain, he says, will be very attractive – considered
by itself – when he's done with it, but personally I couldn't
stand the slummy village atmosphere encroaching so closely.
Outside the abbey all the male population was sitting about,
idle and contented, on chairs – the inevitable Cypriot chairs.

He told me the peasants were extremely friendly and uninhibited towards him in the expression of political opinion. In
his view, there's a great deal of emotional fantasy about the
enosis business: natural enough, but he doesn't believe it goes
very deep, and is only fanned into an unwilling flame by the
implacable priests (priests meddling in politics have always
roused my hackles.)

St Hilarion is a staggering sight. The road rises so sheer out
of the plain, it's like climbing in an aeroplane to go up, and I
felt suddenly giddy and insecure. On the way up, a shepherd
sitting under a tree, surrounded by his flock, greeted us gaily.
Asphodels, and glowing yellow ranunculi within the keep.
Again a very small boy emerged from nowhere and had just
instituted himself our guide when the official guide turned up
(much to his disgust). There are bewildering, beautiful views
to north, west and east: Kyrenia looks like a tiny model harbour, a child's toy. How on earth did the crusader knights
exercise themselves when they spent all the summer up here?
As with so many mediaeval buildings, abbeys, cathedrals,
forts, castles, I am amazed at the daring of the conception,
the strength and thoroughness of the execution. Bellapais abbey
is just the same.

After St Hilarion, we went down to a little beach Larry
and his friends have discovered, with a welcoming lap of sand
among the rocks, the water warm, buoyant and flawlessly clear.
As usual there were beachcomber dogs hanging about, panting
for stones to be thrown for them. An immediate emotion of
distress rose in me when I caught sight of them, but they did
not seem to be starved or broken in spirit. My favourite is the
one who always has a wet bottom, from sitting in the waves.

Tuesday 28th. Famagusta

Sunday morning I left Kyrenia for this place, driving along
the coast with its dazzling panorama of rocky bays and blue
water turning to green as it comes in shore. Then we turned
south over the Levkoniko pass, swiftly changing sharp outlines
of hills with gnarled ancient olive trees and shepherds with
their flocks under them. Again we passed green fields of corn

with purple primuli sword lilies growing wild among the poppies, and everywhere banks covered with giant pink convolvulus and yellow wild chrysanthemums. At last we began to twist down into the plain, towards Famagusta and the other side of the sea.

We made a stop at Salamis, which stirred my imagination more deeply than anywhere else on the island. Salamis, a purely Greek town, was once – as early as the sixth century BC – the most important city on the island, boasting an excellent harbour and a flourishing mercantile community. All one sees at first is a scrub-waste of mimosa-wattle lying towards the sea cliff; and sand dunes. Then one drives through the mimosa, and suddenly one comes to a hollow scooped out of the sand, to see marble pillars, some still standing with their carved capitals, some fallen, fragments scattered everywhere. And everywhere, if one scoops up the soft sand and sifts it through one's hands one finds broken shards and bits of marble. Further on, one comes upon half-excavated temples and a market-place, and more tumbled columns hiding in the mimosa. I can't believe that great treasures are not still lying buried only a little way below the dunes. Dust-coloured lizards and small snakes slither away. The sense of a forgotten, once teeming city, a lost obliterated civilization, of something now forever irrecapturable and stillness after clamour is almost oppressive. I went down to the beach, absurdly to see if I could glimpse the other ruins said to be still lying on the sea-bottom. No, nothing. I kicked the pebbles about, looking for more pottery shards, while a gipsy leading a donkey passed me.

On to Famagusta, the hotel edging on to the sandy beach and the surf. In the distance, down the coast, an army rest-camp (service men on leave from Suez) with its line of tents; and nearby a little bay with all the gaiety of sailing and fishing boats and bathing. From the window of my room I can catch a glimpse of the ruined sandy-coloured cathedral that has been turned into a mosque, the merchant ships and war-ships laid up in the port, and the pointy-prowed sailing boats in front of them. The line of Kyrenia's hills in the distance.

After dark, and before, dinner, in the moonlight, I made a first prowl into the old town, in a different way almost as disturbing and strange as Salamis. There was scarcely anyone about – it might have been under curfew. I could only detect occasional movements and murmurs behind the shutters of the little houses which let out their chinks of light. All around me the towering massive fortifications, and against the moonlit sky the dark outlines of tall palms and the half-ruined, hollow shapes of abandoned churches and the buttresses of the cathedral. An extraordinary ghost-like impression of the east invading the west, of the skeletons of history.

Bill's friend, the gentle, good-looking young painter Valentinos Charalambous, who has studied in London, full of charm and fun, took me to see another aspect of life last night in the old town. Two young Royal Marines were sitting in Pop's Bar, getting steadily sozzled. One, from London, good-looking in a cheeky-boyish way, was full of grins and winks at me, while his friend from Yorkshire gave the barman advice on how to do his pools. Outside the door, two smudgily painted whores, of incredible squalor, kept on leering and beckoning to them. . . . Later, he took me on to the new town, to a street that reminded me of the 'gut' in Malta, where we plunged into a bar called the Spitfire. A ridiculously bad fifth-rate floor-show was going on, displaying some wretched lost girls from (I would guess) Budapest and Vienna and Syria. Little tables and chairs were packed into the room, which was crowded with English soldiers in civvies, sailors and marines in uniforms, and a sprinkling of Cypriots. One big, heftily built black-haired young marine, of straightforward English good looks, was pretty far gone, happily and fatuously bestowing drunken smiles all round the room, and trying to imitate the movements of the dancers, allurements and wrigglings and mock embraces, offering to kiss his pal who was desperately trying to keep him in order. Several times he suddenly collapsed on the floor, waving a feeble arm towards one of the girls, but was propped up again against the bar before the approaching MPs could spot him.

Maurice Cardiff called for me in his car, and took me out to his little holiday shack down the beach, where Leonora and all his children were camping out. Later, we went to the house of Ghiorgiou the painter, where we met Harold Cadman and his Cypriot wife. A Turkish house of considerable beauty, with old chests in corners and old plates hung on walls, and Ghiorgiou's paintings hung closely everywhere else – some of them, of ancient Byzantine churches and street scenes were, I thought, very much more attractive than the figure paintings. His old mother sat in a chair in the corner, heavily draped in black.

A letter from Rosamond, to whom I had written about her new novel *The Echoing Grove*, which I had read while I was in Italy. She wrote from Ireland:

'Thank you for writing so fully and sympathetically about *The Echoing Grove*. I won't write back about it so exhaustively. Staying as I am (for a week) in the bosom of Eire, surrounded by Celtic manifestations such as the lapping of lake water, the rustle of rain, the powerful odour of 3 immense and benign labradors mingled with the pervading corpse-like odour of dry rot, in a wing of this melancholy and romantic Georgian house, my faculties, such as remain to me, are fast dissolving. I am half-asleep all day, only rousing to take slow dream-like walks along the lake. . . . It's wonderful to feel anonymous, have no telephones to answer, etc, etc, and sink down totally into time-less vapours and soft greenery and large silent fur presences. I wish I need never come back. I can't really stand the *attack* of London life, with no protection – though part of me enjoys it. I'm keeping reviews for you. They are controversial as I expected – but the *contradictions* of opinion are bewildering and I get the impression I must be reading about some book I never read, let alone wrote. The critics on the air were over-whelmingly *pro* – Veronica Wedgwood leading off backed up by Tom Hopkinson and two other dear gents. As a matter of fact, apart from Veronica and Vita S-W my most fervently favourable critics have all been male, which pleases me of course. The only violently hostile voice so far had been that of Honor Tracy in the N.S. . . . I'm very sorry you feel the reconciliation and forgiveness in the *Grove* don't come off at the same level. I find that opinions about this roughly cancel each other out. *Everybody* has seen both Rickie and the women differently, so I can only conclude that in matters of sexual rela-tions everybody judges with a pre-disposal or biased eye. . . .'

Here, in my new room, I am finding, as I hoped, that I can write poetry. I began roughing out some poems in Platres, and now suddenly they are beginning to flow, at a rather faster than my usual slow rate. I am working especially on a poem which tries to express the change in the nature of reality caused by the atom bomb – by the apocalyptic nature of our age. . . .

> The public voices make believe
> Reality is still as square
> As what our fingers fastened on
> When there was more in air than air,
> Too deep in consequence to see
> The cities where the treasures lie
> Have learnt the impermanence of leaves
> Under the spell of this goodbye. . . . .

Friday, May 1st.

Yesterday I went out on the Salamis Road, to see Valentinos' family pottery workshops, where they have been working for generations. The old father and his assistants were busy at their wheels – I watched feeling the eternal fascination of the pottery wheel and the shaping fingers – turning out jugs and bowls on an immeasurably old, traditional pattern: while inside, with his up-to-date electric kiln, Valentinos was intent on producing modern stuff, for a more sophisticated public (and yet V's designs were a subtle modernized version on ancient themes more often than not.) As usual, the atmosphere of a craftsman-artist's working place completely captured me, seemed like home. Valentinos, in his blue jeans, took me down through the enormously long grove of oranges, lemons and bitter-oranges, to the water-tank at the end where he plans to make his own little secret hideaway out of a derelict out-house. . . .

> A stranger, sailor, stops beside the yard,
> Who has come from Salamis, the buried town.
> His eyes are fathomless, wondering,
> As he watches the shaping hands intent,
> The keen, fixed glance and the contented frown.
> And attitude and aspect please

With some pure quality that's dropped its guard
The sunburnt painter in blue jeans
Who comes out of the shadows and smiles, beckoning,
Leading him through the orange trees
Brushing the scented branches as they go
To the hidden barn. . . . .

I am appalled to learn that when the Suez Canal was being
built, enterprising get-rich-quick traders plundered Salamis
(and perhaps other sites in Cyprus) and shipped enormous
cargoes of marble off to Egypt. It is something to know that
all that happened before we took over suzerainty of the island
from the Porte, though heaven knows we haven't done much
about the exploration of the sites since. Let sleeping dogs –
and treasures – lie, seems to have been our Imperial motto
for most of the time.

If I were to try to order my impressions of Cyprus for a
serious article or broadcast, I would say that these are the features that strike me in the main. First, the extreme orderliness
and quiet of the island. Whether the Cypriots like it or not
(and there's no particular reason why they should like it) they
are better administered than they have been since Roman
times. The villages have been cleaned up, the farms are fruitful, the roads extended, the mountain forts protected, justice
is uncorrupted. There are moments when it seems as if it is
all but a little paradise. Second, when one gets out into the
country, only a few miles from the towns, the absence of
crowds. One motors for hours along roads where one meets
almost no one, compared with the English countryside or even
Italy or Greece, only flocks of goats and goat-herds and an
occasional high-piled village bus, with the lonely, awe-inspiring
ranges of mountains and isolated peaks on the horizon. And
one finds bay after bay of heavenly warm golden sand where
one can sunbathe and swim without a sign of another human
being. Third, the extreme beauty of nature, the wildflowers
in all their beauty at their season, the groves of oranges,
lemons, tangerines, grape-fruits, with the rich colour of earth,
sea and sky burning through them. Fourth, the astonishing
abundance of pretty little painted Byzantine churches wherever one goes. Fifth, the fact that the bones of everything that

happened in history seem to be here: the ruins of prehistoric and classical Greek settlements, Roman aqueducts, Byzantine cities, crusader castles, Venetian forts, Turkish mosques. The folly and strangeness of all the imperial adventures that have passed across the island without it ever finding its true identity; down to the British, which has produced an extraordinary fusion or mixture of English and Mediterranean cultures, much more extraordinary than in Malta, with British orderliness superimposed on Mediterranean mess.

I am haunted by the ghosts of Richard Coeur-de-Lion and Rimbaud.[1] An odd pair. The saints here seem to have a peculiar brand of humour.

Saturday, May 2nd

Yesterday I had an almost perfect bathe, at Dhavos after visiting Kantara's ruined castle, perhaps the most marvellous bathe of my life, so that it transcended bathing and became a symbolic poetic act. . . .

I began to think again that I could *escape*. What prevented me keeping a small pied-à-terre in London, and coming out to Greece, to Cyprus, buying a plot of land and building a little villa in the sun, living as I had increasingly longed to live, in a Mediterranean atmosphere? I had no publishing firm to look after now, no magazine since the end of *New Writing*, no radio programme since the end of *New Soundings*. The literary world, the young writers could look after themselves, without any stirring and pushing from me. Instead of looking after others, I would look after myself at last, write poetry, memoirs, begin the novels I had long cherished as phantasmal shapes at the back of my mind. Instead of being de-humanized by the business rat-race and the artificial pressure of modern metropolitan civilization, I would re-discover the ancient rhythms of life in these countries where they had never been entirely destroyed. I had made myself miserable with fruitless struggles. Now I would be re-born and live in

---

[1] Arthur Rimbaud worked as a labourer on the island for some months in 1879, and then again in 1880 as foreman in charge of a gang building the Governor General's summer residence.

le vrai. I would grow my own grapes, figs, peaches, lemons, exotic flowers far more abundantly and simply than I ever could in England. I would acquire a mahogany-coloured body and a pagan calm of spirit. . . .

Yes, *what* prevented me? It was no good; or no good *yet.* My restless temperament, my tattered ambitions answered me: I had been defeated, or outmanoeuvred twice, three times, I must try my luck once more. I was still young enough, I still cared very much about what happened in the world of literature and art. I believed I could still influence and stimulate the creation of great work. That vanity had not entirely left me, nor had the voices of others telling me I was still needed. No, I had not done enough, done enough, done enough. . . .

So this internal argument has gone on during this holiday, reviving in the intervals between writing poems, in discussions that have followed marvellous expeditions, in reflections late at night as I have re-read letters from England. At Dhavos a moment of temptation or illumination had come to me, as it came to Mr Lucas at Platanisti; but not on the road to Colonus. Dhavos was one of the stations where I might have changed trains, as at Heiligenkreuz before the war. My star has blessed me; but cursed me too.

Monday 4th. Nicosia.

Today to Nicosia and the last stage of this holiday, the lecture and the 'official' meetings.

Yesterday, in Famagusta, I made the last long sight-seeing trip, with Harold Cadman, up to Stavrovoumi. We passed through valleys where the corn was already being threshed, fields dotted with olive trees whose gnarled and twisted shapes suggested incalculable antiquity, then climbing round perilous hairpin bands wide enough only for one car, up into the heat of the pure mountain air, while H. C. entertained me with hilarious petronian stories of GHQ Cairo during the war. We came at last to the little rock-perched monastery, proud of its alleged fragment of the True Cross. Sceptical always of these authentic relics, knowing what cynical big-scale faking of them went on in distant centuries, I found much greater interest in a

beautiful, finely carved and silver-encased cross on the altar.
The old abbot came out to greet us, the poverty of his neglected establishment evident in the vulture-like hunger with
which he pounced on our sandwiches and cigarettes and wine.
Then a young novice came out to serve us, silent and shy,
with sallow dark face and slightly sprouting beard. He brought
us coffee and looked at us like a sad, caged wild animal: I
tried to imagine his life in this lonely place with the handful
of monks still left there, and shuddered. They have very little
to support them, a small terrace of artichokes and a few vines.
The young novice was suddenly engaged in a violent quarrel
with one old monk, and then turned to us and asked us to
take him to the other monastery, lower down, which we had
passed on the way up. It's not that kind of life I envisage, in
my dreams of Mediterranean re-birth.

This evening I talked about Demetrios, and the Greek poets
and artists he had introduced me to, at the British Institute.
There was a full, very attentive, and I thought very apprecia-
tive audience, including podgy Loizos who seemed very much
moved. The young poet Sophroniou read the originals of
Seferis and Elytis.

Tuesday, 5th

Today, as a follow-up to yesterday's lecture, Maurice invited
Sophroniou and me to lunch. We talked for a long time over
our wine about the problems of poetry in general, and the
problems of his poetry in particular. And tonight I attended
a party with the editor of *Kupriaka Grammata*. He is an ultra-
nationalist and adviser to the Ethnarchy on literary affairs;
and as he could not have shown himself more hospitable,
genial and good tempered, Maurice considered the whole
episode a remarkable coup to have brought off. The other
painter people talk about here was there, Diamantis. He was
charming, diffident, troubled that with his schoolmastering
preoccupations he didn't find the time he wanted to devote
himself to his art. He carried me off to his flat and studio to
see his pictures; they impressed me by their naturalness, their

absolute verity-to-the-Cypriot-scene without affectation, and their rich colour.

Tomorrow I leave for London, an all day air journey by the new Viscount service.

So my holiday interim, of recuperation and re-thinking, came to an end. And already, in this strange, unsettled period of ends and beginnings, a new door was opening, whose invitation I was to find I could not refuse.

Part Six

I

In the middle of September, the year before, while I still had control of my publishing firm and my radio programme, I received a telephone call from my old friend John Hayward.

To my astonishment, he told me that he had a tycoon friend and neighbour, who was much bothered about the dearth of literary magazines in England. He had read with concern the frequent complaints that were aired in the 'posh' Sunday papers and weeklies about their mortality, and the serious gap they were leaving in our literary garden; the destruction, one might say, of the greenhouses. John had encouraged him in his botheration, and mentioned my name. He was ready to think about helping to build a new one. Obviously he had the means, as his name was Cecil Harmsworth King, Grand Panjandrum of the *Daily Mirror* and the *Sunday Pictorial*.

In some excitement, tinged with a little dread at what might be thrust upon me at that particular moment when my fortunes had begun to look so confused, I went along one afternoon to the flat in Carlyle Mansions, which John still shared at that time with Tom Eliot, to meet the tycoon.

Cecil King is a tall, heavily built man, fair, with penetrating blue eyes and a large, rather gloomy bloodhound's face that rarely lights up in humour except when (in his view) *The Times* has made an ass of itself. Evidently I was expected to spout a piece about the need for a new literary magazine, and my own preparedness to run one if the opportunity arose. This I did to the best of my ability, though as always when I have been asked to blow my own trumpet my words sounded to me lame and grotesque. I was keenly supported by John, who appeared privileged to adopt a slightly bullying tone with the tycoon. Nevertheless, we spoke cautiously and in the most general way. Cecil King listened attentively, without saying very much, except occasionally to drop in a pertinent question about the potential audience, circulation, highbrow level, and so on. At the end, he said he would think it over, and let us know if he thought further conversations were worthwhile.

In my innocence, and usual restless impatience, I rather expected decisions to be taken in the next few weeks. As it turned out, however, the project went on ice.

It was not till after I had returned from my Mediterranean trip, and Queen Elizabeth's Coronation had taken place, that I suddenly heard the news from my sister Rosamond, who happened to have been dining with Cecil King, that it was 'on' again. Cecil King had, I think, solved various problems in his vast and complex organization that left him at last with a freer hand than he had had in the autumn. Also he had probably been subjecting me to a little quiet vetting behind the scenes. In any case, it was probably a good thing that there had been a delay. My hands were comparatively empty, for the very good reason that almost everything had been snatched out of them. Only a few days before, Bob Maxwell had sadly told me that efforts to salvage any of my 'belongings' from Purnell's – books or contracts with which we could start again – seemed definitely to have failed. In addition, I felt fresher and more relaxed after my holiday.

I went to see Cecil King in the City office of the *Daily Mirror*, and we had a friendly and practical discussion. I was left with the impression that he really intended the project to come off. I promised to get out some estimates, with the help of James Shand of the Shenval Press, also a 'mock-up' or dummy, and to propose a list of people who could – and in my opinion would – act on an advisory board. The next day I visited John Hayward again, told him of the discussion that had taken place, and got him to promise to keep King up to the mark. The chief problem still to be settled was whether the new magazine should be a quarterly, bi-monthly, or monthly. The more we talked, the more we came round to the belief that a proper impact could only be made with a monthly. Could I get enough material? I said I felt quite certain, and that the magazine's existence would be self-propagating, that is

unknown people would begin to send their work in just as soon
as it appeared on the bookstalls and they could judge its quality. Also, I said, I intended to continue the policy with which
New Writing had been associated, of publishing American authors and translations from Continental authors. I wanted it
to be mainly for creative writing – that seemed to me where
the absence of a magazine was felt most keenly – but proposed also to have a serious critical section that would provide
'second thought' reviews of the most important literary books
as they came out.

John began to be caught up in the excitement that the preparations were generating. Barring some totally unforeseen
mishap, neither of us believed the plans could collapse now.
A few days later I went down to Fetter Lane again to report
progress, and to get, if possible, a final clear-cut agreement.
I told Cecil King that, for a name, I had been hesitating between the *London Review* and the *London Magazine*, but finding
the former already in use I had plumped, with John's approval, for the latter. I presented him with the new estimates
and the dummy. He sniffed rather about the smallness of the
latter, but I persuaded him that it would be unwise to be
more lavish. We then discussed the question of choosing a
young assistant to myself: all through he had been most
anxious that the younger generation should be actively involved. I told him I had interviewed Mark Boxer from Cambridge and David Hughes from Oxford, and asked them if
they knew of any young man at either university who would
be ideally suitable. I had come to the conclusion that neither
could suggest anyone more suitable than David himself, whose
engagement and enthusiasm I already knew from *New Soundings*. Cecil King seemed satisfied with this. To stand at his side
with her long experience and instinctive knowledge of the
literary scene, especially of my own views, and enthusiasms
and idiosyncracies, Barbara Cooper was a must to join the
new set-up.

A slightly comic scene then developed over the composition
of the Advisory Board. John Hayward's was the first name I
put forward, as in honour bound, and that was agreed without argument. Was Rosamond to come on? He shared my

hesitation about having more than one Lehmann on the bridge (though both of us would dearly have loved to have her), and thought Elizabeth Bowen an excellent choice if Rosamond didn't join. He then suddenly announced that he wanted Raymond Mortimer. I said that I was devoted to Raymond, but as he was at least a dozen years senior to me, did he quite fit in with the general plan he had in mind? . . . Raymond nearly sixty? Nonsense. A furious flurry through the pages of *Who's Who* followed, and then a rather grim acceptance of the truth of my claim. Emboldened by this passage, I suggested the names of Rex Warner and William Plomer. . . . Who on earth? Never heard of them. A telephone call was put through to John Hayward. Faintly, I heard John's voice raised in sharp sardonic protest at the great man's ignorance, He was not entirely convinced by this, but when I stuck to my guns and insisted that they both had sound critical judgment in their various spheres as well as imagination, and knew me well enough both to get on with me and keep me in order, he yielded gracefully. The Sitwells, any of them, were rejected with a wild laugh. Could Tom Eliot be associated with the project? I said that it must be clear that he was far too grand to be on the board, but I would try to persuade him to write for our first number.

So it was that the tricky problem of the editorial set-up for the *London Magazine* was settled. I must add that King was good-tempered and genial throughout; and as he had never dealt in business with anyone like me before, I thought it a good omen that everything was concluded so amicably. At the same time, I hoped that such violent objections as he had voiced about the editorial board would not be repeated every time he saw the monthly contents list. A nagging anxiety about this persisted at the back of my mind; but in fact he played fair, and only growled on occasions about the number of pages and the level of expenditure.

A fortnight later I met Tom Eliot at a meeting of the Alliance Française, over which he presided at that time, and told him about our plans (of which he had probably already heard from John Hayward). To my delight, he agreed to write an introductory letter for our first number. I told him that Cecil King would be extremely pleased, as he was one of the few contemporary highbrow authors he admitted having heard of. He chuckled, and said: 'That's what comes of having become part of the entertainment industry.'

Tom remarked that he thought it essential that the new magazine should be a monthly, especially in the light of his experience in running a quarterly. And so in fact it was agreed; and that the first number should come out on January 15th (for February), with copies ready before Christmas. Finally, a generous maximum limit of loss was also agreed, which allowed me to pay my contributors on a reasonable scale. 'Poets have always lived on a crust in garrets,' grumbled Cecil King; but he did not press the point, and I realized with relief that I should not have to persuade authors to contribute for reasons of charity, prestige, or obligation. In fact, I would not have undertaken the job if I had. Except for the few top best-selling names, writers have always been underpaid, and their comparative remuneration has got steadily worse. As a writer myself, I had no intention of being party to any scheme (and there has always been an abundance of such schemes) to exploit them even further.

Now at last our preparations went into top gear. It was a headily exciting time, with the wind behind us. Every now and then I was assailed by sudden qualms and doubts, as I had always been in the past in such periods; but as in the past they did not last long. There were other moments, to balance them, when it seemed to me almost too good to be true that, after all my reverses, this opportunity had fallen into my lap of creating a new literary magazine. It was only when the first number was finally printed and published, that I woke one morning to ask myself where all my energy and enthusiasm had come from, and what it had all been in aid of. Why had I bothered? Where was it all leading? I remembered that I had experienced almost exactly the same backwash of feeling after the first number of *New Writing* had come out.

For the time being our office was to be at my house in Egerton Crescent. It was to open in October; but there was plenty to do meanwhile. I set myself to think out even more clearly what kind of magazine I wanted – what kind of magazine *was* wanted. As I had said to Cecil King, I intended above all to avoid being narrowly British, even if our basic aim was to provide room for new and developing talents, and to make that room a place of stimulus and creative ferment. There must be writers from the rest of Europe among the contributors, above all writers little known in our country; and from America as well. At the same time, it seemed to me important not to devote ourselves exclusively to the young, or to a coterie or group of writers, however excellent a group we might uncover. As the magazines where any good writing could appear had grown so few, it seemed to me proper that our pages should be open to all authors who were still making discoveries in their work, who were still growing creatively, irrespective of their age. It also seemed to me important to decide about the balance of imaginative and critical work. In *New Writing* the balance had always been tipped well in favour of poems and stories and imaginative documentaries. On this occasion, though it was far from my intention to establish a critical side that was inspired by any more rigorous rules and attitudes than those of lucidity, freshness and seriousness of approach, I wanted there to be not only a book review section in which the critics could spread themselves more amply and less hurriedly than in the daily and weekly papers in general, but also space for longer critical estimates of contemporary writers, and such articles as John Wain's in the last Penguin, that provoked and stimulated imaginative writers and not merely other critics. I was on the whole against the French fashion for extracts from novels, though I was ready to make one or two concessions in order to include certain authors I thought it essential to represent, as I did not believe the English reader really liked such titillation. Painting, music, architecture, Cecil King ruled out. He said that to support literature was the priority at that moment, and we would only just have enough room to do that adequately. I did not disagree with him, though I had a twinge of regret for what had been such fun to do in the latter life of *Penguin New Writing*.

Having made my mind clear about this, and got the general assent of my editorial board to the pattern, the next most important thing was to write round to all the authors whose sympathy and cooperation I felt was important. And to nose round as hard as a dog hunting truffles for new poems and stories.

At this moment an event occurred which looked for a moment as if it was going to knock our backers off their perch. Stephen Spender had told me confidentially some months before that the Congress for Cultural Freedom had at last agreed to back a new monthly magazine in England, and to put him in as co-editor with an American beside him. I wished him well: I told him that there was plenty of room, in my opinion, for more than one new monthly, and as in addition his was to be as much political and sociological as literary, I didn't see how we could clash. No rows and no jealousies arose, to my immense relief, as I was tired of them. John Hayward and the tycoon were aware of this imminent arrival on the scene, but the concrete appearance of the first number in September, beating us by several months, caused perturbation. *Encounter* did not, at its birth, receive an all too favourable welcome from the press – the reviews in *The Times Literary Supplement*, the *Listener* and the *Spectator* were chastening – but the *Economist*, rather exceptionally, was enthusiastic in its praise. It so happened that this was just the weekly that Cecil King read with attention. He rang me up one day in some agitation. I calmed him down by saying I wasn't worried, and that as far as the literary side went we'd produce something as good, if not better. 'I don't fear competition, do you?' I asked him. 'Well, I don't here,' he replied, 'I've got my rivals but I've licked the lot of 'em.' 'Have a word with John Hayward about it.' 'Well, I do ring him up, but he always says he's too busy to speak to me – well, *I'm* a busy man too.' He added that he'd heard they gave a big launching party, and that seemed to him a bad thing, splash champagne about the place, bound to make some of the advertisers think they're being charged too much, etc. Nevertheless, when it came to the point, the *London Magazine* also gave a big launching party. By that time we had reason to feel a little reckless.

I began to warm to Cecil King. Things were going well, and I think he was warming a little to me. Some days later, he came down in his super Rolls-Royce to see the office we had opened in Egerton Crescent, and to be introduced to Barbara Cooper, who had returned as one of my editorial assistants, and David Hughes. He was in rollicking form, and made himself very agreeable to everyone. He talked with me for a long time, but more about politics than the *London Magazine*; in particular about Churchill. 'Most extraordinary man, would always see me at once during the war if I rang up for an interview, but some of his colleagues had to wait three months.' He went on to say that in his view what Churchill cared about was not so much power as *position*. Once he was in office as prime minister, he didn't mind if he carried a lot of duds in the cabinet with him, he felt he could look after them. But, he added, he simply couldn't bear being criticized, in spite of all the attacks he'd made himself on other people when out of office. 'Curious thing,' he concluded, 'these attackers can't stand being attacked themselves. Look at Nye Bevan: he always rang up if so much as a word of his speeches was criticized in the *Daily Mirror* or *Sunday Pictorial*.'

A little later, when the *London Magazine* was a going concern, I had lunch with him at the *Daily Mirror* offices, and found him almost entirely absorbed in the success of his *Junior Mirror*. As usual, he was very amusing about the efforts of his rivals in the popular newspaper world to outdo him. As we finished our meal, we were talking about the *Economist*, and he said: 'The really lucky man is the chap who runs the paper he *wants* to run, and makes other people like it.' So I said: 'Well, what about you and the *Daily Mirror*?' He immediately replied: 'Oh, no, no, no. What I'd like to run is something nobody'd buy.' 'What exactly do you mean?' 'Well, something that had, first of all, first-class articles on economic and business affairs.' 'Like the *Economist*?' 'Oh no, *far* more elaborate and detailed.' 'And what about the arts?' 'Well, books, yes, plenty about books, but not about the theatre or the cinema – I'm no good at the entertainment world.' 'Well, what else?' 'There's the whole world of science – and not merely physics and chemistry and all that, because I believe they've had their day, but archaeology, psychology, telepathy – yes, all those sciences that have scarcely begun, that deal with intuition and what's called instinct.'

At the same time, I made it my business to see as much as possible of my editorial advisers, and also of other friends I hoped would be sympathetic contributors or observers. Cyril Connolly, who for the greater part of a lunch we had together was extremely amusing about the history of recent literary magazines and the prospects of *Encounter*, promised a series of parodies of current literary favourites. Alas, they never materialized. Christopher Isherwood, who had just finished *The World in the Evening*, wrote: 'I hope you will come to the U.S. before long, in search of new authors. I think it's wonderful that both you and Stephen have magazines. One really helps the other. Everybody here is pleased about it, as things are very quiet on this side.'

I went down to see William Plomer at his home in Rustington, a few miles from the Sussex coast near Worthing. He was very keen that we should include, as a distinct feature in the *London Magazine*, personal stories, or confessions from contemporary authors: an idea which eventually crystalized in the series *Coming to London*. He was looking bronzed and well. We went for a walk along the seashore with Lottie, who immediately plunged with abandon into the grey, seaweed-tangled waves and floated like a sea-monster, much to William's entertainment. As we passed down the rows of extraordinary bungalows on our way to the sea, he rattled on at a tearing speed about the oddities of the people who lived in them, the famous local characters and the eccentricities of the neighbourhood. While we were walking along the beach, he picked up two white stones with strange holes in them, and said he would have to send them to Herbert Read after he had mounted them on plinths. He told me that people often discovered Roman coins round there; a few moments later he picked up a piece of swollen seaweed and remarked: 'And here's a Roman letter.'

When I left, he handed me a poem he had just finished, called 'The Bungalows'. I have always thought it one of his best, in its mixture of mocking observation and serious imaginative vision:

Begrudging vulgar fantasy
To cheap and ordinary homes,
Discrimination might deplore
That concrete frog, those whimsy gnomes,
Nor see them as blind tribute to
The rule of dreams, or as a last
Concession to the irrational,
The old, wild, superstitious past. . . .

'The Bungalows' appeared in the third number of the *London Magazine*.

2

A few days later, I went over to stay with Elizabeth Bowen at Bowen's Court in County Cork. I was overcome at once by the green rural make-believe of the Irish countryside. The pace and pattern of life there might, I thought, have belonged to any time between 1700 and the year we were in. I felt I was sinking into, being absorbed by the deep quicksands of peace, the soft air among the huge trees of the old park. This lulling quiet was only disturbed, every dawn and dusk, by the rooks, who put on the most extraordinary Farnborough air display of their own on their way to and from the harvest fields. Thousands of them packed the sky, as they dived, planed, soared, swooped and circled in formation. In some odd way, in the long twilights, I felt I could understand their language, another language, without any intervening barrier at all.

The house was not, from the outside, strikingly beautiful, a square, grey stone Georgian block with large windows; but it was not ugly, and the distinction it undoubtedly revealed was enhanced by the delightfully elegant and discreetly classical door-front. The rooms which Elizabeth was using in the house – she found it too extravagant to refurbish and domesticate them all – were large and handsome in their proportions, with doors, fireplaces and cornice ornamentation in admirable classical style. I was particularly struck by the hall, with its

rich red damask wallpaper; and by one of the most beautiful
sofa-tables, in coromandel wood, I had ever seen. My (slight)
disappointment was to find the animals so few: only an evasive
cat, a rather disdainful pony mare of fourteen, and a gardener's
spaniel of soulful intensity.

This visit gave me the very welcome opportunity to get to
know Elizabeth much more intimately than before. We talked
without stop, at meals, after dinner by the fire in the big drawing room, while she walked me round the old walled garden
full of dahlias and fruit bushes, and drove recklessly about
the countryside. She aired her literary prejudices, I aired
mine; and we came to a general agreement about the kind of
review we wanted the *London Magazine* to be. All she had for
me at the moment, she said, was a section from the novel she
was at work on that might stand by itself; but at the same
time she promised me an article on Eudora Welty, and some
of the short stories which were already cloudily moving in her
imagination, as soon as she put them down on paper.

I began to draw a portrait of her, as I observed her in the
midst of these activities and arguments. I would have liked to
capture her stylish, rather masculine carriage, as if about to
settle on a shooting stick and lift binoculars – her narrow face
with its high cheek-bones, not prominent but making the
cheeks below them rather flat – her strong nose (always a
mark of character and energy when not betrayed by a weak
chin) and her wide mouth whose laugh seems so often and so
strangely just short of a leer – the wrinkled lines of amusement puckered all round her pale green, arresting eyes. I
noticed that she had almost completely conquered her stam-
mer. Above all, I was captivated again by the quality she displays almost more abundantly than anyone else I know, of
making one feel completely at ease, of immediately establishing
rapport by a flow of uninhibited conversation which mingles
sympathy, charm, wit, and shrewd intellectual comment. And
her energy! She moved about the house like a young man setting out for a football match; all morning she worked in her
study at her letters, her review articles and her current novel;
in the afternoon she took tireless, striding walks about the
estate or the surrounding countryside, talking all the time, or

motored like one possessed, mainly on the wrong side of the
the road, for shopping or sight-seeing purposes; in the late
afternoon, after tea, and again after dinner, she was engaged
in drawing out her guests and friends, while she embroidered
or hunted in her library for books our discussion referred to.
On the first morning of my visit, she questioned me closely
about the failure of Aer Lingus to carry me on from Dublin,
a lapse which had resulted in my late arrival the previous
evening, and then proceeded to write an indignant letter of
protest to the management. The whole house palpably pulsa-
ted with the unfolding periods of this four-page masterpiece.

I decided that the new British writers I wanted to give space
to in my first number should be Elizabeth Jennings and Thom
Gunn as poets, and Hugo Charteris as fiction writer. All three
had appeared in my *New Soundings*.

I did not meet Thom Gunn until May of the following
year, in Cambridge. I was struck by the rather tightly drawn
mouth, the slightly Punch-like nose and chin which seemed to
me to indicate willpower and obstinate conviction but were
qualified by the imaginative dark eyes and the sensitive readiness of his laughter. I had an extraordinary feeling, at this
first meeting, that here was a young poet who had it in him to
become for his generation what Wystan Auden or Stephen
Spender had been for our generation of the 'thirties. This feeling deepened as our friendship developed. I remember how
only a few months later I took him and David Hughes out to
dinner in London, and Thom scarcely drew breath the whole
evening, talking about poetry, Shakespeare and our contemporaries. He turned out to be a fan of Christopher Isherwood,
and also a boyhood enthusiast for *Penguin New Writing*.

Elizabeth had just published a first collection of poems, and
received an Arts Council prize for it. Hugo Charteris, unknown when I presented him in *New Soundings*, had published
his first novel, *A Share of the World*. To celebrate the appearance of this novel by her brother, Annie Fleming, the former
Lady Rothermere and by then married to 'James Bond' Ian
Fleming (a contemporary and friend of mine at Eton) gave
an evening party. I remembered that, when my publishing

firm had been breaking up, I had one day met Mark Bonham Carter – who had begun to work for Collins – in the Brompton Road, and said to him: 'Go for Hugo Charteris, Rosamond and I think he's jolly good.' Now this advice, such as it was, had borne fruit.

I arrived at the party after dinner, expecting (as Annie had given me to believe) just a few literary people. Instead, I found a vast concourse of guests, both literary and social, packing the little house in Victoria Square. Their tongues were already loosened by the abundant champagne, and the noise was deafening. Only Evelyn Waugh, still sitting at the cleared dinner table downstairs, with Jennifer Ross at his side to soothe and encourage, seemed indifferent to the jollification intensifying upstairs, and muttered both to Rosamond and me: 'Never heard of you.' (This did not prevent him writing to me some months later, from Cairo, to congratulate me on the first number of the *London Magazine*, saying that he had enjoyed it enormously.)

Every week-end at Lake Cottage my thoughts were filled with schemes and preparations. I decided I must have new French authors for the magazine as well as British, and as early as possible. Towards the end of October, therefore, I decided to go to Paris, to tie up my connections there. During two sunblest days of mild autumn weather, with showers from dark cloud masses blowing over at rare intervals, I worked out a plan of action. All the time golden coins of leaf sailed, twirled and fluttered down from the oak trees and silver birches and sycamores, and lay like a becalmed armada on the black, bright lake below. The last, large leaves from the fig tree had fallen yellow on to the michaelmas daisies, the rich crop from the pear espalier beside it had been plucked, a few clusters of purple grapes still hung in the greenhouse. Day and night, one heard the 'thuck' and 'plop' of the falling acorns, and until light failed the squirrels frisked about in the high branches, while Lottie gambolled below, picking up stick after stick to bring in for the fire.

I thought that when I returned from my visit to Paris the branches would almost be bare of leaves, the dahlias and double begonias dug up for storing, and the chrysanthemums all cut. The end of a season again; but this time it was not melancholy I felt.

Paris was cold and rainy, and late autumnal already. I saw a great many old friends and several new young authors, and I left a number of fuses burning for the future of the *London Magazine*. I set off by visiting Plon and Gallimard. At the latter great factory of literature in the rue Sebastien Bottin, I had a long talk with Jean Dutourd, author of *A Dog's Head*, who put me on to several possible young contributors, and followed the visit by drinks with Dionys Mascolo and Marguerite Duras at the Hotel Pont Royal next door. Mascolo, as usual, was all charm, showed great keenness to help, and was inclined to contrast the gloomy stagnation in Paris with what struck him as signs of active literary revival in London. It was the first time I had met Marguerite Duras, whose *Barrage Contre le Pacifique* I had much admired: small, raven-haired, with a large, attractive round face she was altogether different from what I had expected from the book. She spoke with warm affections of Sonia Orwell, whom I found she already knew intimately: a subject in common soon broke the ice, and she gladly promised to let me see her short stories as soon as they were ready – as a collection – in French.

Apart from Marguerite, the most rewarding results of these meetings and discussions was getting to know Pierre Gascar and Felicien Marceau and their works. Pierre Gascar struck me as one of the most original and exciting writers to appear in France for a long time. I read what he gave me at once, and arranged to take his short story 'The Animals' for my first number. (Just as we were going to press, I heard that he had been awarded the Prix Goncourt for the volume.) Felicien Marceau, painter, critic, and dramatist as well as fiction writer, agreed to let me have his short story 'The Armistice in Venice' for the second number.

On many previous visits I had made a habit of talking over the literary situation with the poet Pierre Emmanuel, to whom I had become very devoted. A tall, dark man of tortured sensibility and extreme charm, a brilliant and provocative speaker, he had changed his name to Emmanuel during the war as a gesture of sympathy towards the Jews. He had been brought up in America, though of French middle-class parents, and told me with amusement that when he returned to America to lecture after 1945, the 'best families' of Boston had received him with the most cordial politeness, but had subsequently completely dropped him because they assumed he really was a Jew. He invited me to lunch on this occasion in his flat in the rue de Varenne, where I met for the first time his beautiful Indo-Chinese wife and two boisterous young step-children. Pierre lamented that, in contrast to England, there were far too many literary reviews in France, and not nearly enough talent to go round. He also voiced the complaint – which I was to hear more and more often as the years went by, in Italy as well as France – that literature was being ruined by the proliferation of new '*prix*', and the rather shady, publisher-wangled exploitation of second-rate or third-rate talents which accompanied it.

I had let Marguerite Caetani know that I was going to be in Paris, and her loud, decisive, eager New England voice was on the telephone almost every morning. I made several visits to her famous apartment in the rue du Cirque, where the floors and tables were always piled with a vast jumble of books, manuscripts and letters, like the débris left in the wake of a flood, and where she was apt to be surrounded by an adoring group of young expatriate American would-be writers whom she was supporting, or considering supporting through *Botteghe Oscure* – and hoped I might also support through the *London Magazine*.

Before I left I went to see Marie-Laure again. It was on this occasion, I think, that she showed me the designs-on-stone she had begun to make. She picked up these stones and pieces of wave-worn pottery, she told me, mainly on the beach at Hyeres by her summer home, and then painted eyes or other human features on them, as the shape of the stones inspired her. I was completely captivated by them, and tried to per-suade her to let them be seen in London. Her reply was to present me with one of the most imaginative.

There was a young man at lunch that day whom she was befriending at the time, a small, blond, attractively smiling American composer: Ned Rorem. It turned out that he knew several of my friends, including Paul Bowles, and we became attached to one another. Later, he set to music, very beautifully, several of Demetrios Capetanakis's poems.

3

The first luncheon party of the editorial board of the *London Magazine* took place at No. 31 very soon after my return from Paris. It turned out to be a very animated and stimulating occasion, with all present: Elizabeth Bowen, Veronica Wedgwood, Rex Warner, William Plomer and John Hayward. I told them of the general plan, as it had finally emerged from discussions between myself and the various persons Cecil King had designated to help me at Geraldine House, what contributions I had already got lined up, what other writers had agreed to contribute in the future, the results of my Paris visit, and the successful beginning of our campaign to get advertisers. There was a good deal of discussion about *Encounter*, and our determination to remain purely literary without any political bias whatsoever was reinforced by the general dislike or suspicion of the political line to which *Encounter* was committed by its genesis and its backers. I put forward the view that the more distinct we were in that way, the easier it would be to co-exist, even though literary contributions were bound to overlap from time to time.

It was, I think, at this first meeting that several members pressed for literary reminiscences as a fairly regular feature. Writers should be encouraged, they said, to commit to paper all that they could remember of their contemporaries and the literary world of their time, before all memory had faded. I had thought this an excellent idea when William Plomer had suggested it to me in Rustington, and was impressed by the general enthusiasm. As I have already said, out of it eventually grew the series we called 'Coming to London', with its precious recall of historical scenes and characters. We broke up on a distinctly sanguine and even boisterously merry note.

Meanwhile, the technical organization was developing apace. Once the printers had been chosen – and we were fortunate in having worked out a satisfactory arrangement with my old friend James Shand and his excellent Shenval Press – and the format settled, the most urgent priority was to get the support, on as permanent a basis as possible, of the publishers – or rather, of those publishers who could be said to be seriously interested in literature. We wanted as much 'prestige' advertising as possible from kindly disposed insurance companies, banks and other giants of the commercial world. I looked to the *Daily Mirror* to deal with that, though I soon realized that just because they were the rich *Daily Mirror* some reluctance (much more than I found a few years later when I was on my own, carrying around a hopeful begging bowl) would be shown. The publishers, however, were my home ground. If, after all the talk there had been about the necessity of having a literary magazine, the publishers were not ready to cooperate, well, things were in a pretty bad way. Luckily, they rallied round for our birth with a cynic-shaming enthusiasm. And Ian Parsons of Chatto & Windus rang me up one day to say that he and his fellow directors took the new magazine very seriously, and wanted to book a special position facing the first contribution for at least six months. *That* was indeed the generous gesture I had scarcely dared hope for. Incidentally, it was by no means the last of the generous gestures Ian Parsons made towards the *London Magazine* before, seven years later, I relinquished my editorial chair.

With all due respect to the highly trained advertising bloodhounds of the *Daily Mirror* (nice, as all bloodhounds are if tickled behind the ear), I think I knew a great deal more about how to get advertising revenue out of the book world than they did; and after listening politely to all the talk they let off about 'punch' and 'drive', I went out and got it myself in my own way.

Another tricky problem that refused to be solved at once was that of distribution. A magazine needs someone *in the trade* who will take the orders from booksellers and other vendors, deal with the subscriptions, and see that the copies go out on time. Obviously, this was no job suited to a daily newspaper. At first I had thought that Bob Maxwell and his wholesale organization in Simpkin Marshall might help us. To my great disappointment, he came to the conclusion in early November, no doubt rightly, that it was too risky for him to handle – in his special relationship to the book trade. Where to turn? At five minutes to twelve, I was like a train without an engine: all cars assembled, passengers in their seats, but no one to draw it out of the station.

Here again, Ian Parsons came to the rescue. It was decided that Chatto & Windus should, technically, be the publishers, and handle all the complex, dirty work of distribution. Cecil King was delighted to have such an excellent imprint, and was impressed by Ian's practical and professional helpfulness, while John Hayward and the rest of my editorial board were full of congratulations that we had found such an expert and experienced outfit to mediate between us and the booksellers and public.

Ian went into the whole situation with me with characteristic thoroughness, and came to the conclusion that our preliminary prognostications about circulation were far too low. Rather than lose hundreds of pounds on the first number, he said we might even make a few pennies.

Cecil King's delighted squeal of amusement when I told him over the telephone still rings in my ears.

Pleasant, however, though this experience of unexpected promise of public success was at the time, I cannot help feeling, now that I look back on it all, that it was unfortunate. Cecil King had said, in the course of our early negotiations, that as he saw it the *London Magazine* would have a circulation of two or three thousand, and would be largely unintelligible to himself. I replied, yes, that summed up the situation very nicely; and we laughed. Now, however, with the *Daily Mirror's* machine behind it, it looked as if we were going to produce another circulation success. This immediately took it out of the prestige-charitable class into the potential money-making class. A disaster: for it meant that all the bloodhounds who surrounded King lost interest and heart when, after a few numbers, the *London Magazine* settled down to a far more modest circulation – though still well above our original idea. One of the bloodhounds even suggested to me at this time sending an advance complimentary copy to President Eisenhower. I managed to cool that extravagant impulse down; but it was clear to me that he was dreaming of a minimum 50,000 circulation, as a kind of eventual rival to the *Reader's Digest*.

4

Just at this time, when our plans were coming to the boil, an event occurred in the literary world which created, in the words of James Michie (who was firmly sat on for his remark by the Leavisite critics), 'something like a panic': the death of Dylan Thomas. But James, I believe, was right: it was the death of a Pan figure, the only and probably the last in our lifetime.

I realized at once that we must do something about it, far advanced though our plans were. I persuaded James Michie to write, as a younger poet just outside the range of his contemporaries, the excellent letter from which I have already quoted. As James so well said, Dylan 'stayed outside coteries, beyond argument, and apart from self-explanation. As every modern poet must, he kept on friendly terms with the various official god-fatherly institutions of culture, but he never kow-towed or sold out. He published little, threw away a lot, wrote nothing to order.' What stays most clearly in my memory, however, from James's letter, is one of those chance asides, glimpses of history that can mean more than any sober assessments. 'I can remember,' he wrote, 'how the early poems with their mesmeric iambic pentameters took the ear by storm much as Swinburne's did in their day. We had a game of shouting out favourite lines to each other when we met. "I see you boys of summer in your ruin," someone would say. "I sit and watch the worm beneath my nail wearing the quick away," a second would reply. While a third added gravely "My father's ghost is climbing in the rain." '

R

As luck would have it, Louis MacNeice, engaged on a much longer work, devoted a whole canto – the eighteenth canto – to Dylan; and this he offered to us at the last moment. We were able to make space for it, and treat it as a major contribution that was both topical and timeless. Among many memorable lines, I remember particularly his description of Dylan as

> . . . a spruce and small
> Bow-tied Silenus roistering his way
> Through lands of fruit and fable, well aware
> That even Dionysus had his day
> And cannot take it with him. . . .

Edith Sitwell wrote to me from New York, giving me a hair-raising description of Dylan's last days and the aftermath of his death among his hangers-on, 'everyone accusing everyone else', for the circumstances of his death, and describing the desperate demonstrations of his wife Caitlin 'the only person he ever loved' over his dying body. 'Complete strangers rang me up ceaselessly,' she added. 'And one poet sent me a batch of poems in one of which he claimed that owing to Dylan's death he (the author) had become *transparent*. Do you suppose that can be true? If so, it is too horrible. . . . I *cannot* believe my dear Dylan, whom I loved, as well as knowing him to be a really great poet, is dead. I just feel a dreadful numbness.'

Dylan's death in fact, though one could not clearly discern it at the time, was the beginning of a change of mood and intention in contemporary English poetry, in which his ideals, and the style of writing favoured by himself, and also in different fashion by Edith, were to be violently attacked by some of the younger critics.

Christmas passed, and when the New Year came we were in the full flood of launching excitement. Orders for the first number rose from day to day. We were changing our print order at shorter and shorter intervals. First of all it was 20,000 (far higher than we had dreamed of when we started work); then 22,000; then, though it seemed a bit of a risk, 25,000. Almost immediately after, however, we had to raid the 1,000 we had set aside for first subscriptions; and then within a few hours we saw that it was no good, we should have to order a repeat. We thought at first 3,000 would be enough; but the torrent overtook us, and Ian Parsons emphatically advised 5,000. Whenever I rang Cecil King up in his office, chuckles greeted me. I went to see him to present one of the first of the finished copies: his delight was immense, and his congratulations pursued me by letter afterwards. The members of my editorial board sent their enthusiastic messages, except for John Hayward who devoted a long telephone conversation to unearthing minute misprints and complaining that we dated this first number February 1954 whereas it actually appeared on January 15th (a practice we continued to pursue, after careful consultations with the booksellers and bookstall managers.) My constant and faithful friend on the *Evening Standard*, Eric Hiscock, said it 'smelt of success on every page', while the friendly publishers, Jamie Hamilton, Billie Collins, Mark Longman and several others, promised boundless support after reading this first number.

Meanwhile, news of the new literary magazine had begun to get around, and contributions began to trickle in. The trickle soon swelled to a full stream: by March over 100 a week were arriving, and many of them from writers well-known, or at least known to me. The trade reported high-speed sales. In a whip-round of the bookstalls at Victoria and Waterloo stations just after publication, I found copies going out all the time. Mr Hoyle, the manager at Waterloo, had covered his big stall with copies and displays to be seen from every angle. At Hatchards I listened to loud laments that they had ordered far too few and had been badly caught out. I was made to sign copies by eager young assistants.

The celebration party at No. 31 was a huge affair, with 120 guests and every reception room in the house – dining-room and morning-room as well as study – thrown open. Champagne slopped over free copies of the first, blue-coated number of the new magazine. Barbara Cooper and David Hughes, aided by the young student Hans Tauchnitz (grandson of the famous Leipzig publisher of the first continental paperbacks), worked like Trojans to support the staff from the caterers. To my amusement, several spies from the Beaverbrook papers appeared, to keep an eye on what their Geraldine House rivals were up to.

I could not help being pleased by this 'smell of success'. Nevertheless, even in the midst of the popping champagne corks and telegrams of congratulation, I sensed how much a sheer curiosity about the combination of the *Daily Mirror* and my highbrow self contributed to the occasion, and knew that the hard work really lay ahead.

In my 'Foreword', I had taken a 'middle' position, saying: 'No "ideologies" are likely to help writers today to write. It is the obstinate will to create, whatever form it takes, that must be fanned and fed, like a fire when the rain has been coming down the chimney all night. . . . We would like the *London Magazine* to represent the best that the England of our day can show to the world in literary endeavour, both creative and critical; mindful, however, of the fact that without some sense of its European perspective English literature and thought have always in the past tended to be sorely impoverished, and that today and in the future the world perspective is necessary beyond the European. . . .'

In his 'Message', Tom Eliot reinforced my plea for a non-partisan, non-parochial attitude. 'The first function of a literary magazine, surely,' he wrote, 'is to introduce the work of new or little known writers of talent. The second is to provide critical valuation of the work of living authors, both famous and unknown. The third is to be in the best sense *international*. . . .'

Earlier on, he had made a prophetic statement about a phenomenon which I had myself seen approaching, and which was to loom even larger as the years went by, deeply affecting the fortunes of the *London Magazine*: 'It is undoubtedly a scandal that we have had, in London, since the end of the war, no literary magazine to compare with those which have sprung up in other countries. There are half a dozen, on the Continent, for which we have no equivalent. As for America, I am aware of a common Anglo-American danger of abandoning the central position for those of two extremes: the Academic and the Popular Educational. The type of magazine from the lack of which we suffer is neither that which provides a vehicle of expression for critics occupying university posts nor that which elevates the Public Taste. What we need is the magazine which will boldly assume the existence of a public interested in serious literature, and eager to be kept in touch with current literature and with criticism of that literature by the most exacting standards.'

I would have liked to add as a postscript: 'We propose to be the *London* Magazine, and not the Magazine of Oxford, or Cambridge, or Redbrick, or any other, smaller partisan circle. There is, after all, centred in our great civilized capital of London, which we love so much, what Dr Johnson called "the common reader", "uncorrupted by literary prejudices, after all the refinements of subtilty and the dogmatism of learning." And he rejoiced to concur with it.'

5

Writing as I do now, at an interval of a dozen years from the foundation of the new *London Magazine*, I see that many hopes were fulfilled but many others disappointed: perhaps by my own deficiencies, perhaps by a real dearth of first-class new literary talent in our country at that particular time, perhaps partly also by sudden changes in taste and fashion, under-currents over which the individual has very little control, if any at all.

The seven years during which I edited the *London Magazine* were full of stimulus and interest for me, if also bringing a share of vexation and discouragement. I like to believe that they were of value to the continuity of literary creation in our country. Equally, I am certain that it would have been un-wise for me to carry on beyond 1961, even if I had found a Maecenas who would stoically have endured the lean years and judged with a sceptical eye the fat. One plays one's part on a certain stage; it is good if one can be aware of the signs which indicate that a new generation of players is impatient to take one's place. I never wanted to linger on as a grotesque from an earlier generation, held in place only by compassion and respect for past achievement.

The death of Dylan also seemed to mark the beginning of a new period, during which the writers of the 'thirties and the 'forties were spurned (at least temporarily, and with certain exceptions) by an up-and-coming generation who affected, in their early manifestos, to be scandalized by the romanticism and cosmopolitanism of their immediate predecessors. The vogue for a new kind of social realism and a picaresque style in the novel indicated much more effectively, I thought, a genuine shift in the social structure of our country, the first results of post-war Welfare State building, than the move towards a kind of humdrum 'consolidation' in poetry. In so far as both these tendencies were parochial and against the European mind, they seemed to me reactionary and to be deplored, even to be absurd in the circumstances of the world in which we have lived since the first atom bomb exploded. Already, however, the so-called 'Movement' has disintegrated, and the authentic talents have pursued their own diverse paths ignoring the slogans with which they were launched.

In curious contrast, the new movement in the theatre which began with the first night of John Osborne's brilliant *Look Back in Anger*, rapidly expanded into an interest in foreign theatrical developments, the experiments of Brecht, Ionesco, Beckett and Durrenmatt. There was a certain irony in this return to the symbolical and surrealist elements in our modern intellectual heritage just at a time when they appeared to be anathema to the novelists and literary critics.

I found this new phase in the theatre sympathetic and often exciting, and believed it could have a fertilizing influence on the whole literary scene. It was my constant regret while I was editor of the *London Magazine* that it was impossible in such a review as mine to do much to help or blow wind into the sails. I felt that for some years the most vital imaginative currents would be moving towards the drama, and that young authors who had something urgent to say would be much more likely to want to write plays rather than short stories or poems, perhaps even rather than novels.

This is not, however, the place or the moment for me to attempt to write in detail or pass judgment on those developments that coincided with the founding of the *London Magazine*. It is also, I must admit, still painful to me to write of years which saw the death of so many writers and artists, dear friends of mine, admired and often loved by me, who were prominent in the intellectual activity of that time. Even while I have been writing, their number has been swelled by the deaths of Tom Eliot, Edith Sitwell, and Louis MacNeice. If I were editing a magazine today, again and again when asking myself the regular question 'now who should write about this, or that?' I know that the names of the dead would come to my mind first.

My mother's death also took place in those years: my mother, who had helped me to support *New Writing* at more than one crucial point, who helped me to find the money to start my publishing firm, and supported me again when the *London Magazine* lost its original backers. She died in the fulness of years, in greater calm and detachment than she had known through all her middle age, but leaving such a gap that still today, nine years later, when I am abroad on a holiday I cannot change the impulse that makes me want to write the first postcard or letter to her.

I remember how we celebrated her eightieth birthday at Egerton Crescent. My three sisters, Helen, Rosamond and Beatrix, had taken her to the theatre, and late supper was laid out in my newly decorated dining-room, with its black and gold furniture, on their return. We drank her health in champagne from the exquisite cut-glass goblets that had been specially made for my grandfather in Bohemia in the last century, and ate from the oriental dishes he had brought back from his Far Eastern trip nearly a hundred years before. She seemed at the top of her form, as young as any of us in comment and appreciation. It seemed to me that at the end she retired happily into a world of her own, reflecting perhaps with amused satisfaction on the phenomenon of being surrounded by all her children on such a night of celebration, after two world wars, in a London so much changed from the city she had known when she first came over from New England with my father more than half a century before.

Everyone who has enjoyed a game which he has played, with some success and effect, for over quarter of a century, and who is eventually obliged to give it up because he finds the forces arrayed against him too great for him to control, must have some bitterness among his recollections of past pleasures and achievements. I must confess that a certain sour taste of frustration has been in my mouth, while I have watched authors, whose hopeful beginnings or revivals I encouraged, pass on to the lists of other publishers, or individual books of rare merit, which originally appeared under my imprint, be re-issued with little or no mention of how they first came to the light. So the waves of time sweep away all the sandcastles we spend our mornings with such expenditure of energy and enthusiasm in erecting.

If I were not by nature a poet, endowed with some measure of philosophy, all this would be much harder to bear. But my career has made me reflect on the increasing difficulties which individual ventures in publishing and editing are bound to contend with in our time. Gone are the days when a young man, or a young couple, with keen literary interests and a feeling for the production of books could start a publishing business with a few hundred pounds in the bank, and with a certain amount of luck favouring could establish it as of national importance and make a modest living out of it within a decade. And yet those days are only as far away as the years between the wars. Gone are the days when it was not too difficult to find a private patron who would support a literary magazine. Heavy taxation, and the increasingly rigorous rules under which the Inland Revenue judges what can be allowed as expenses before taxation, have almost eliminated such patrons, except in the rare cases of great riches deliberately dedicated to such enterprises. My own career has, I think, been a kind of demonstration experiment of the problems of finding a patron in our time. I can only hope that in the future the only patrons left will not be public and official bodies. Immense though their value may be, I have never believed that they – or the great commercial enterprises which for prestige reasons care for a time and then lose interest – could in any way replace the private patron with a hunch.

I have written in my previous volumes of the 'fertile dilemma' which seemed to rule my life: the way in which the course of events, with diabolical and repeated ingenuity, made it impossible for me to decide to devote my energies finally either to writing, or to the presentation and encouragement of other people's writing. Part of my mind, when I was running a literary magazine or a publishing enterprise, always regretted the time I could have devoted to my own poems and books. And yet, as soon as such an enterprise came to an end, the opportunity arose to start a new one which I felt I could not refuse. A few weeks of creative work, and the notebooks had to be abandoned again for the new editor's or publisher's desk.

Curiously enough, in a quite unexpected way, a partial resolution of this problem came when one day, early in the fifties, Mark Longman suggested to me that I should write my autobiography for his ancient and distinguished publishing house. One or two other publishers had mentioned the possibility to me before; but now Mark came along, full of enthusiasm and with concrete proposals. The first volume of this trio, which I now conclude, was not published until 1955, but it occupied me increasingly after the end of my publishing career. The very friendly reception which *The Whispering Gallery* was accorded made me feel that to make a work of art out of the story of how I had through all my adult life been unable to choose finally whether to make works of art myself or be the impresario of others engaged in this difficult life, was a gift that my good angel had held behind his back all those years and only gave me now with an ironical smile.

At the same time, I would be both foolish and hypocritical if, having looked back, I pretended that I had not found great rewards in my life of tension between these two poles. I think of all the friends I might never have met, all the stories of adventure, suffering and joy I might never have heard, all the discoveries in other people's lives I would never have made, all the journeys I would never have set out on; above all, of those moments of pure delight when I found a book, a story or poem that I knew was the real thing and could be shown by me to the public to be the real thing. If it has been a weakness in me not to have been ready to accept the more restricted and austere life of the artist struggling in his own darkness, I cannot altogether say that I am sorry I failed to be strong.

Now I face a different life, with all those strange and turbulent ends and beginnings behind me. Only the future will tell whether I shall still find keys to other rooms along the long corridor that is always in shadow just ahead of one's steps; or whether my good angel will have at last to admit that both his hands are empty.

APPENDIX

It may be of some slight historic interest to append a complete list of the books published in my *Modern European Library*:

ANDRÉ CHAMSON: A Mountain Boyhood
JACQUES LEMARCHAND: Geneviève
ERNST JUENGER: On the Marble Cliffs
IVAN BUNIN: Dark Avenues
RAYMOND QUENEAU: A Hard Winter
JEAN-PAUL SARTRE:
    The Diary of Antoine Roquentin
ENNIO FLAIANO: Mariam
ROBERT MERLE: Week-end at Zuydcoote
JEAN-LOUIS CURTIS: The Forests of the Night
RAYMOND QUENEAU: Pierrot
JEAN DUTOURD: A Dog's Head
JACQUES LAURENT: Goribon's Folly
ANDRÉ MALRAUX: The Walnut Trees of Altenburg
CESARE PAVESE: The Moon and the Bonfire
MARIO SOLDATI: The Commander Comes to Dine
NIKOS KAZANTZAKIS: Zorba the Greek
JEAN-LOUIS CURTIS: Lucifer's Dream

INDEX

Aberconway, Christabel, Lady 132

Abrahams, William, 82

Ackerley, Joe, 102

Acton, Harold, 38, 87, 156–9; Italian home, 157–8; *Memoirs of an Aesthete*, 157

Adlington, William, 22

Algren, Nelson, 72

Alliance Française, 99, 100, 242

Amalfi, Italy, 209–10, 212–14

Ariel series of poems, 100

Arts Council, 34, 250

Ashton, Sir Frederick, 96, 125

Askwith, Betty, 145

Athens, Greece, 58–9, 61, 63, 64–5, 215, 216, 217–18, 219; British Embassy, 59

Attlee, Lord, 46, 164

Auden, Wystan, 28, 29, 82, 107, 127, 128, 250

Austria, 42, 47–8, 49, 56; zonal frontiers, 55; *see also* Vienna

Avilov, Lydia, *Chekhov in My Life*, 146–7

Ayer, Frederick, 186

Ayrton, Michael, 74, 124, 170

B.B.C., 20, 109, 123, 165, 191–2, 198, 202–3, 206, 211; European Service, 47, 123; North American Service, 202; Third Programme, 191, 192, 196

Bacon, Francis, 74

ballet, 33, 34, 37, 73, 125–6, 170; U.S., 87

Balzac, Honoré de, 172

Banting, John, 23

Barbirolli, Sir John, 55

Barker, George, 'Letter to a Young Poet', 205–6

Barrymore, Ethel, 97

Baxter, Walter, 200

Beaconsfield, 26, 133, 135, 136; *see also* Fieldhead

Beauregard, Comtesse Costa de, 135

Beckett, Samuel, 262

Bellapais Abbey, Cyprus, 226

Bellow, Saul, 72, 81; *Dangling Man*, 20, 23, 82; *The Victim*, 20

Beneš, Dr, 46

Benthall, Michael, 137

Berenson, Bernard, 158–9

Berlin, Sir Isaiah,, 215–16

Berlin, Germany, 118, 198

Betjeman, John, *Sun and Fun*, 201

Bevan, Aneurin, 246

Bingham, Henrietta, 87

Biro, B. S. (Val), 173–4, 184, 185

Blake, Martin, 47

Bloomsbury, 162–3

Boakie (cat), 19

Bohemia, 43, 48, 263

Bonham Carter, Mark, 251

Book Centre, 17, 181n

Book Society, 40, 153, 178

Bookseller, The, 185, 186

Boston, U.S.A., 77, 83–4, 253; Harvard Club, 84

Botteghe Oscure, (Italian magazine), 155–6, 253

Tsarouchi, Greek painter, 58, 67, 217
Tuohy, Frank, 72

Uhlman, Frederick, 113
United States of America, 17–18, 29–30, 31, 32, 40, 97, 108, 118, 125–6. 201; author visits, 77–87; literature in, 121; *see also* place names
Ustinov, Peter, 110

Valaoritis, Nanos, 21, 217
van Thal, Herbert, 176
Vaughan, Keith, 18, 23, 32, 35–6, 41, 74, 113–14, 124, 171; mural in Dome of Discovery, 113; *A View of English Painting*, 74
Venice, Italy, 48, 159–61, 163
Vidal, Gore, 79–80, 148–9; *The City and the Pillar*, 79–80, 149
Vienna, Austria, postwar, 47, 49, 50–57, 65, 121; music in, 7, 65, 121; author's flat in; 49, 50–52; University, 55; music in, 55
Voigt, Frederick, 162

Wain, John, 72, 196, 203, 206; article in *PNW*, 72, 196, 244; *Mixed Feelings*, 196
Wanger, Walter, 87
war, in Europe, 49–51; effects of, 13, 30–31, 52–3
Warburg, Frederick, 132
Warner, Barbara, (*née* Hutchinson), 135–6, 137, 138
Warner, Lucy, 136
Warner, Rex, 21, 242, 254; in Greece, 58–60, 66, 217; in Oxfordshire, 135–6, 137, 138; *Views of Attica*, 60, 135
Washington, U.S.A. 31, 82, 85–6

Watkins, Armitage ('Mike'), 81, 82, 87
Watkins, Vernon, 155–6, 193, 196, 199
Waugh, Evelyn, 251
Wedgwood, Dr Veronica, 230, 254
Welch, Denton, 116–18, 124, 172; *Journal*, 103; *A Voice Through A Cloud*, 117, 118; *A Last Sheaf*, 117
Wellington, Duke of, 94–5
Welty, Eudora, 72, 108–9, 249
Wessely, Paula, 55
West, Paul, 192
Weybright, Victor, 201–2
Weygand, General, 93
White, Eric Walter, 34–5
Wilde, Leading Electrical Mechanic, 193, 200
Wilde, Oscar, 101–2, 105, 149
Williams, Emlyn, 105–6
Williams, Tennessee, 72, 109–10, 115, 155; plays, 80–81, 82, 110
Willingham, Calder, 197; *End as a Man*, 81
Wilson, Angus, 186, 200
Witherby, Diana, 201
Wood, Kenneth, 204
Woolf, Leonard, 13, 15, 20, 146, 170, 179
Woolf, Virginia, 13, 74, 170; *To The Lighthouse*, 195
World Review, 75
Wydenbruck, Countess Nora, 101; *Rilke*, 101, 146, 170

Yorke, Henry, *see* Green, Henry

Zenkevitch, Comrade, 38
Zorza, Dalla, 74